A Letter to Teachers

Hello! Our world is a wonderful, wonder-filled place. Sooner or later, each of us will be warmed by a glowing sunrise, cooled by a gentle rain, transfixed by a dancing butterfly, or rocked by crashing thunder. Making sense of these extraordinary events is the crucial first step to understanding our world and our place in it. Knowledge comes from wondering and then becomes the foundation on which we construct both who we are and who we will become.

Is your heart filled with a passion to bring the wonders of the world to your students? If so, you have likely come to these conclusions about what is needed to share that passion with your students:

1. I need straightforward science activities in the physical, life, and earth and space sciences for my students.

2. I need ideas that will help me tie science to language arts, mathematics, and the arts.

3. I need some stimulating science questions to initiate student discussions and independent study projects.

4. I need a book that reflects current National Science Education Content Standards.

Whizbangers and Wonderments has been prepared to meet these needs. In each chapter, you will find straightforward, easy-to-use science activities organized in a three-step format: 1. Get Ready, 2. Do and Wonder, 3. Think and Write. Each activity ends with an Explanation, which provides a brief discussion of the science content involved, along with any relevant Safety Tips.

Each chapter also includes ideas on how to integrate science with language arts, mathematics, and the arts. Two or three activities in each of these subjects are provided in sections named Word Play, Magnificent Math, and Art Connections. Each chapter ends with a section called Amazing but True! Brainstretchers, which is a collection of puzzling questions and answers that will help stimulate class discussions and serve as the basis for student research projects. A few science jokes are included in these sections, just for fun!

Finally, all the science activities in the entire book are correlated to the National Science Education Content Standards for grades K–8. To help you address these standards in your planning, I have created bracketed codes to identify the relevant standard for each activity. You will find these codes listed with the activity titles in the Contents and in each chapter-opening outline.

I hope this book will help you create a classroom in which the walls echo with choruses of "oohs" and "aahs" from young people who are surprised by their own discoveries. It will be up to you to build on that fascination as you help students experience more fully and deeply the wonders of our wonder-filled world!

Many thanks to the following individuals, who reviewed this book for Allyn and Bacon: Lorraine Gerstl, Santa Catalina School (Monterey, CA); William Hughes, Ashland University; Eileen Madaus, Newton (MA) Public Schools; and Lucy J. Orfan, Kean University.

Joseph Abruscato

Whizbangers and Wonderments

Science Activities for Young People

Joseph Abruscato

University of Vermont

Allyn and Bacon

Boston London Toronto Sydney Tokyo Singapore

For young Gregory and Catie,
who in this twenty-first century will see things yet unseen
and dream things yet undreamed. May they use
the wisdom of the ages and the eyes of the young
to wonder, to explore, to wisely choose, and to become.

Vice President, Editor in Chief, Education: Paul A. Smith
Series Editor: Norris Harrell
Editorial Assistant: Bridget Keane
Director of Education Programs: Ellen Mann Dolberg
Marketing Manager: Brad Parkins
Editorial-Production Administrator: Annette Joseph
Editorial-Production Service: Susan Freese, Communicáto, Ltd.
Text Design and Electronic Composition: Denise Hoffman
Composition Buyer: Linda Cox
Manufacturing Buyer: Suzanne Lareau
Cover Administrator: Jenny Hart
Cover Designer: Suzanne Harbison

Library of Congress Cataloging-in-Publication Data
Abruscato, Joseph.
    Whizbangers and wonderments : science activities for young people
/ Joseph Abruscato
        p.   cm.
    Includes index.
    ISBN 0–205–28409–4 (alk. paper)
    1. Science—Experiments.   I. Title.
Q182.3.A27   2000
507'.8—dc21   99–28639
                                                   CIP

Printed in the United States of America

10 9 8 7 6 5 4 3 2 1   04 03 02 01 00 99

Contents

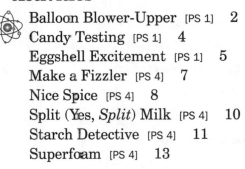
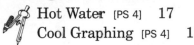
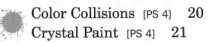

Part II

Creepers and Peepers
(Life Sciences)

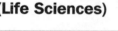

STANDARDS:	Life Science [LS]
	Science in Personal and Social Perspectives [SPSP]
	History and Nature of Science [HNS]
	Science and Technology [S&T]

Chapter 4
Plants

Chapter 5
Critters Small,
Monsters Tall

Chapter 6
Amazing You

Chapter 1
Kitchen Chemistry

Activities

Balloon Blower-Upper   [PS 1]
Candy Testing   [PS 1]
Eggshell Excitement   [PS 1]
Make a Fizzler   [PS 4]
Nice Spice   [PS 4]
Split (Yes, *Split*) Milk   [PS 4]
Starch Detective   [PS 4]
Superfoam   [PS 4]

Word Play

Wanda, Wally, and the Wacky Water   [PS 4]
The Drama in a Drop   [PS 4]

Magnificent Math

Hot Water   [PS 4]
Cool Graphing   [PS 4]

Art Connections

Color Collisions   [PS 4]
Crystal Paint   [PS 4]

Amazing but True!
Brainstretchers   [PS 1–6]

Part I Fizzers and Poppers

Matter and Energy

Activities

Balloon Blower-Upper

Would your friends be amazed if you showed them a balloon that could blow itself up? In this activity, you'll discover how to make an automatic balloon blower-upper. When you show it to your friends, they'll wonder how it works!

1▶ Get Ready

Clean, empty, plastic 2 liter soda bottle
Round balloon that will inflate to at least 9 inches
    (about 23 centimeters) across
1 cup white vinegar
2 tablespoons baking soda
Enough aluminum foil to wrap around bottle
Funnel
Plastic bowl or tray

2▶ Do and Wonder

Place the bottle upright in the plastic bowl or tray. Add the vinegar to the bottle.

Inflate and deflate the balloon a few times until it becomes easy to blow up.

Using the funnel, put the baking soda in the balloon. Put the open end of the balloon over the top of the soda bottle; the part containing the baking soda should be hanging down along the neck of the bottle. Be careful not to spill any of the baking soda into the bottle. What do you predict will happen if you pull the balloon up and spill the baking soda into the vinegar?

2

Pull the balloon up, and then step away from it. Write down your observations.

To show your invention to your friends, first wrap the bottle in foil so no one will be able to see the vinegar and baking soda reacting.

3▶ Think and Write

Write a short paragraph that answers these questions: What changes did you observe in the bottle? What do you think caused the balloon to blow up? How could you make the reaction go faster or slower?

Explanation

Baking soda reacts with vinegar to produce carbon dioxide gas and other compounds. The gas increases the pressure inside the bottle, which causes the balloon to inflate.

Safety Hint

Be sure to place the bottle in the bowl or tray in order to catch any liquid that might squirt out.

Activity 1.2

Candy Testing

When you look at a piece of red or purple candy, does it look
completely red or completely purple? This activity will show that
your eyes can be fooled.

1▶ Get Ready

Three dark-colored pieces of
   M&M or Smarties candies
White paper plate
Tablespoon

Water
White coffee filter
Scissors
Candy wrapper

2▶ Do and Wonder

Cut three strips from the coffee filter; each should be about 3
centimeters (1 inch) wide by 15 centimeters (6 inches) long.

Spread about 1 tablespoonful of water around the center of
the paper plate.

Moisten each candy in water, and place it near the center of
the plate. None of the candies should touch. Place one drop
of water on each candy. Why do you think it's important to
moisten the candy?

Place each coffee filter strip so that one end touches the drop
of water on the candy and the other end hangs over the edge
of the plate. Observe what happens as water travels from each
candy along the paper strip.

3▶ Think and Write

Write a short paragraph that answers these questions: What
colors were you able to get from each piece of candy? What
colors do you find in the list of ingredients on the candy
wrapper? Did you find the same colors that were on the list?
If you found different colors, why do you think this might
have happened?

Explanation

The dyes used to make candy are *soluble* (sol-u-bul), which
means they can be absorbed in water. Dark-colored candies
are made using more than one dye. In this activity, the dyes
from each candy were absorbed into the water, moved along
the filter paper, and eventually left behind. Since the dyes are
different chemicals, they left the water at different places
along the paper strip.

Activity 1.3

Eggshell Excitement

One way scientists learn about matter is to study how different substances react. You can make some of your own discoveries about matter without using any special chemicals or equipment. To learn some interesting things about eggshells, all you need are eggshells, water, and white vinegar.

1▶ Get Ready

Two eggshells
Porcelain cup
½ glass white vinegar

½ glass water
Hand lens (magnifying glass)
Tablespoon

2▶ Do and Wonder

Thoroughly rinse out the eggshells. Then remove the thin membrane attached to the bottom of each shell, and put the shells in a warm place to dry.

After the shells are completely dry, put them in the cup. Use the back of the tablespoon to crush the shell pieces until you've made a coarse powder.

Write down what you think will happen if you sprinkle a small amount of the powder on the water.

Now sprinkle a little powder on the water. Use your hand lens to carefully observe the surface of the water. Take notes about what you observe. Also make a diagram to show how the tiny bits of eggshell are reacting. Is there any evidence of a gas being formed during this reaction? If so, what do you think the gas might be?

Predict what you expect to observe if you sprinkle a small amount of the powder on the vinegar.

Now sprinkle a little powder on the vinegar. Repeat the observations and notetaking you did before.

3▶ Think and Write

Answer these questions in a short paragraph: What changes did you see when you sprinkled the powdered eggshell onto the vinegar? Compare what you observed when you added the eggshell to the water and the eggshell to the vinegar. Do you think the reaction would have happened more quickly or more slowly if you used pieces of eggshell instead of a powder? Do you think the same reaction would happen if you added eggshell to lemon juice?

Explanation   An eggshell is made of a compound called *calcium* (cal-see-um) *carbonate* (car-bon-ate). Vinegar is a weak acid called *acetic* (ah-see-tick) *acid*. When acetic acid and calcium carbonate react, one of the compounds produced is the gas carbon dioxide.

Activity 1.4

Make a Fizzler

If you wanted to cool down a liquid, you would probably put it in a cold place. If you wanted to warm it up, you would probably put it in a warm place. In this activity, you'll discover that certain chemicals can change the temperatures of liquids.

1▶ Get Ready

Three Alka-Seltzer tablets
Three large glasses that can each hold at least ½ cup of water

Kitchen thermometer
Water

2▶ Do and Wonder

Break each tablet in half.

Add ½ cup of water to one of the glasses. Take the temperature of the water in the glass. Predict what might happen to the water temperature if you put half an Alka-Seltzer into it.

Drop half an Alka-Seltzer into the water. Wait 30 seconds, and then take the temperature of the water again. Observe the reaction that occurs.

Pour ½ cup of hot water in one glass and ½ cup of the coldest water you can get in the other glass. (You can use the hot and cold water from the faucet.) Do you expect the reaction of the Alka-Seltzer with the hot water to be the same or different from the reaction of the Alka-Seltzer with the cold water? Write down your predictions.

Put half an Alka-Seltzer in each glass of water.

3▶ Think and Write

Make a list of the active ingredients found on the Alka-Seltzer package. Next to each item, write down your best guess about what that ingredient is supposed to do for the person taking the Alka-Seltzer.

The starting temperature of the water may have had something to do with the speed of each reaction. Based on what you observed, would you say that a high temperature makes the reaction happen more quickly or more slowly?

Explanation

Alka-Seltzer contains crystals and powder. When you put a tablet in water, the chemical reaction uses up some of the water's heat energy, which makes the water temperature drop.

Nice Spice

This activity uses a common spice and a few other kitchen items
to explore chemical reactions. You'll have fun observing these
reactions, since some of them may cause color changes.

1▶ Get Ready

¼ teaspoon turmeric (a food-coloring powder/spice usually
   found in the spice section of the supermarket)
¼ cup rubbing alcohol
¼ cup white vinegar
¼ cup water
¼ cup water plus 1 teaspoon baking soda (mixed together)
¼ cup glass-cleaning liquid
Six small, clean jars (about the size of baby food jars)
Four strips cut from a white coffee filter, each 1 inch
   (about 2½ centimeters) wide by 2 inches
   (about 5 centimeters) long
Masking tape and marker

2▶ Do and Wonder

Use small pieces of masking tape to put labels on the jars.
Then use the marker to label the jars as follows: "Soaked
Strips," "Alcohol," "Vinegar," "Water," "Water plus Baking
Soda," and "Glass Cleaner."

Put the "Soaked Strips" jar aside for now. Pour one of the
liquids into each of the remaining jars, following the labels.

Dissolve the turmeric in the alcohol, and let it stand for a few
minutes. Change the label on the jar to read "Turmeric plus
Alcohol."

Hold each strip of coffee filter by one end, and soak half of it
in the turmeric and alcohol solution. Store the four strips in
the jar labeled "Soaked Strips."

Make a chart to write down what you will observe later in the
activity, when you will dip each soaked paper strip in one of
the remaining liquids. Also write down your predictions for
what you think will happen with each liquid.

Dip one strip in each liquid, and write down what you observe on the chart.

What do you think will happen when you spray the strip with glass cleaner? Try it.

3▶ Think and Write

Turmeric is an *indicator*, which means that it changes color when it touches certain substances. Turmeric is usually used to give rice and other foods a yellowish color. If you wanted to create a yellow-colored salad dressing using vinegar, would adding turmeric make this happen? Explain your thinking in a short paragraph.

Explanation

Adding turmeric to a substance indicates whether a chemical called a *base* is present. The yellow turmeric-soaked strip turns reddish when placed in a base. We see the color change because the color of light reflecting from the molecules changes when the molecules do. This happens when the turmeric and base react. Baking soda in water is a weak base. Common glass-cleaning spray contains ammonium hydroxide, which is also a base. Turmeric does not react with acids.

Safety Hints

Be sure to keep the liquids away from your eyes. Also try not to breathe in any of them.

Rinse out the jars thoroughly before using them.

Wash your hands thoroughly when you're done.

Activity 1.6

Split (Yes, Split) Milk

Do you think there's a mistake in the title of this activity? Do you think the word *split* has accidentally been substituted for *spilled*? If you do, you're wrong! This activity will show you how to take ordinary milk and break it apart.

1 ▶ Get Ready

½ cup skim or lowfat milk   Spoon
4 tablespoons white vinegar   Coffee filter and funnel
Two glasses

2 ▶ Do and Wonder

Put the milk in one glass and the vinegar in the other.

In a minute, you're going to slowly pour the vinegar into the milk. What do you predict will happen?

Add the vinegar to the milk by slowly pouring it down the inside of the glass. Observe what's happening at the surface of the milk by looking through the side of the glass.

Next you're going to stir the liquid. What do you predict will happen?

After 5 minutes, stir the liquid using the spoon. What do you observe?

Pour the liquid through the coffee filter, and observe how the parts separate.

3 ▶ Think and Write

If you left ordinary milk in a warm area for a day or two, it would get sour. You wouldn't need to add anything to it. Knowing this, what would you guess to be one of the substances produced when the bacteria in milk consume the natural sugars found in it?

Explanation

By adding vinegar to the milk, you made instant sour milk! The vinegar is a weak acid that causes a change in the proteins that are part of the liquid. They start to stick together, forming a solid. The solid is called *curd,* and the liquid is called *whey.*

Activity 1.7

Starch Detective

Detectives are always looking for clues. Chemists sometimes act like detectives when they search for clues to tell them what certain substances are. In this activity, you'll be a detective searching for clues that tell whether a food contains starch.

1▶ Get Ready

1 teaspoon of each of these: flour, laundry starch, instant mashed potatoes, powdered milk, salt, baking powder
Six small jars, each filled with ½ cup warm water
1% iodine solution
Eyedropper
Masking tape and marker
Teaspoon
Paper towel

2▶ Do and Wonder

Make a chart to write down your predictions and observations about whether each substance contains starch.

Add 1 teaspoon of flour to one of the jars containing warm water. Stir thoroughly. Using the masking tape and marker, label this jar "Flour."

Add 1 teaspoon of each remaining substance to one of the remaining jars of warm water. Label each to identify the substance it contains. (Be sure to wash, rinse, and dry the teaspoon each time you use it.)

Write down on the chart your observations about the contents of each jar.

What do you predict will happen if you add a drop of iodine to each jar? Write down your predictions on the chart.

Now add one drop of iodine to each jar. Write down your observations on the chart.

3▶ Think and Write

Which substances do you think contain starch?

Imagine that an alien who visits Earth is from a planet where everyone is allergic to starch. Design a testing kit the alien could use to test Earth foods for starch.

Explanation   Starch is a substance found in plant cells. Like sugar, starch contains energy. Our bodies are able to change the starch we eat to sugar and then make the sugar release energy. Scientists can test substances to discover whether they contain starch. Iodine can be used to do this because it turns blue/black or dark brown when mixed with starch.

Safety Hints   Iodine is used as an antiseptic and a poison. Be sure to keep it away from your eyes and to put it away and out of the reach of young children as soon as you're done using it.

Also thoroughly wash and rinse the teaspoon and all the jars when you're done.

Remember that you only need *one* drop for each test in this activity.

Activity 1.8

Superfoam

If you've ever eaten lemon meringue pie, you've seen one way that egg whites are used in cooking. The meringue—the white substance on top of the pie—is made using egg whites. In this activity, you'll use egg whites to cause a chemical reaction that produces something that looks just like meringue.

1▶ Get Ready

Clean 1 liter (about 1 quart) plastic container
Three egg whites
½ cup water
2 teaspoons baking soda
½ teaspoon citric acid crystals (used for food preservation;
    get this at any store that sells home canning materials)
Three drops food coloring
Fork
Sink

2▶ Do and Wonder

Look at the list of ingredients above. What do you predict will happen when they're all mixed together?

Add all the ingredients to the plastic container *except* the citric acid. Briskly stir the contents of the container with the fork. What do you observe?

What do you predict will happen when you add the citric acid crystals?

Add the crystals, and stir them into liquid. Observe what happens. How did your predictions and observations compare?

3▶ Think and Write

Citric acid and vinegar react to produce carbon dioxide. What role do you think this reaction plays in producing the foam?

Explanation

By beating the egg whites with other substances, you have actually created a *polymer-* (poly-mur) like substance. A polymer is made when simple molecules bind together to form long, chainlike molecules. These long chains act like the fibers in a fabric, trapping the carbon dioxide released during the chemical reaction. The carbon dioxide puffs out the polymer to form bubbles of superfoam.

Word Play

Wanda, Wally, and the Wacky Water

What would life be like if water molecules didn't behave the way we expect them to? Write a story about the adventures of Wanda and Wally, who visit a planet that's exactly like Earth except for one thing: the very strange behavior of the water.

1▶ Get Ready Paper and pencil

2▶ Do and Wonder Describe the adventures of Wanda and Wally as they visit the planet Retaw. Use at least five of the following ideas in your story.

On the planet Retaw:

1. Ice sinks.

   Story Ideas:

   How people would skate on a lake

   How a glass of iced tea would look

   How submarines would avoid icebergs

   How polar bears would hunt seals

2. On Mondays, Wednesdays, Fridays, and Sundays, water doesn't stick to anything.

   Story Ideas:

   How to use a towel to dry off after swimming

   How to walk during a rainstorm

3. On Tuesdays, Thursdays, and Saturdays, water sticks to everything.

    Story Ideas:

    How a duck would swim to shore and then walk around on dry land

    How to take a shower after doing gymnastics

4. Water doesn't dissolve anything.

    Story Ideas:

    How to wash a dog

    How to make iced tea

3▶ Think and Write   Let your friends read your story about Wally and Wanda's visit to Retaw. Then use some of your friends' ideas to write brand-new adventures for Wally and Wanda.

Explanation   Without water, life could not exist on Earth. *All* life depends on it. Living on our planet would be difficult or impossible if water didn't behave exactly the way it does.

Word Play 1.2

The Drama in a Drop

Have some fun telling others what you know about the behavior of water molecules! Imagine that a molecule has a very interesting adventure and tells its story in a newspaper article. Here's one way to write that story.

1▶ Get Ready   Paper and pencil   Reference books (if needed)

2▶ Do and Wonder   Write a three-paragraph newspaper story about the adventures of a traveling water molecule. Tell the story as if *you* were the molecule. Be sure you describe how the molecule and the molecules around it move from place to place. Here's an outline of what should happen to the molecule in each paragraph:

Paragraph 1: The molecule is in a slowly melting chunk of ice.

Paragraph 2: The molecule is in a slowly evaporating puddle of water.

Paragraph 3: The molecule and its neighbors are in the air. They are part of the gas we call *water vapor.* The air begins to cool, and the gas changes to tiny water droplets.

3▶ Think and Write   Work with a friend to turn your story into the script for a short play or skit. Perhaps you can even create a "Water Molecule Dance" that tells the story through movements that go with the script.

Explanation   The molecules in water are always moving. In solid water, the molecules vibrate back and forth. In liquid water, they actually move by each other as they travel from place to place. In the gas form of water (water vapor), the molecules move by each other and spread out to fill the container.

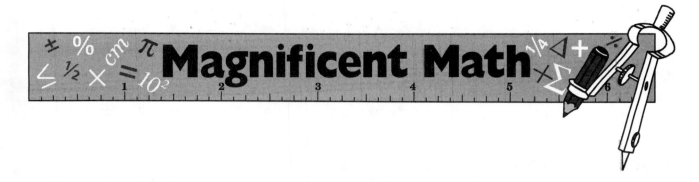

Magnificent Math 1.1

Hot Water

If someone asked you to name the boiling point of water, what would your answer be? Would you say 212 degrees Fahrenheit or 100 degrees Celsius? Even though either would seem to be the right answer, you would be wrong. The correct answer is "It depends!" In this activity, you'll use your graphing skills to discover why this is the only correct answer.

1 ▶ Get Ready

Graph paper   Ruler
Pencil

2 ▶ Do and Wonder

Draw one vertical and one horizontal line on your paper, connecting them at the bottom to form a big L. These are the *axes* (ax-eez) of the graph. You'll chart temperatures along the vertical axis and altitudes along the horizontal axis. So write "Temperatures" to the left of the vertical axis and "Altitudes" below the horizontal axis.

Table 1   Altitudes and Boiling Points

Altitude in Feet	Boiling Point in Degrees Farenheit	Altitude in Meters	Boiling Point in Degrees Celsius
Sea level	212	Sea level	100
1,000	209	300	99
5,000	203	1,500	95
8,000	197	2,500	93
10,000	194	3,000	90
12,000	190	3,600	88

Prepare a graph using the data from Table 1. If you're using Fahrenheit temperatures, use *feet* as your altitude unit. If you're using Celsius temperatures (sometimes called *Centigrade* temperatures), use *meters* as your altitude unit.

3▶ Think and Write

After looking at your graph, form a *hypothesis* (a good guess) that explains why an increase in altitude causes a decrease in the boiling point of water. Write down your hypothesis.

Here's another fun thing to think about: If the boiling point of water decreases as the altitude increases, would the tea you make on top of a mountain be as hot as the tea you make at the bottom of a mountain? Write down your answer.

Explanation

How easily a liquid boils depends on two things: (1) the amount of heat added and (2) the air pressure. If the air pressure is reduced, less heat energy is needed to make the liquid boil. Boiling water on the top of a mountain will take less heat energy than boiling water at the bottom of a mountain. This happens because the height of the column of air is less at the mountain top than at the mountain bottom.

Magnificent Math 1.2

Cool Graphing

If you've ever had a vaccination, or shot, you may remember that the doctor or nurse rubbed alcohol on your skin before giving you the injection. Alcohol is used because it has some ability to kill germs. Alcohol also does something else that you may have forgotten from your visit. This activity will help you understand one very interesting thing about alcohol molecules.

1▶ Get Ready

Two eyedroppers   Scissors
Rubbing alcohol   Thermometer
Water   Small rubber band
Graph paper
Two small pieces of cotton or paper towel
Two colored pencils or fine-tipped markers of different colors
Watch with a second hand or digital watch that shows seconds

2→ Do and Wonder

Make a graph that has "Temperature" along the vertical axis and "Time in Seconds" along the horizontal axis.

Wrap the bulb of the thermometer with a thin layer of paper towel or cotton. Hold the towel or cotton in place with the rubber band.

Record the temperature of the water, the alcohol, and the air at the start of your experiment.

Place 10 drops of water on the cotton or paper towel. Observe the temperature every 20 seconds for 5 minutes.

Remove the wet paper towel or cotton from the thermometer, and replace it with a dry piece.

Now repeat the experiment using alcohol instead of water. Place 10 drops of alcohol on the cotton or paper towel. Observe the temperature every 20 seconds for 5 minutes.

Chart the results of both experiments on the graph. Use one of the colored pencils or markers to connect all your data for the water experiment. Use the other colored pencil or marker to connect the alcohol data.

3→ Think and Write

After studying your graph, write a hypothesis that explains why alcohol molecules might be more or less attracted to one another than water molecules.

Explanation

It takes energy to cause molecules of a liquid to leave your skin. This energy comes from your skin and causes molecules to break away from one another. Water molecules are attracted to each other more than alcohol molecules. This means that alcohol molecules use more energy, since so many of them can evaporate in a short time. The evaporation of alcohol molecules lowers our skin temperature more than the evaporation of water molecules. The rate of evaporation is also affected by the number of molecules of a certain substance that are in the air. Since normal air doesn't contain alcohol molecules, the alcohol molecules on your skin are able to enter the air easily.

Safety Hints

Don't touch your eyes or nose while you're working with the alcohol.

Be sure to wash your hands thoroughly after this activity.

Art Connections

Art Connections 1.1

Color Collisions

Have you ever washed dishes? If you have, you were using the ability of soap molecules to stick to water. In this activity, you'll observe this happen in a beautiful and colorful way.

1▶ Get Ready

Shallow bowl
Milk
Three bottles of food coloring

Liquid hand soap
Teaspoon

2▶ Do and Wonder

Pour about 1 inch (almost 3 centimeters) of milk into the bowl. Then place two or three drops of each color of food coloring at various places on the surface of the milk.

Now add 1 teaspoon of liquid soap to the surface of the milk along the edge of the bowl. What do you observe happen on the milk's surface?

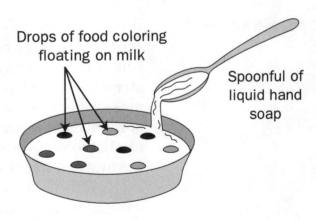

Drops of food coloring floating on milk

Spoonful of liquid hand soap

3▶ Think and Write

In a short paragraph, describe any changes you observed on the surface of the milk. Also write down anything you might do differently in the activity to create even more interesting color movement and mixing.

Explanation   As the soap molecules spread out across the surface of the milk, they twist and turn so one part of each molecule points toward a water molecule and another part points away. The rapid action moves some of the food coloring around to create beautiful patterns on the surface of the milk.

Art Connections 1.2

Crystal Paint

In this activity, you'll see a beautiful design that's left behind when an Epsom salts solution evaporates. You'll be using the solution to paint on paper. The design you see will be made of tiny crystals.

1▸ Get Ready

Sheet of black construction paper
Sheet of white construction paper
Hand lens (magnifying glass)
Pencil
Scissors
Paintbrush

Cellophane tape
Tablespoon
Warm water
Epsom salts
Paper cup

2▸ Do and Wonder

Cut a circle from the white paper that's 6 inches (about 15 centimeters) across.

Fold the circle in half, and then fold the half in thirds. The shape of the folded paper should look like a wedge of pie.

Now fold the wedge in half the long way, and cut a pattern into the fold. If the paper is too thick to cut easily, unfold it once and cut the pattern into the previous fold.

Open the white paper to reveal the design. Flatten out the paper, and tape it to the black paper.

Next prepare your "paint": Mix 3 tablespoons of Epsom salts into about 1/8 cup of warm water.

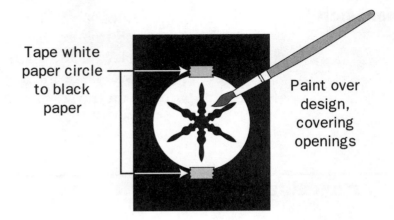

Tape white paper circle to black paper

Paint over design, covering openings

Use the Epsom salts mixture to paint over the design in the white paper, covering the openings where the black paper shows through.

Put the papers in a warm place. When the black paper is dry, paint over the design again.

After the black paper has dried again, carefully remove the white paper from it. Then use the hand lens (magnifying glass) to carefully observe the black paper.

3▶ Think and Write

In a few sentences, describe what you observed in this activity. Did you see crystals on the black paper? If so, describe their size and shape.

Suggest some other "paint" solutions you might make using cooking ingredients and what types of designs they might produce.

Explanation

The "paint" you made was really a solution of Epsom salts in water. As it dried, the water molecules left the surface of the black paper and entered the air. The crystals you may have observed were formed by molecules of Epsom salts that were left behind on the paper.

Amazing but True!
BRAINSTRETCHERS

1.1 If ice is solid water, why does it float?

1.2 Is there another form of matter besides solids, liquids, and gases?

1.3 What is an element's *atomic number*?

1.4 How many different elements are there?

1.5 Are any elements liquid at room temperature?

1.6 Does our universe contain more of one element than any other?

1.7 Is there more hydrogen on Earth than any other element?

1.8 What is osmium?

1.9 Why are metals cold to the touch?

1.10 Why are silver, gold, and platinum so valuable?

1.11 What does a chemist do?

1.12 Why did people who were looking for gold find copper instead?

1.13 Did the first chemists have "secret recipes" for making gold?

1.14 What are diamonds made of?

1.15 Why are diamonds so shiny?

1.16 What is the stuff around us made of?

1.17 What are molecules and atoms?

1.18 What are crystals?

1.19 Which would burn longer: a white candle or a blue candle?

1.20 What gets wetter the more it dries?

1.1 If ice is solid water, why does it float?

Ice floats because solid water is less dense than liquid water. In other words, more molecules of liquid water can fit into a space than can molecules of solid water. In solid water, the molecules are arranged in a pattern with more space between them. Water is one of the few substances that is more dense as a solid than as a liquid. If this wasn't true, ice would sink. That sure would make ice skating difficult. You would have to ice skate wearing scuba-diving gear!

1.2 Is there another form of matter besides solids, liquids, and gases?

Yes. There is a fourth state of matter, called *plasma* (plahs-ma), which is a mixture of electrons and positively charged atoms. Plasma can be found in fluorescent light bulbs, in places where nuclear bombs have exploded, and in and around the sun and other stars.

1.3 What is an element's *atomic number?*

This is an easy question to answer. An element's *atomic number* is simply the number of protons in the nucleus of its atom.

1.4 How many different elements are there?

It depends on how you count them. Ninety-two elements occur in nature; uranium is the element with the atomic number 92. However, there are at least 17 other elements, which include those created by humans. So if you ask this question tomorrow, there may be even *more* elements.

1.5 Are any elements liquid at room temperature?

There are just a few, including these two: Mercury (symbol Hg, atomic number 80) and bromine (symbol Br, atomic number 35).

1.6 Does our universe contain more of one element than any other?

Definitely. The big winner in any atom count would be the element hydrogen (symbol H, atomic number 1), which makes up about 75% of the total mass of the universe. If you counted every atom in the universe, you would find that 90% of them were hydrogen.

1.7 Is there more hydrogen on Earth than any other element?

No. There is more oxygen (symbol O, atomic number 8) on Earth than any other element. Oxygen makes up 50% of the mass of the outer layers of the Earth, the water, and the atmosphere.

1.8 What is osmium?

Osmium (oz-me-yum) is a very heavy metal. A chunk of it would weigh twice as much as a piece of lead the same size. Osmium is twice as dense as lead and about 23 times as dense as water. Since your body is made up mostly of water, you could estimate how much you would weigh if you were made of osmium. Just multiply your weight times 23—and don't step on a scale!

1.9   Why are metals cold to the touch?

This is a tricky question. If you found a chunk of copper outside and brought it indoors, it would soon become the same temperature as the room. However, it would still *feel* cold. The reason for this is that metal is an excellent heat conductor. When you touch metal, some heat leaves your finger and enters the metal. The metal carries the heat away from the place that was touched, so your fingertip will feel cold.

1.10   Why are silver, gold, and platinum so valuable?

These metals wouldn't be valuable if you could just find chunks of them lying around on the ground. Instead, they have to be mined from deep in the ground, which involves a lot people and machines and therefore costs a lot of money. These metals are also valuable because there is a big demand for them. For example, jewelry makers need these metals because people like how they look bright and shiny, and computer makers need these metals because they are good conductors of electricity. In general, when many people want something that there is very little of, its price will go up. So, these metals are valuable because many people want them and they are difficult to remove from the earth.

1.11   What does a chemist do?

A *chemist* is someone who studies how different substances can be broken down or put together. Some of chemists' discoveries are used to make materials that you use every day. For instance, the plastic in your pen, the dye in your clothes, and the rubber in your sneakers are all made using substances discovered by chemists.

1.12   Why did people who were looking for gold find copper instead?

The first so-called chemists were ancient Egyptians, who discovered that by heating a green-colored rock we now call *malachite* (mal-a-kite), they could release copper. Unfortunately, they were trying to make gold!

1.13   Did the first chemists have "secret recipes" for making gold?

They certainly did, but none of them really worked. One of the recipes they tried was to mix and heat rocks containing mercury, gold, and iron with coal and egg yolk. Another even more interesting recipe was to heat rocks containing metals with mercuric oxide, alum (something used to make pickles), and horse manure!

1.14 What are diamonds made of?

A *diamond* is a crystal form of carbon, an element that we usually see as coal or charcoal. If you burn a diamond, it will form the gas carbon dioxide and your diamond will disappear!

1.15 Why are diamonds so shiny?

Diamonds are dug up from deep inside the earth and only look shiny after they've been washed and polished. But they *really* shine and sparkle after a gem cutter has carved many small surfaces into them. When a diamond is cut properly, the light that enters the top surfaces reaches the bottom surfaces and is reflected to your eyes.

1.16 What is the stuff around us made of?

The stuff around us—every book, pencil, fly, rock, and person—is all made of matter. *Matter* is anything that occupies space and has weight. And all matter is made of *elements,* of which there are over 109 different types. Everything you can see, smell, and touch is made up of one or more of these elements. In fact, *you're* made of some of the same elements that stars are made of. Not only that, but the atoms of elements in your body were once part of stars that exploded. So, you're actually made of "star stuff!"

1.17 What are molecules and atoms?

Molecules and *atoms* are types of matter that are so small, they are invisible to your eye. In fact, they are even invisible to an ordinary microscope. Molecules are made of atoms. Atoms contain protons, neutrons, and electrons. Protons and neutrons are made of quarks. Scientists aren't sure if there are any particles smaller than quarks.

1.18 What are crystals?

If you've ever looked at grains of table salt under a microscope, you've seen crystals. A *crystal* is made of atoms and molecules that are lined up in a certain way. The crystals of various minerals all have their own unique patterns. A salt crystal, for example, is made of sodium and chlorine atoms all lined up to form cube-shaped crystals.

1.19 Which would burn longer: a white candle or a blue candle?

Neither. They would both burn shorter.

1.20 What gets wetter the more it dries?

A towel.

Chapter 2
Matter and Motion

Activities

Boro Slime: Make It, Test It [PS 1]

Starch Slime: Make It, Test It [PS 1]

Oobleck—Regular and Alien:
Make It, Test It [PS 1]

Who? What? Rosalyn Yalow and
Marie Curie [HNS 2]

When? Where? A Matter-and-
Motion Puzzle [HNS 3]

Word Play

Pyramid Power [PS 5]

Match It [PS 5]

Magnificent Math

Marbles and Surfaces [PS 2]

Bicycle Adventure [PS 5]

Art Connections

Seashell Mobiles [PS 2]

Colorful Kites [PS 5]

Amazing but True!
Brainstretchers [PS 1–6]

Activities

Boro Slime: Make It, Test It

Have you ever watched people throw slime at each other on television? In fact, that slime is actually a harmless substance. It's even sold in toystores! You'll make some slime of your own in this activity, but you won't be throwing it at anyone. Instead, you'll be studying it like a scientist does, since slime is a type of matter that behaves very strangely.

1▸ Get Ready

Box of Borax or Boraxo laundry booster
Container of white, nontoxic Elmer's Glue-All
   (7.58 ounce/225 milliliter size)
Two small plastic bowls that can each hold at least 2 cups
   (about ½ liter) of liquid
One larger plastic bowl that can hold at least 5 cups
   (more than 1 liter) of liquid

Water	Paper and pencil
Measuring cups and spoons	Newspapers
Stirring spoon	Access to a sink

2▸ Do and Wonder

Cover your work surface with newspapers.

To make the slime, you'll need to prepare two liquids:
(1) a glue mixture and (2) and a Borax solution.

First make the *glue mixture:* Pour the full container of glue into one of the small bowls. Then refill the empty glue container with water, and add that water to the bowl. Stir the glue/water mixture thoroughly, and then pour it into the larger bowl.

28

Next make the *Borax solution:* Pour 1 cup (about 250 milliliters) of warm water into the other small bowl. Then stir in 2 teaspoons (about 10 milliliters) of Borax. If all the Borax dissolves, stir in a little more until you see Borax crystals at the bottom of the bowl.

Now make the *slime:* Slowly add the Borax solution to the glue mixture. Stir the mixture as you pour and then for another minute or two. Congratulations! You have made Boro Slime. Remove it from the bowl, and squeeze out the excess liquid.

Test the Boro Slime to discover its properties. Try to poke, stretch, and pour the slime. Invent other tests and try them, too.

Find out if the Boro Slime can bounce. Form a tiny ball of slime by pinching off some and rolling it in your hand. Predict how high the ball will bounce if you drop it from a height of 20 inches (about 50 centimeters). Drop the ball from this height, and compare the results with your prediction.

❸ Think and Write

In one paragraph, tell how you tested your slime and what you learned about its properties.

In another paragraph, invent a practical use for the slime you just made.

Explanation

Slime is a special kind of fluid. Like all fluids, it takes the shape of its container. It also can be slowly poured from one container to another. Slime changes its behavior when you apply a force to it. Pushing, pulling, or striking slime makes it act like a solid. Scientists have a name for any fluid that acts in these very strange ways: It's called a *non-Newtonian fluid.* Isaac Newton was the first scientist to write about this type of fluid, which is how it got its name.

Safety Hints

Don't taste the slime.

Thoroughly wash and dry all your equipment when you're done.

Dispose of the cups.

Wash your hands after completing the activity.

Activity 2.2

Starch Slime: Make It, Test It

If someone says that an object is *slimy,* what does he or she mean?
Does it mean the item is gooey or that it sticks to things? Would it
flow if you poured it? In this activity, you'll make a slimy substance
from starch and glue. Then you'll study this Starch Slime to learn
its characteristics.

1▶ Get Ready

Small (at least 1 quart, or about 1 liter) container of
    liquid laundry starch
Container of white, nontoxic Elmer's Glue-All
    (7.58 ounce/225 milliliter size)
Salt shaker
Two sturdy and disposable paper or plastic cups
Measuring cups and spoons
Food coloring
Stirring spoon
Paper and pencil
Pencil
Newspapers
Access to a sink

2▶ Do and Wonder

Cover your work surface with newspapers. (You'll be making a
bit of a mess!)

Put 2 tablespoons (about 30 milliliters) of glue into one of the
cups.

Put ¼ cup (about 60 milliliters) of liquid laundry starch into
the other cup. Add ½ teaspoon (a little less than 4 grams) of
salt to the starch. Stir well.

Pour the starch/salt mixture into the glue, stirring as you
pour. What do you observe happening?

Take your mixture over to the sink. Remove the Starch Slime
from the cup, and rinse it under running water.

Squeeze and knead the Starch Slime until it feels like soft
dough. If it's too wet, add a small amount of salt to the
mixture.

Test the Starch Slime to discover its properties. Try to poke, stretch, and pour the slime. Invent other tests and try them, too. Write down your observations.

Find out if the Starch Slime can bounce. Form a small ball of slime by pinching off some and rolling it in your hand. Predict how high the ball will bounce if you drop it from a height of 20 inches (about 50 centimeters). Drop the ball from this height, and compare the results with your prediction.

3▶ Think and Write

In one paragraph, tell how you tested the slime and what you learned about its properties.

In another paragraph, invent a practical use for the slime you just made. (Throwing it at people is not a practical use!)

Explanation

Slime is a special kind of fluid. Like all fluids, it takes the shape of its container. It also can be slowly poured from one container to another. Slime changes its behavior when you apply a force to it. Pushing, pulling, or striking slime makes it act like a solid. Scientists have a name for any fluid that acts in these very strange ways: It's called a *non-Newtonian fluid*. Isaac Newton was the first scientist to write about this type of fluid, which is how it got its name.

Safety Hints

Don't taste the slime.

Thoroughly wash and dry all your equipment when you're done.

Dispose of the cups.

Wash your hands after completing the activity.

Oobleck–Regular and Alien: Make It, Test It

Wouldn't it be fun to experiment with something that's really strange? In this activity, you'll do just that. First you'll make a very strange substance—called *Oobleck*—out of cornstarch and water. (You can even make it any color you choose!) Then you'll get to test the Oobleck to see how it behaves.

1 Get Ready

Two 1 pound (454 gram) boxes of cornstarch
Water
Food coloring
Measuring cups and spoons
Sturdy stirring spoon or wooden ruler
Two bowls that can each hold about 2 cups (1 liter) of liquid
Scissors
Ruler
Aluminum pie plate
Newspapers
Hammer

2 Do and Wonder

You'll mix the materials to make two kinds of Oobleck: regular and alien.

Regular Oobleck

Put 2 tablespoons (about 30 milliliters) of water into one of the bowls. Add 4 tablespoons of cornstarch a little at a time. Gently stir the cornstarch into the water. The result will be a stiff dough.

Add a little more water to the mixture, and stir it again to form a very soft dough. (It should be so soft that when you tip the bowl slightly, you can see the dough flow against the edge of the bowl.) You have made Oobleck! Write down your observations of this substance.

Remove the Oobleck from the bowl. Test it by poking, stretching, and bouncing it.

Make a small ball of Oobleck, and gently press a fingertip into it. (If it's too soft to form a ball, add a little more cornstarch.) Write down what you observe.

Now put the small ball on a solid surface, and strike it with the hammer. What do you observe?

Alien Oobleck

Prepare the same recipe as above, but add 3 drops of food coloring to the water before adding the cornstarch.

Test the alien Oobleck the same ways you tested the regular Oobleck. Write down your observations.

Mass Production

Now you're ready to make a large quantity of either regular or alien Oobleck. Before you begin, clean out one of the bowls so it's ready to receive the ingredients. Then look at the recipe for Regular Oobleck. Notice that it says to use about *twice* as much cornstarch as water. (You may find that you need a little more or a little less cornstarch to make a soft dough.) Now make a large quantity of Oobleck. (Remember to add the cornstarch a little at a time and to gently stir it into the water.)

Test this batch of Oobleck as you did the smaller batches.

Take a small amount of Oobleck, and roll it into a ball. (If it's too wet to form a ball, add a little cornstarch.) Test how well the ball bounces from a distance of 20 inches (about 50 centimeters) above the desktop. What happens when you drop the ball from this height?

Take another small amount of Oobleck, and try to stretch it. (You may have to dry it out a bit by adding some extra cornstarch.) What do you observe?

Try to cut the strand of Oobleck with a scissors. What happens?

Put some of the Oobleck in the pie plate. Step back and slap the surface of the Oobleck with the back of a spoon. What do you observe?

Now very slowly and gently press your opened hand into the Oobleck. Does it feel like a solid or a liquid? Write down your observations.

Now quickly force your hand into the Oobleck. Does it behave differently?

3▶ Think and Write   In one paragraph, tell how you tested the Oobleck and what you learned about its properties.

In another paragraph, invent a practical use for the Oobleck.

Explanation   Oobleck is a special kind of fluid. Like all fluids, it takes the shape of its container. It also can be slowly poured from one container to another. Oobleck changes its behavior when you apply a force to it. Pushing, pulling, or striking Oobleck makes it act like a solid. Scientists have a name for any fluid that acts in these very strange ways: It's called a *non-Newtonian fluid*. Isaac Newton was the first scientist to write about this type of fluid, which is how it got its name.

Safety Hints   Don't taste the Oobleck.

Thoroughly wash and dry all your equipment when you're done.

Wash your hands after completing the activity.

Activity 2.4

Who? What? Rosalyn Yalow and Marie Curie

Are you curious about things? Do you ask a lot of questions? If you do, then you think just like a scientist! In this activity, you'll find out some interesting things about a famous scientist who asked a lot of questions—Rosalyn Yalow or Marie Curie. Then you'll share what you learned with others.

1▶ Get Ready

Paper and pencil	Two sheets of poster paper
Ruler	Felt-tipped markers in assorted colors
Resource books and/or	
access to the World Wide Web	

2▶ Do and Wonder

In this activity, you'll do two things: (1) Gather a lot of information about the life and discoveries of a scientist, and (2) create two posters that will show what you learned.

Pick one of these scientists for your research: Rosalyn Yalow or Marie Curie.

To begin, read the brief biography of this scientist in the Explanation section at the end of this activity. Then use resource books and/or the World Wide Web to find more information about your scientist. Take as many notes as you can about the individual and her discoveries.

Now you're ready to create your posters.

Poster 1

Write the scientist's name at the top of the poster, and draw a picture of her below it.

Write down when and where the scientist lived.

List important facts about her life.

Poster 2

At the top of the poster, write the problem or question the scientist worked on.

Draw the kinds of equipment she used to make her discoveries.

If you could ask the scientist two questions about her life and discoveries, what would they be? Write them down.

3▶ Think and Write

Imagine that the scientist you selected was going to visit your classroom. What would you like her to bring to show you and your classmates? What science questions do you think you and your classmates might ask the scientist? What are two things the scientist might tell about her life and work?

Write one or two paragraphs about the scientist's visit to your classroom, describing what she would show and tell you and your classmates.

Explanation

Rosalyn Yalow

Rosalyn Yalow was born in 1921 in the Bronx, New York. She received her Ph.D. in physics from the University of Illinois. Trained as a physicist (a person who studies matter and energy), she began her work by trying to use physics in the field of medicine. Much of her research was done with a medical doctor, Solomon A. Berson. Dr. Yalow and Dr. Berson worked as a team on a project that measured the amount of insulin circulating in the human body. While working on this project, they realized they had made a discovery that would change medical research forever: They had invented a method of measuring *any* substance carried in the body's fluids. This amazing discovery earned Dr. Yalow and Dr. Berson the Nobel Prize in physiology and medicine in 1977.

Marie Curie

Marie Curie was born in Warsaw, Poland, in 1867. Her father, who was a professor of physics and mathematics, encouraged her to be interested in science and to work hard at her studies. She later married a chemist, Pierre Curie, and together with A. H. Becquerel, they worked on experiments with the radioactive element uranium. In 1903, the three scientists were honored with the Nobel Prize for physics. And then, in 1911, Marie Curie received a second Nobel Prize, this time in the field of chemistry, for separating the elements radium and polonium from uranium. Marie Curie is still the only woman to have won two Nobel Prizes. She died in 1934.

When? Where? A Matter-and-Motion Puzzle

Which do you think was invented first: a submarine or a bus? a bow and arrow or ice skates? You'll have to do some very careful thinking about all these things in this activity, in which you'll try to figure out the order in which they were invented. Think of this activity as a puzzle. When you're done solving it, you can have some fun discovering whether adults can solve it, too!

1▶ Get Ready

20 index cards
Pencil
Resource books and/or access to the World Wide Web

2▶ Do and Wonder

Take a look at the following list of inventions. Write the name of each on the front of an index card. Then put the cards in a stack, with the names of the inventions facing upward.

Airplane
Automobile
Bow and arrow
Cannon
Catapult
Electric train
Gunpowder
Horse-drawn bus
Hot air balloon
Ice skates
Jet airplane
Jet engine
Liquid-fueled rocket
Railroad locomotive
Reusable space vehicle
Sailing ship
Space satellite
Steam engine
Submarine
Supersonic jet passenger plane

Now spread the cards out on a table so you can see each one. Think about which item was probably invented first, second, third, and so on. Here are some hints: Think about how early in history humans would have needed each invention. The inventions that use energy such as gas or electricity were probably invented fairly recently. Some of the inventions use ideas that came from previous inventions.

Put the cards in order, from the oldest invention (at your left) to the newest (at your right).

Check your work. Look at the Explanation at the end of this activity. There, you'll find a list of the inventions, including information about when each was invented, who invented it, and what country the inventor was from. The inventions are listed in order from oldest to newest. Use this information to check the order of your index cards. How did you do?

Now it's time to see how well an adult can put the inventions in order! Find an adult family member or someone at school who's willing to try. Mix up the cards, and challenge the adult to put them in order, from oldest to newest. When he or she has finished, check the order of the cards. Then ask the adult if any of the dates surprised him or her. Also ask about what ideas he or she used to put the cards in order.

▶ Think and Write

Write a paragraph about how *you* did in solving the puzzle. Did you have the oldest invention in the correct place? The most recent invention? How about the inventions in between? When you checked the order of your cards against the correct information, what surprised you? Why?

Write another paragraph about the *adult's* success at arranging the cards.

Explanation

For each of the following inventions, see the approximate time it was invented, who invented it, and what country or region the inventor came from:

Bow and arrow (around 30,000 B.C.E.*)—Inventor unknown; probably North Africa

* The abbreviation B.C.E. means "before the common era" (which is equivalent to B.C., or "before Christ").

Sailing ship (4,000–3,000 B.C.E.)—Inventor unknown; probably Egypt and/or Mesopotamia

Catapult (around 400 B.C.E.)—Inventor unknown; probably Greece

Ice skates (around 200)—Inventor unknown; Northern Europe

Gunpowder (around 950)—Inventor unknown; China

Cannon (around 1280)—Inventor unknown; China

Submarine (1624)—Cornelius Drebbel (who was Dutch); England

Horse-drawn bus (1662)—Blaise Pascal and others; France

Steam engine (1765)—James Watt; Scotland

Hot air balloon (1783)—Joseph and Etienne Montgolfier; France

Railroad locomotive (1803)—Richard Trevithick; England

Electric train (1879)—Inventor unknown; Germany

Automobile (1885)—Many inventors in various countries were designing and testing automobiles the same time; Karl Benz of Germany usually gets the credit

Airplane (1903)—Wilbur and Orville Wright; United States

Liquid-fueled rocket (1926)—Robert Goddard; United States

Jet engine (1928)—Frank Whittle; England

Jet airplane (1939)—Ernst Heinkel; Germany

Space satellite (1957)—Designed by many scientists and engineers; Soviet Union

Supersonic jet passenger plane (1976)—The Concorde, designed by many scientists and engineers; England and France

Reusable space vehicle (1981)—The space shuttle, designed by many scientists and engineers; United States

Word Play 2.1

Pyramid Power

How did they do it? That's the question most people ask when they visit the pyramids in Egypt. They wonder how these enormous monuments, rising hundreds of feet above the desert floor, could possibly have been built. It's even more amazing when you consider that the pyramids were constructed 3,000 to 5,000 years ago, long before machines like cranes were invented. In this activity, you'll learn the secret of the pyramids!

1▶ Get Ready

Paper and pencil
Ruler
Resource books and/or access to the World Wide Web

2▶ Do and Wonder

Use the resource books and/or the World Wide Web to gather information about how the Egyptian pyramids were built. Try to discover information about the use of simple machines, such as levers, pulleys, and inclined planes. Take careful notes that you can use later to explain pyramid construction.

Make rough drawings that show how these simple machines were used in building the pyramids.

3▶ Think and Write

Write a paragraph or two about how the pyramid builders solved these problems: How did they carve the enormous stone blocks? How did they move the heavy blocks across the soft desert sand? How did they get the huge blocks to the tops of the pyramids?

Make labeled drawings to go with your explanation.

Explanation   The pyramids are wonderful, mysterious places. One of the
biggest mysteries about them is how people of so long ago
were able to carve the huge stone blocks, move them across
the desert, and then lift them high above the earth's surface.
Of course, thousands and thousands of people worked on the
pyramids for many years. But the ancient Egyptians made
this work easier by coming up with clever ways to use simple
machines.

Word Play 2.2

Match It

In order to share their discoveries with others, scientists must learn
how to use words very carefully. In this activity, you'll have a chance
to see if you know how to use words about matter and motion properly.

1▶ Get Ready   Pencil

2▶ Do and Wonder   Read all of the items in each column. Then draw a line
connecting the word(s) in the first column to the phrase
in the second column that best explains it.

Word(s)	**Explanation**
1. Force	a. Two inclined planes
2. Melting ice cube	b. An inclined plane that winds around in a spiral
3. Machine	c. A machine that has a turning wheel and string, rope, or chain
4. Chemical change	d. Anything that makes work easier
5. Pulley	e. A liquid becoming a gas
6. Freezing	f. The turning point of a lever
7. Boiling water	g. Push or pull
8. Fulcrum	h. A solid becoming a liquid
9. Screw	i. A sheet of burning paper
10. Wedge	j. A liquid becoming a solid

3 ▶ Think and Write

Check your work, using the answers provided in the Explanation.

Make a list of the matches that you missed and study them. To show that you understand what each word means, write a sentence using it.

Explanation

Check your matches using this list:

1. g
2. h
3. d
4. i
5. c
6. j
7. e
8. f
9. b
10. a

Magnificent Math 2.1

Marbles and Surfaces

Press your hands together. Now rub them back and forth quickly. Did you feel your hands get warm? You probably did because *friction*—the force that keeps your palms from just sliding over each other—caused your skin to heat up. In this activity, you'll discover that friction can do more than just heat things up!

1▶ Get Ready

Two plastic rulers
Marble
Book about 2 inches (5 centimeters) thick
Waxed paper 70 inches (178 centimeters) long
Paper toweling 70 inches (178 centimeters) long
Aluminum foil 70 inches (178 centimeters) long
Clear tape
Paper and pencil

2▶ Do and Wonder

You're going to use the rulers and the book to make an inclined plane. The marble will roll down the rulers onto the table top.

To make the inclined plane, put the book on the floor. Place the rulers next to each other, with one end of each on the book and one on the floor. Then push the rulers apart slightly, so the marble can roll between them without falling on the floor.

Predict how far the marble will travel across each of these surfaces: the bare floor, the waxed paper, the foil, and the paper toweling. Make a chart to record your predictions. (Also include a place to record your actual results later.)

Now let the marble roll down the rulers and over each surface. For each different surface, measure how far the marble rolls. To do so, record the distance from the bottom of the inclined plane to each stopping place. Write down your results on the chart. How do your results compare with your predictions?

3▶ Think and Write

Write a few short paragraphs that answer these questions: Were you surprised by any of your results? When you compare how far the marble rolled across the different surfaces, what do you think caused it to slow down and finally stop? What could you have done to make the marble roll a longer distance? How do you think your results would be different if you used a cube-shaped object instead of a marble?

Explanation

No surface is perfectly smooth. Although you probably can't see them, each surface has tiny hills and valleys that get caught in the hills and valleys of any other surface that comes in contact with it. This creates friction. Smooth surfaces have less high valleys and less deep hills than rough surfaces. This means that contact with smooth surfaces creates less friction than contact with rough surfaces. And objects that are round produce less friction when they move, since only a small part of the object ever touches the surface it rolls on.

Magnificent Math 2.2

Bicycle Adventure

If you've done much bike riding, you know that traveling from one place to another on a bicycle can be a lot of fun. But it can also be tiring! In this activity, you'll use a map to find how long it would take to bicycle from one city to another. You'll also compare the speed of traveling on a bicycle with the speeds of other types of transportation.

1▶ Get Ready

Map showing major North American cities
Paper and pencil

2 **Do and Wonder**   Locate these cities on the map:

United States	Canada
Los Angeles, California	Toronto, Ontario
Dallas, Texas	Vancouver, British Columbia
Des Moines, Iowa	Montreal, Quebec
New York, New York	

Using your ruler and the legend on the map, figure out the distance you would travel on a trip between each of these pairs of cities:

Vancouver to Toronto

Toronto to Montreal

Los Angeles to Dallas

Dallas to New York

Suppose that on an average day, you can ride your bicycle for 9 hours and travel 36 miles (about 58 kilometers). What is your speed (in miles per hour or kilometers per hour)?

Imagine that you can ride at that speed every day. How long would it take you to ride from Los Angeles to New York? From Vancouver to Montreal?

Now imagine that you are in a car that travels at a speed of 50 miles per hour (about 80 kilometers per hour) for 9 hours a day. How long would each trip take by car?

Suppose that you are in an airplane that travels 400 miles per hour (about 645 kilometers per hour). How long would each trip take by plane?

3 **Think and Write**   Where does the energy come from that moves the bicycle? The car? The airplane?

What pollution problems are caused by each vehicle?

Explanation   An object's speed is the distance it moves in a certain amount of time—say, 20 miles in 1 hour, or 20 miles per hour. This means that if we know the distance traveled and the time it took to get there, we can find how fast we were going.

Art Connections

Art Connections 2.1

Seashell Mobiles

As you probably know, a mobile is a collection of hanging objects that move as the breeze blows through them. Think of it as a moving sculpture! In this activity, you'll make your own mobile using seashells and twigs.

1➤ Get Ready

Spool of string
Assortment of seashells
Assortment of sticks, branches, and twigs between 1 and 3
   feet (between 30 and 90 centimeters) in length
Flat board of any length
Masking tape
Hand-operated drill with a bit less than ¼ inch
   (about 7 millimeters) in diameter
An adult helper

2➤ Do and Wonder

Tape the seashells to the board to hold them in place. Then use the hand drill to make a hole in each shell.

Find the longest stick or twig. This will be the top of the mobile.

Take two seashells. Thread a length of string through the hole in each shell. Then attach each string to one end of the twig.

Find the balance point of the twig. Tie a string to it; secure it by tying a knot.

Now find the second-longest twig. Thread two more lengths of string through two more seashells, and tie the strings to the ends of the twig. You may also tie some strings at other places on the twig.

Find the balance point of this twig. Attach the string from your first twig to the balance point of the second twig. Secure it by tying a knot.

Find your third-longest twig. Thread several more seashells on strings, and attach them to the twig. Find its balance point, and attach it to the second twig.

Find a place to hang your seashell mobile

3▶ Think and Write

Does where you attach the shells to the twig affect the location of the balance point?

Suppose you notice that one of the twigs is hanging at an angle. What can you do to get it to hang straight? Can you get it to hang straight without adding or removing a seashell?

Explanation

The horizontal sticks in a mobile act like simple levers, so you can think of the places the strings are tied as fulcrums. You can change the balance point by changing either the weight of the balanced objects or their distance from the fulcrum of the horizontal stick.

Safety Hints

Have an adult assist you with this activity.

Remember to tape down the seashells before drilling holes in them.

Of course, never hold a seashell as it's being drilled.

Art Connections 2.2

Colorful Kites

Have you ever flown a kite made from a paper bag? You'll create a colorful paper bag kite in this activity using some very simple materials. And if you live where strong breezes blow, you'll be able to watch your kite travel high in the air.

1▶ Get Ready

Large paper bag (the kind you would get at a supermarket)
Masking tape
Assortment of colored markers
Scissors
Spool of kite string
Single-hole punch

2 **Do and Wonder**

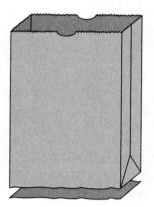

Cut off the bottom of the bag, and throw it away.

Lay the bag flat on the table, so you can work on one side. Use the ruler to measure about one-third down from the center of the top edge of the bag. Make a small X at that spot. Then draw a line from each corner of the bag to the X.

Notice that the surface of the bag now has four triangles drawn on it. Cut off the top and bottom triangles, and throw them away.

Throw away

Throw away

Fold the two remaining triangles back toward opposite sides of the bag. Tape the inside portions of these triangles to the sides of the bag. You should see the tops of two triangles sticking out.

Run a strip of masking tape down the long edge of each triangle, from the top to the bottom of the bag. (This will reinforce the folds in the bag.) Also put a square of masking tape on the point of each triangle. (This will reinforce the part that's sticking out.) Punch a hole through each square of tape about 1 inch (2.54 centimeters) in from the point of the triangle.

Use the ruler to measure and mark about 4 inches (10 centimeters) up from the bottom of the kite. Use the paper punch to make six evenly spaced holes straight across the bottom. (These are vents to let some trapped air out when the kite flies.)

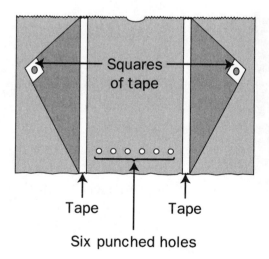

Squares of tape

Tape   Tape

Six punched holes

Cut a length of string about 40 inches (1 meter) long. Thread one end through each wing hole, and tie a knot to secure it.

Gently pull up on the string connected to the kite to find its center point. Connect this point to your spool of string by tying another knot. Be sure it's secure!

Use colored markers to decorate your kite. Make it special so you'll be able to tell your kite from all the others when they're up in the sky!

To make your kite fly more upright, tie some short strings with ribbons or small pieces of construction paper to the vent holes.

Go outside and fly your kite!

3▶ Think and Write   In a short paragraph, explain why the kite rises and then stays in the air.

Explanation   Many forces affect how well a kite flies. Air moving over its top and bottom surfaces produce *lift*, which moves the kite upward. At the same time, gravity pulls the kite down toward the earth. Changes in a kite's weight and shape, whether it has a tail, and how strong the wind is blowing will also affect how well your kite will fly.

Amazing but True!
BRAINSTRETCHERS

2.1 Where is Einstein's brain?

Although Albert Einstein's body was cremated, his brain is in Wichita, Kansas. Why, you might ask? Well, after Einstein died in 1955, the doctor who did the autopsy removed the brain and placed it in a jar containing a liquid that stops tissue from decaying. After all, this was the brain of a great genius! People who have observed Einstein's brain, however, have said that it looks pretty much like any other brain that's been in a jar for about 50 years!

2.2   Why was Einstein so famous?

Albert Einstein might very well have been the most brilliant thinker of the twentieth century. Although many of his ideas shocked people, who thought they couldn't *possibly* be true, most have been proven correct. One of the most amazing things Einstein discovered was that matter and energy are the same thing, which means that matter can be changed into energy and energy into matter. Einstein also discovered that empty space is curved near objects that have a lot of mass. That idea might not make sense to you or me, but it did to Einstein, who proved it was correct. If during your life, you come up with ideas that are as brilliant as Einstein's and if you are very, very lucky, your brain might also wind up in a jar in Wichita, Kansas!

2.3   What are springs, and how do they work?

Springs are coils of metal used inside things like bicycle seats, car seats, sofa cushions, and mattresses to provide cushioning or support. Springs provide this effect because whether they are stretched out or pushed down, the coils return to their starting position. When you stretch a spring, you are forcing the molecules of the metal apart from one another. When you let go of the stretched-out spring, the attraction of the molecules for one another pulls the spring back together. Imagine having a mattress with no springs inside it. When you lay down on it, you would sink right in, and when you got up, you would see the shape of your body molded into the mattress top!

2.4   Is there really such a thing as a jumping bean?

Absolutely! If you held a small pile of jumping beans in your hand and watched them for awhile, you would see them move around a bit. The reason the beans jump is that the larval stage of a moth lives inside each one. When the beans are placed in a warm place, the larvae begin to move around. And as they do, the beans move.

2.5   If you ride a bicycle really fast on a smooth road and suddenly jam on the brakes, you might get thrown over the handlebars. Why don't you just stop along with the bicycle?

Isaac Newton, a famous scientist, figured this out a few hundred years ago, long before the bicycle was ever invented. Newton discovered that an object that's moving at a constant speed in a certain direction will keep moving at that speed and in that direction until a force acts on it—for instance, something that makes it change direction or stop. Suppose you are on your bicycle, riding down the sidewalk at a constant speed. Both you and your bicycle are moving in the same direction and at the same speed.

When you put on the brakes, it applies a stopping force just on the *bicycle.* You're not really connected to the bicycle; you're just sitting on it. So even though the bicycle will be stopping, your body will keep going forward. And if you're going fast enough when you hit the brakes, your body will be thrown forward over the handlebars.

2.6   When a horse runs, does it ever get all four feet off the ground at the same time?

People have argued about this question for a very long time! The answer was finally learned when motion pictures, or movies, were invented. Looking at slow motion pictures of a galloping horse showed that the answer is yes. A gallop follows a pattern in which a horse first has three, then two, then one, and finally all four feet off the ground. This pattern repeats again and again. So you could say that a horse at full gallop is actually flying for part of the time!

2.7   Why are golf balls made with bumps all over them? Wouldn't they travel further if they were smooth?

Golf balls are covered with tiny bumps, called *dimples,* for two reasons. First, the dimples tend to catch and hold onto small amounts of air, which smoothes out the path of the ball as it moves through the air. The dimples also make it easy for the ball to develop a backspin—in other words, a spin opposite to the direction the ball is moving. This backspin creates an area of low pressure on top of the ball. Because the air pressure is higher everywhere else around the ball, it's pushed upward. This means that the ball will stay in the air a long time. So if you see golfers washing their golf balls before or during a tournament, don't think they're just being very neat and clean. They're removing the dirt from the dimples to make sure their balls will travel as far as possible.

2.8   How does a pitcher throw a curve ball in baseball?

In fact, there are two kinds of curve balls. Most pitchers throw a curve that moves downward. To do so, they throw the ball forward with topspin, which means the ball spins clockwise when you look at it from the right-hand side. When the ball spins like this, the stitches on the surface of the ball carry a little layer of air around them. This spinning layer of air causes lower air pressure on the bottom of the ball, making the ball dive. To throw the ball so that it also has a slight sideways curve, the pitcher has to release it from the right, not from his or her usual overhead position. Pitchers who throw curve balls are really clever!

2.9   Who were the first humans to fly?

If you think it was the Wright brothers, you're wrong! The first humans to fly were some Frenchmen, the Montgolfier brothers. In 1783, they managed to get themselves off the ground by climbing into a basket attached to the bottom of a hot air balloon. They made it across the English Channel, which separates France and England, without getting wet in 1785. (The Wright brothers didn't make their first flight until 1903. Read on!)

2.10   How long was the first trip in an airplane?

Count to 12 slowly. Now you know how long the first trip in an airplane was. That's right. The first trip—which was by Orville Wright on December 17, 1903, in Kitty Hawk, North Carolina—took exactly 12 seconds and traveled only 120 feet (about 37 meters). Orville's brother Wilbur stayed on the ground and watched. It was easy for him to keep track of his brother's flight because the airplane never got higher than 12 feet (less than 4 meters) off the ground!

2.11   Airplanes are much more dense than air, so why don't they fall out of the sky?

Airplanes stay in the air because of the shape of their wings. If you took a slice out of a wing, you'd see that the bottom of the slice is flat and the top is curved. As the wing moves, the air traveling over its curved top travels further than the air moving over its flat bottom. However, the air moving over the top and bottom get to the back of the wing at the same time, which means the air moving over the top must be going faster. This creates a low-pressure area on top of the wing and a high-pressure area under the wing, which pushes the wing straight up. The force that pushes up is called *lift*. Pilots can change the lift by adjusting how the air flows over the wings of the airplane. For instance, they can change the direction in which the front of the wing hits the air by moving the elevators (flaps at the back edge of the horizontal tail section) up or down. Pilots also can do some things that actually change the shape of the wings while the plane is in the air. For example, by adjusting the wing flaps (ailerons), they can make the path that air travels over the top of the wing longer or shorter, producing more or less lift.

2.12   If lift is caused by an airplane's wings, then why are engines needed?

Engines turn the propellers, which move air backward, causing a forward force on the airplane called *thrust*. The thrust moves the plane—and, of course, the wings attached to it—straight ahead. As long as the plane is moving, air is traveling over its wings. And the movement of the wings through the air produces lift on the wings' top surface.

2.13   Why don't jet planes have propellers?

Jet planes don't need propellers. They get their thrust by burning fuel and oxygen from the air to produce hot gases. The gases shoot out the back of each engine with a great deal of force. This moves the plane forward because an equal and opposite force is created by the force of the gases going backward. This idea of "equal and opposite" has actually been around for hundreds of years. Isaac Newton developed a scientific law that says that for every action, there is an equal and opposite reaction. For a jet plane, that reaction is thrust, which moves the plane forward.

2.14   Who invented the wheel?

The wheel was invented so long ago that no one really knows who came up with the idea. Archaeologists know that wheels were in use at least 5,000 years ago, which was long before the first person jumped on a skateboard! But then and now, the ability of a wheel to roll made it useful in moving things from place to place. Imagine how hard it would be to cruise down a hill if your skateboard didn't have wheels. You certainly wouldn't get very far!

2.15   How did the ancient Egyptians move those enormous blocks of stone to the tops of the pyramids they were building?

Of course, no one knows for certain, but many experts think the ancient Egyptians built ramps up to and around the pyramids and slid the huge blocks of stone to their tops. A ramp has the exact shape as a simple machine you probably know about: an inclined plane. Somehow, the Egyptian pyramid builders must have been able to get the blocks of stone on wooden sleds or possibly logs that would roll. Doing this, they were able to pull and push each stone up the ramp. As the pyramid became taller, the workers would build new ramps to reach the new height.

2.16   What would you use to stick blocks of ice together?

Ig-glue.

2.17   How can you make a hamburger roll?

First, find a very smooth surface. Then put the edge of the hamburger on the surface and push it forward very gently.

2.18   What shellfish makes the best weight lifter?

Mussels.

Chapter 3
The Energies

 Activities

Spectacular Spectrums   [PS 3]

Weird Lenses   [PS 3]

Racing Ice Cubes   [PS 3]

Whisper Tubes: The Sound Bouncers   [PS 6]

Who? What? Maria Goeppert-Mayer
and Chen Ning Yang   [HNS 2]

When? Where? An Energy Puzzle   [HNS 3]

 Word Play

The Battery-Powered Skateboard
and Much More   [PS 6]

Word Wonders   [PS 6]

 Magnificent Math

Measuring Magnet Power   [PS 3]

Smart Battery Shopping   [PS 3]

 Art Connections

Rainbows Outside *and* Inside   [PS 3]

Solar Energy Prints   [PS 3]

 **Amazing but True!
Brainstretchers**   [PS 1–6]

Activities

Spectacular Spectrums

Light is stranger than you might think. Light from the sun, a flashlight, or almost any other source consists of many different colors—but you usually can't see them. In this activity, you'll experiment with ways to break up ordinary light to make its invisible colors visible!

1▶ Get Ready

Flashlight (A MAG-LITE, an EXCELL, or another brand of focused-beam flashlight will work best, but others will work, too.)
Audiocassette case made of clear plastic
Clear plastic cup or glass
Water
Two sheets of white paper
Transparent tape
Large assortment of colored markers or crayons
Stack of books taller than flashlight
Small table
Partner

2▶ Do and Wonder

In this activity, you'll try to break apart white light. To do that, you'll aim a beam of light through water in one container and then another and try to capture the spectrum each produces on a sheet of white paper. Your partner will use colored markers or crayons to draw each spectrum.

Shining Light through a Glass Containing Water

Move the table so it's against the wall. Then arrange the books on the table so they're stacked flat against the wall.

Fill the glass about three-fourths full with water. Set it on top of the stack of books so part of the glass is over the edge.

Darken the room.

Your partner should be prepared to tape a sheet of white paper to the wall where the spectrum is produced.

Turn on the flashlight and hold it close to the part of the glass that extends over the edge of the book stack. Move the flashlight back and forth and up and down until you see a pattern of color somewhere on the wall or floor. (The pattern won't be very large and will probably be at the edge of a circle of white light.)

Your partner should tape the paper on the wall where the pattern appears. Then he or she should take a minute to memorize the colors in the spectrum and how they're arranged.

When your partner is ready to draw, turn the lights back on. After he or she has finished drawing, turn the lights off again and check the pattern and colors. Do this a few times to make sure the drawing of the spectrum matches what you see on the wall.

Shining Light through an Audiocassette Case Containing Water

You'll be using only the top part of the case (that is, the part the cassette slides into). Remove all parts of the label on the case. Hold the case upright, so that the small enclosed part is at the bottom, and carefully add water until it's almost filled.

Darken the room again.

Your partner should once again be ready to tape a piece of white paper on the wall where the spectrum appears.

Pick up the audiocassette case and move it near the wall. Turn on the flashlight and hold it near the case, aiming the light into the water. As you did earlier, move the flashlight up and down, back and forth, and over and under the container until you see a spectrum somewhere on the wall or floor. It will be a small patch of colors. (Hint: Be sure to look in back of you as you search!)

When you find the spectrum, give your partner a little time to study and memorize it. Then turn the lights back on, and have him or her draw the pattern using the colored markers or crayons. Turn off the lights and check the spectrum a few times to make sure the drawing matches the pattern on the wall.

3▶ Think and Write   Study the drawings of the spectrums. In a short paragraph, describe how you could use what you learned in this activity to invent a way of making white light by putting the colors back together. Imagine that you have as much equipment as you need! Make a labeled drawing to show how your idea would work.

Explanation   White light is actually a mixture of many different colors, but they aren't visible until the light is broken up. You can do this with a triangular piece of glass called a *prism* or any clear container of water. The light that leaves the prism or water forms a pattern of colors called a *spectrum*.

Activity 3.2

Weird Lenses

Did you know each of your eyes has a lens in it? The lens focuses light rays to form images on your retina. Cameras, magnifying glasses, telescopes, and microscopes also contain lenses made of plastic or glass. In this activity, you'll make some lenses out of something that might surprise you—water!

1▶ Get Ready

Hand lens (magnifying glass)
Single-hole punch
Index card
Transparent tape (should be as clear as glass)
Small amounts ("pinches") of salt, pepper, and sand
Medicine dropper
Water
Clear, empty plastic soda bottle with cap
Sheet of newspaper
Paper and pencil
Ruler

2▶ Do and Wonder

You'll make and use two different lenses: One will be a drop of water, and the other will be a plastic soda bottle filled with water.

Water Drop Lens

Punch a hole in the center of the index card. Place a small strip of clear tape over the hole. (The tape must be flat against the card.)

Use the medicine dropper to put one small drop of water on the tape over the hole.

Look at the drop of water from the side, and draw its shape.

Carefully move the index card so it's close to the newspaper. Find a letter *e* somewhere in the print of the newspaper. Hold your water drop lens above the *e,* and move it toward and away from your eye until the letter is in focus. Draw what you see.

Following the same steps, use the lens to look at the grains of salt, sand, and pepper.

Hold your lens over a photograph or drawing in the newspaper. Move the lens up and down. Write down your observations.

Change the size and shape of your lens by carefully adding another drop or two of water. Draw its new shape, and then experiment with it to see how well it works.

Soda Bottle Lens

Fill the soda bottle completely with water, and screw the cap on it.

Hold the bottle sideways, with one hand at each end. Move it up and down over the newspaper. Look through the bottle at the print. What do you observe? Now put the bottle over a headline or any large print on the page. Does the soda bottle act as a lens? Move the bottle up and down. Does the image you see change? By moving the bottle, can you get the image to look upside down?

Hand Lens (Magnifying Glass)

Try the same experiments you did with the water drop and the soda bottle using your hand lens.

3▶ Think and Write

Which of your three lenses worked the best?

Each of the lenses you used was thicker at the center than at the edges. These lenses are all *convex* lenses. Think of a way to make a water lens that's *thinner* at the center than at the edges. (Hint: If a bottle of water had an air bubble in it and you looked through it at something, what would be the shape of the *water* lens you were looking through?)

Try making this kind of lens and experiment with it. Describe your results.

Explanation

Anything that can be used to bend light is a *lens*. The bending of light by a lens is called *refraction* (ree-frak-shun). There are two types of simple lenses: concave and convex. Concave lenses spread light beams apart, and convex lenses bring light beams together.

Activity 3.3

Racing Ice Cubes

Imagine that it's pitch black outside! You're a scientist, riding in
a small plane that's cruising high above a jungle pond. You're
watching tigers in the dark by using equipment that turns an
invisible form of heat energy called *infrared radiation* into light.
All living things send out this radiation, so you can use it to follow
the tigers. You'll do some tests in this activity to discover ways to
stop the flow of heat energy from place to place.

1▶ Get Ready

Four ice cubes (all about the same size)
Four disposable paper or plastic dishes (all the same color)
Three pieces of cloth, each large enough to cover one dish
    (some dark colored, some light colored)
Sheet of aluminum foil large enough to cover one dish
Clock or watch
Access to a sunny window
Paper and pencil

2▶ Do and Wonder

Move the table so rays of sunlight shine directly on it. Then
arrange the plates on the table so they all receive sunlight.

Put an ice cube in the middle of each plate. Quickly cover three
of the plates with pieces of cloth and the fourth one with foil.

Write down the time. Predict which ice cube will be completely
melted in the shortest amount of time.

Observe and quickly re-cover each ice cube every 2 minutes.
Write down the time at which each ice cube is completely melted.

3▶ Think and Write

In a short paragraph, compare your results with your predictions.

Write a few hypotheses that might explain the results you
observed.

Explanation

Heat energy can move from place to place as waves of infrared radiation. Even though it's invisible to our eyes, beams
of sunlight contain some infrared radiation. When it strikes
a surface, some of the heat energy is reflected and some is
absorbed. Absorbing this energy heats up the material. In this
activity, some infrared radiation traveled through each piece of
cloth or foil and was absorbed by the ice cube, causing it to melt.
(Of course, heat energy in the air also caused some melting.)

Whisper Tubes: The Sound Bouncers

Did you ever whisper a secret in someone's ear? If you did, you were aiming sound waves toward his or her eardrum. In this activity, you'll make some devices that will let you whisper to someone without speaking into his or her ear!

1 ▶ Get Ready

Four cardboard tubes from rolls of paper towels
Masking tape
Cookie sheet
Book
Table near a wall
Paper and pencil
Partner

2 ▶ Do and Wonder

First make two whisper tubes. To make each, put the ends of two cardboard tubes together and tape them very tightly. Use plenty of tape to do this so the tubes don't bend or sag in the middle.

Move the table against a wall. Put the cookie sheet on the table so it's vertical and pressed right against the wall. Use the book to hold the cookie sheet in this position.

Next you'll be aiming sound waves toward the cookie sheet. Lay both whisper tubes side by side on the table, so they're pointing toward the cookie sheet. Then move together the ends of the tubes nearest the cookie sheet, forming a V shape. The bottom of the V should be about 1 inch (2.5 centimeters) from the cookie sheet.

Have your partner put his or her ear up to the open end of one tube while you whisper into the open end of the other tube. Adjust the positions of the tubes until your partner can hear your whispers coming from the tube. Try softly whistling into one tube while your partner listens from the other.

Switch roles and repeat the experiment.

Make a labeled diagram that shows the source of the sound waves and the path they took from one whisper tube to the other.

3► Think and Write   Write a hypothesis that explains echoes. Here are some hints to help you: An echo needs a solid, flat surface for the sound waves to bounce off. If you're standing far away from a wall and yell toward the wall, you'll hear the sound made in your own voice box *immediately*.

Explanation   Sound waves carry energy from one place to another. When sound waves hit a surface, they bounce off it. The direction they come from determines the direction they will bounce. Using a whisper tube, you aimed sound waves at a reflecting surface—the cookie sheet. If you put the tube you whispered into in the right place, the sound waves traveled through your tube, bounced off the cookie sheet, and entered your partner's tube. That's how he or she was able to hear you!

Activity 3.5

Who? What? Maria Goeppert-Mayer and Chen Ning Yang

Individual scientists are curious about a lot of different things! The scientist you'll learn about in this activity—Maria Goeppert-Mayer or Chen Ning Yang—studied the energies needed to hold the parts of an atom's nucleus together and the particles and energy released when the nucleus breaks apart. Both of these scientists were so successful that they won Nobel Prizes for their work.

1▶ Get Ready

Paper and pencil   Two sheets of poster paper
Ruler   Felt-tipped markers in assorted colors
Resource books and/or
    access to the World Wide Web

2▶ Do and Wonder

In this activity, you'll do two things: (1) Gather a lot of information about the life and discoveries of a scientist, and (2) create two posters that will show what you learned.

Pick one of these scientists for your research: Maria Goeppert-Mayer or Chen Ning Yang.

To begin, read the brief biography of this scientist in the Explanation section at the end of this activity. Then use resource books and/or the World Wide Web to find more information about your scientist. Take as many notes as you can about the individual and his or her discoveries.

Now you're ready to create your posters.

Poster 1

Write the scientist's name at the top of the poster, and draw a picture of him or her below it.

Write down when and where the scientist lived.

List important facts about his or her life.

Poster 2

At the top of the poster, write the problem or question the scientist worked on.

Draw the kinds of equipment he or she used to make his or her discoveries.

If you could ask the scientist two questions about his or her life and discoveries, what would they be? Write them down.

3→ Think and Write

Imagine that the scientist you selected was going to visit your classroom. What would you like him or her to bring to show you and your classmates? What science questions do you think you and your classmates might ask the scientist? What are two things the scientist might tell about his or her life and work?

Write one or two paragraphs about the scientist's visit to your classroom, describing what he or she would show and tell you and your classmates.

Explanation

Maria Goeppert-Mayer

Maria Goeppert-Mayer was born in Germany in 1906, and her interest in science began when she was quite young. She learned about fossils and plants by taking walks with her father, who encouraged her to study hard and have a career. Maria Goeppert-Mayer did both of those things, proving her wonderful abilities in mathematics and physics. She moved to the United States in 1930 and taught these subjects at several famous universities. She also carried out research that explained what held together the neutrons and protons in the nucleus of an atom. In 1963, she and two other physicists, H. D. Jensen and E. P. Wigner, were awarded the Nobel Prize in physics for their work on this topic. Maria Goeppert-Mayer died in 1972.

Chen Ning Yang

Chen Ning Yang studied the form of energy that holds together the parts of the nucleus of an atom along with the energy needed to break apart the nucleus and the particles that leave it. He was born in Hefei, China, in 1922 and received some of his education in China. However, his advanced studies were done at the University of Chicago, where he also taught for awhile. Eventually, he was invited to do research at the Institute for Advanced Study in Princeton, New Jersey. Later in his career, he was awarded the position of Albert Einstein Professor of Physics at the State University of New York. Chen Ning Yang's study with another professor, Tsung Dao Lee, about the energy and behavior of tiny particles released from the nucleus, was so important that they were awarded the Nobel Prize in physics in 1957.

Activity 3.6

When? Where?
An Energy Puzzle

Have you used a telephone today? Did you watch any television yesterday? If so, you have used energy of one kind or another. You might think that these energy-using inventions were all created at about the same time, but they weren't. In this puzzle, you'll put a list of these and other inventions in the order in which they were invented.

1▶ Get Ready

15 index cards
Pencil
Resource books and/or access to the World Wide Web

2▶ Do and Wonder

Take a look at the following list of inventions. Write the name of each on the front of an index card. Then put the cards in a stack, with the names of the inventions facing upward.

Battery	Gas engine
Black-and-white television	Gas stove
Color television	Lightning rod
Dynamite	Magnetic compass
Electric light bulb	Magnifying glass
(first successful)	Telephone
Electric motor	Thermometer
Eyeglasses	35 mm camera

Now spread the cards out on a table so you can see each one. Think about which item was probably invented first, second, third, and so on. Here are some hints: Think about how early in history humans would have needed each invention. The inventions that use energy such as gas or electricity were probably invented fairly recently. Some of the inventions use ideas that came from previous inventions.

Put the cards in order, from the oldest invention (at your left) to the newest (at your right).

Look at the Explanation at the end of this activity. There, you'll find a list of the inventions in order, including information about when each was invented, who invented it, and what country the inventor was from. Use this information to check the order of your index cards. How did you do?

Now it's time to see how well an adult can put the inventions in order! Find an adult family member or someone at school who's willing to try. Mix up the cards, and challenge the adult to put them in order, from oldest to newest. When he or she has finished, check the order of the cards. Then ask the adult if any of the dates surprised him or her. Also ask about what ideas he or she used to put the cards in order.

3▸ Think and Write

Write a paragraph about how *you* did in solving the puzzle. Did you have the oldest invention in the correct place? The most recent invention? How about the inventions in between? When you checked the order of your cards against the correct information, what surprised you? Why?

Write another paragraph about the *adult's* success at arranging the cards.

Explanation

For each of the following inventions, see the approximate time it was invented, who invented it, and what country or region the inventor came from:

Magnetic compass (1090)—Inventor unknown; probably China or Arabia

Magnifying glass (1200)—Bishop Robert Grosseteste; England

Eyeglasses (1286)—Inventor unknown; probably Italy

Thermometer (1592)—Galileo Galilei; Italy

Battery (1800)—Alessandro Volta; Italy

Gas stove (1802)—Zachaus Andreas Winzler; Austria

Electric motor (1821)—Michael Faraday; England

Dynamite (1865–67)—Alfred Nobel; Sweden

Lightning rod (1752)—Benjamin Franklin; Colonial United States

Telephone (1876)—Alexander Graham Bell; United States

Electric light bulb (1879)—Thomas Edison; United States

Gasoline engine (1884)—Gottleib Daimler; Germany

35 mm camera (1914)—Various inventors in various countries

Black-and-white television (1926)—John Logie Baird; Scotland

Color television (1928)—John Logie Baird; Scotland

Word Play

Word Play 3.1

The Battery-Powered Skateboard and Much More

Did you brush your teeth this morning? If so, what did you use: a regular toothbrush? an electric toothbrush? or maybe one of the new sonic-type gadgets? What do you think your *grandparents* used when they were your age? Better yet, what do you think your *grandchildren* will use? In this activity, you'll use your imagination to think, design, and write about some inventions your children or grandchildren might someday use. Each invention will be a type of transportation—something that will take people from place to place.

1▶ Get Ready

Paper and pencil
Resource books and/or access to the World Wide Web

2▶ Do and Wonder

Here's a list of four vehicles that could move you from place to place (Note that none of them has been invented yet!):

Battery-powered skateboard
Sound-powered bicycle
Heat-powered automobile
Nuclear-powered airplane

Pick any two of these vehicles, and do some research to find out about the energy they use. Try to discover what you would need to do to change the type of energy and actually make the vehicle move.

Use what you've learned to invent two vehicles. Make a drawing of each, labeling its parts. (Important: You may add devices to your invention that can change one form of energy to another.)

3▶ Think and Write   Write one or two paragraphs under each drawing that explain how your invention works. Be sure to tell how the energy is changed so that it moves the vehicle. (For example, how is sound energy changed in the bicycle so it pushes the bicycle forward?)

Explanation   *Energy* is any force that's able to move things. Many of the devices we depend on each day use different types of energy. In this activity, you had a chance to put what you know about energy to work by inventing types of transportation that don't yet exist. Perhaps someday, you'll see an invention just like yours actually working!

Word Play 3.2

Word Wonders

For each of the mystery words in this puzzle, you'll find two kinds of clues: a sentence that tells something about the word and a few of the letters in the word already filled in. To solve the puzzle, you'll need to fill in the rest. To help you do that, here's one more hint: All of the puzzle words are words about *energy!* Good luck!

1▶ Get Ready   Paper and pencil

2▶ Do and Wonder   Using the hints provided, figure out each puzzle word and write in the missing letters in the right-hand column.

Sentence Hints	Puzzle Words
1. We will probably use up the world's supply of this fuel before we run out of coal.	_ _ T R _ _ _ _ M
2. This fuel is made by mixing 90% unleaded gasoline and 10% ethyl alcohol.	_ _ S O _ O L
3. Power plants that use nuclear energy to produce electricity need this as their fuel.	_ R _ N _ U _

Sentence Hints	**Puzzle Words**
4. Making throwaway containers of paper, glass, and plastics uses up raw materials and also needs this.	_ N _ R G _
5. The remains of small ocean creatures sometimes get trapped in the muddy bottom of the ocean floor and form this fuel.	_ _ T R _ _ _ U _
6. The buried, decayed remains of plants and animals in ancient swamps sometimes form this fuel.	_ O _ _
7. Oil, coal, and gas are all this type of fuel.	_ O _ _ I L
8. This heat energy comes from the earth's crust and can be used to heat water and produce electricity.	_ _ _ T H E R _ A L
9. Energy from nuclear power plants is produced by this process.	_ I S S _ _ N
10. People who use this type of energy may have problems during the night and on cloudy days.	_ _ L _ R
11. We have plenty of this fuel.	_ _ A _
12. This source of energy is made from oil.	G _ _ _ L I _ E
13. If you wanted to create a cheap and clean way of producing electricity, you might consider using one of these.	_ _ N D _ I L _

3▶ Think and Write   Check your answers using the list in the Explanation section. For each word you missed, write a sentence using it.

Explanation   Here are the answers:

(1) PETROLEUM   (8) GEOTHERMAL
(2) GASOHOL   (9) FISSION
(3) URANIUM   (10) SOLAR
(4) ENERGY   (11) COAL
(5) PETROLEUM   (12) GASOLINE
(6) COAL   (13) WINDMILL
(7) FOSSIL

Magnificent Math 3.1

Measuring Magnet Power

If you've ever visited a recycling plant, you've probably seen electromagnets. Not only are they much bigger than the horseshoe and bar magnets you've used at school, but they also can be turned on and off! In this activity, you'll make an electromagnet that will let you pick up and drop things.

1▶ Get Ready

Iron nail (Get this in a hardware store; ask the clerk for help, since most of the nails in the store will be steel.)
Piece of insulated copper wire 20 inches long (about 50 centimeters)

Wire strippers	Small box of paper clips
Dry cell (6 volt)	Graph paper and pencil

2▶ Do and Wonder

Have an adult use the wire strippers to remove about 1 inch (2.54 centimeters) of insulation from each end of the wire.

Next you're going to wrap the wire around the nail. First find the midpoint of the wire by folding it in half. Then place the nail at the midpoint, with the wire about halfway down the length of the nail. With each section of wire (that is, above and below the midpoint), make three wraps around the nail. These wrappings or coils should be close together.

Make a small curl at one end of the copper wire, and attach it to one of the terminals on the dry cell.

Put one of the paper clips on the table. Bring the pointed end of the nail near the paper clip. Touch the free end of the copper wire to the other terminal, and hold it there for no more than 2 seconds. What do you observe?

Predict how many paper clips the nail can pick up. Test your hypothesis by touching the free end of the wire to the terminal for just 2 seconds.

Prepare a graph with the labels "Number of Paper Clips" along the vertical axis and "Number of Wire Turns" along the horizontal axis.

Now test your magnet to see how many clips it can pick up. Each time, increase the number of wire turns around the nail.

Make a prediction about the number of clips your magnet will pick up if you add five turns at once. Put an X on your graph at the spot that shows your prediction.

3▸ Think and Write   Write a short paragraph that tells the results of your experiment.

Explain why an electromagnet is more useful than a permanent magnet.

Explanation   When electricity flows through a wire, the space around the wire starts to act as a magnet. In this activity, you made a temporary magnet. By wrapping the wire around the iron nail more and more times, you increased the power of the electromagnet. The magnet loses its magnetism when the electricity is cut off.

Magnificent Math 3.2

Smart Battery Shopping

There are a lot of commercials on television (some, very silly!) that claim certain brands of batteries last the longest. But which brand really *does* last the longest? Since you probably buy batteries for electronic games, radios, tape players, and CD players, you should know. This activity will help you find out.

1▸ Get Ready   Three new "D" cell batteries, each from a different company (Note that all companies sell different quality levels of batteries, such as regular, heavy duty, and alkaline. You should get the same type of battery for each brand.)
Three pieces of insulated wire, each 6 inches long (15 centimeters)
Three new flashlight bulbs   Graph paper and pencil
Cellophane tape

2▶ Do and Wonder

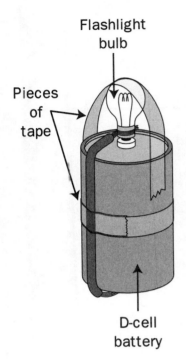

Flashlight bulb

Pieces of tape

D-cell battery

Create a graph that shows the prices of the different brands of batteries. Label the vertical axis "Price," and show units from 10¢ to $3. Label the horizontal axis "Battery Brand," and write the three brand names of batteries along it (with equal space between the names). Record the price of each battery on the graph.

Prepare another graph to record data about battery life. Label the vertical axis "Minutes," and show units from 0 to at least 200. Label the horizontal axis "Battery Brand," and write the three brand names of batteries along it (as you did for the first graph). Now put this graph aside for awhile.

Build three battery testers like the one shown. (Don't light any of the bulbs until you've made all the testers.)

When you're ready to begin testing the batteries, write down the starting time.

Look at your testers every few minutes. Pay close attention when you notice that one or more of the bulbs is starting to dim. Write down the time each bulb completely stops giving off light.

Record your results on the graph.

3▶ Think and Write

In a few sentences, tell what you observed in testing the batteries. Which battery lasted the longest?

Now do some thinking about which battery is really the best *value*. In other words, consider not just how long each battery lasted but how much it cost, too. Which battery cost the least for each minute it kept the bulb lit? (Hint: To find this out, divide the number of minutes each bulb was lit into the price of the battery.)

Explanation

The strength of a battery depends on how well it was made and the types of chemicals used to make it. To find the best buy, you need to know the price of the battery and how long it will work.

Safety Hint

When the current from a battery passes through a wire, the wire may heat up and be hot to touch. Be sure to use insulated wire, which has a protective coating.

Art Connections

Art Connections 3.1

Rainbows Outside and Inside

You can usually find a rainbow outside, up in the sky, when the sun shines during or after a rainstorm. You'll make and observe your own rainbows in this activity— outside *and* inside!

1 ▶ Get Ready

Outside Rainbow
Garden hose with nozzle attached to outdoor faucet
Sunny day

Inside Rainbow

Clear drinking glass
Water
Sheet of white paper
Window that gets direct sunlight

2 ▶ Do and Wonder

Outside Rainbow

Go outside early in the morning or late in the afternoon on a day when the sun is shining. (Choose a time when the sun is low in the sky.)

Turn on the faucet to send water to the hose. Adjust the nozzle on the hose so the water comes out in a fine spray.

Stand with your back to the sun, and spray the water in front of you. You should see the colors of the rainbow in the spray. What colors do you see?

Inside Rainbow

Fill the glass almost to the top with water.

Put the glass on the window ledge. Carefully position the glass so a small part of it extends over the ledge and into the room.

Put the paper on the floor where you think the rainbow will form.

Adjust the position of the glass so the sunlight shines through it.

You should see patches of light on the paper that are the same colors you would see in a rainbow. What colors do you see?

3▶ Think and Write   What do you think causes a rainbow to appear during or after a rainstorm?

Explanation   The colors we see in a rainbow come from sunlight that breaks up as it passes through and bends in water droplets. The colors we would expect to see (from top to bottom) are red, orange, yellow, green, blue, indigo, and violet.

Art Connections 3.2

Solar Energy Prints

The sun's energy can do many things, one of which is to cause chemical changes. In this activity, you'll use Sunprint paper to capture the sun's energy and create images of some natural objects.

1▶ Get Ready   Sunprint paper*
Rectangular pan filled with water
Roll of clear tape
Collection of small objects (such as leaves, pebbles, small twigs, and coins)
Sheet of clear plastic (A transparency will work.)
Sheet of cardboard at least 1 foot (about 30 cm) on the longest edge
Sunny day

*You can get this as part of the Sunprint Kit (which costs $3 or $4) at a well-stocked toystore, science museum store, or any Nature Company Store. You can also order this paper from the Lawrence Hall of Science, University of California at Berkeley, Berkeley, CA 94720, (415) 642-1016.

2▶ Do and Wonder

Begin indoors. Put a sheet of Sunprint paper on the cardboard, with the blue side facing up.

Lay one or more leaves or other small objects on the paper. Then cover the entire paper with the clear plastic sheet. Tape down the corners to keep the plastic flat.

Now take your materials outside, and expose them to sunlight until the paper almost turns white. (Depending on the amount of sunlight, this should take 1 to 5 minutes.)

Take the materials inside again, and quickly remove the plastic and the objects from the Sunprint paper.

Rinse the paper in the pan of water for 1 minute. Flatten it out to dry. What do you see on the paper?

Try the experiment again, this time exposing the Sunprint paper to sunlight for a longer or shorter time.

3▶ Think and Write

In one paragraph, describe two or three ideas you have for other experiments using Sunprint paper. (Here are some hints: Use indoor lighting. Use different colors of light. Put sunscreen on the clear plastic.)

Explanation

The ultraviolet rays that are part of sunlight cause chemical reactions on those parts of the Sunprint paper that aren't exposed to the light. This happens because the paper contains a chemical that absorbs ultraviolet light and changes the blue color to white. By placing leaves and other opaque objects on the paper, you stop sunlight from reaching those parts of the paper, so they stay blue.

Amazing but True!
BRAINSTRETCHERS

3.1 What makes popcorn pop?

3.2 When I banged my knee into a wall, a friend gave me a "cold pack" that she found in a first aid kit. But before giving it to me, she twisted the pack, which made it get really cold. How could something that was at room temperature suddenly get so cold?

3.3 A friend of mine gets aches and pains in her ankles, so she takes a "hot pack" with her when she goes for long bike rides. How does the pack get hot when she needs to use it?

3.4 If it's completely dark outside, how does someone wearing night vision goggles see things?

3.5 Is there a snake that can see in the dark?

3.6 Why are coal, oil, and gas called *fossil fuels*?

3.7 What's the difference between *fission* and *fusion*?

3.8 How much energy could you get from 1 pound of uranium?

3.9 Why do ice cubes crackle when you put them in a glass of water?

3.10 How do fireworks work?

3.11 How do bats use energy to catch insects?

3.12 If a sweater is only at room temperature, why do I feel warm when I put it on?

3.13 Why does a balloon stick to the wall after you rub it on a sweater?

3.14 Why can't a pendulum swing forever?

3.15 I've seen movies in which some of the Bedouins (people who live and travel across the desert) wear black clothing. Doesn't wearing black clothing make them feel hot?

3.16 How do refrigerators make and keep things cold?

3.17 Do the oceans ever freeze?

3.18 If I'm traveling through a tunnel, why can I tune in FM radio stations but not AM?

3.19 Why does cereal make noise when you pour milk on it?

3.20 How could baseball players stay cool on hot days?

3.21 Wool is a great insulator, but wool sweaters are expensive. How many sheep does it take to make a warm wool sweater?

3.1   What makes popcorn pop?

When corn kernels from certain species of corn plants are heated, they explode. This happens because the heat energy reaches small amounts of liquid water in the kernel and makes it rapidly change in state. The outer layer of the kernel holds the water vapor in place until the inside pressure gets high enough to break the kernel apart. The starch in the kernel explodes into bubbles that stick together and form the white solid you see on a fully popped kernel of corn. The liquid water in the kernel first forms steam and then turns to water vapor as it escapes. So popcorn pops because heat energy causes water to change into steam and water vapor. And when there's not enough heat energy to pop every kernel, watch out! If you chomp down on just one kernel of unpopped popcorn, you might hear the awful sound of one of your teeth cracking in two!

3.2   When I banged my knee into a wall, a friend gave me a "cold pack" that she found in a first aid kit. But before giving it to me, she twisted the pack, which made it get really cold. How could something that was at room temperature suddenly get so cold?

A cold pack contains a salt and a liquid (usually water). When the pack is twisted, the salt and liquid are mixed together. It just so happens that the dissolving of the salt in the liquid absorbs energy from its surroundings. This causes the solution to get very cold.

3.3   A friend of mine gets aches and pains in her ankles, so she takes a "hot pack" with her when she goes for long bike rides. How does the pack get hot when she needs to use it?

The hot pack contains a salt and a liquid that produce energy when mixed together. That energy leaves the pack as heat. When applied to your friend's sore ankle, the heat causes the molecules of the skin to vibrate more, which will warm up the area. And even though the energy from the hot pack doesn't make a sound, you might hear your friend say, "Oooooh, that feels good!"

3.4   If it's completely dark outside, how does someone wearing night vision goggles see things?

It's possible to see in the dark with night vision goggles because they don't need light to work. These goggles are able to detect the heat that all people, animals, and objects give off. The goggles receive heat energy, which moves through space as infrared waves, and turn that energy into images that the person wearing them can see.

3.5   Is there a snake that can see in the dark?

No animals can really *see* in the dark, but a snake called a *pit viper* can do the next best thing. It has two organs in its head that are heat sensors. So even if a pit viper can't see its prey on a dark night, it can tell how far away the prey is and in what direction to strike.

3.6   Why are coal, oil, and gas called *fossil fuels?*

The answer is simple: They are made from fossils. Not fossils like the dinosaur bones you might see in a museum, but from the bodies of organisms that lived hundreds of millions of years ago. Very tiny organisms called *phytoplankton* became part of rock layers that formed on the ocean bottom. Over a very long period of time, these layers turned into oil and gas. In a similar way, plants and trees buried by rock and soil can be changed into coal over a long time. So when people use coal, oil, and gas, they are really burning up fossils.

3.7   What's the difference between *fission* and *fusion?*

Fission and fusion are the same in one way but different in many others. They're the same because they're both ways of producing energy from matter. However, they're different in the way they *produce* the energy. During *fission,* uranium atoms split into two parts. One of the parts is an atom of barium, and the other is an atom of krypton. Some other bits of matter are also released along with high-energy gamma rays. Fission reactions are used to produce energy at nuclear power plants. Atomic bombs also work because of fission reactions. In nuclear *fusion,* two light atoms are forced together to form a heavier atom. When this happens, some of the mass of the lighter atoms is changed into energy. Fusion reactions are used to produce the energy released during the explosion of a hydrogen bomb. So far, the energy of nuclear fusion hasn't been used to produce electricity for cities.

3.8   How much energy could you get from 1 pound of uranium?

You could get the same amount of energy as you would get from burning about 3 million pounds (6.6 million kilograms) of coal. Now that's a lot of coal!

3.9   Why do ice cubes crackle when you put them in a glass of water?

The liquid water in the glass is warmer than the ice cubes. The warmer water heats up the outside of each cube. The part of the cube that's being warmed expands and pushes against the colder inside of the cube. And when the different parts of the ice cube press against one another, you can hear a cracking noise!

3.10 How do fireworks work?

Fireworks are made by packing gunpowder and other chemicals into a paper or cardboard tube. A fuse leads from the inside to the outside of the tube. When the fuse is lit, a small fire travels through the tube to the gunpowder. The gunpowder explodes, and the energy contained in its molecules is quickly released. The colors we see in the sky when fireworks explode are produced by the chemicals mixed in with the gunpowder. Fireworks convert chemical energy into light energy in a very short time. They should only be used by responsible adults.

3.11 How do bats use energy to catch insects?

The food bats eat gives them the energy to fly and produce high-pitched sound waves. Those sound waves strike moving insects and bounce back to the bat's ears. When the bat's ears receive some of the sound waves, its brain calculates how long it took for the sound waves to leave the bat, bounce off the insect, and return. This all happens very quickly and gives the bat some of the information it needs to catch insects.

3.12 If a sweater is only at room temperature, why do I feel warm when I put it on?

You feel warm because the sweater lets you warm yourself up. The fibers of the sweater trap pockets of air and keep air from moving around your body. The air conducts heat very poorly, which makes it a good insulator. This means that more of the heat your body produces is kept *in your body*. The sweater just keeps you from losing the heat you're producing.

3.13 Why does a balloon stick to the wall after you rub it on a sweater?

When you rub the balloon across the sweater, the balloon picks up some electrons from the sweater. As a result, the balloon gets a negative charge, and the sweater gets a positive charge. When you bring the negatively charged balloon near the wall, some of the electrons on the wall's surface are pushed away, or *repelled,* by the balloon. This leaves extra positive charges on the surface of the wall. The negatively charged balloon and the positively charged wall surface attract each other with enough force to keep the balloon from falling when you touch it to the wall.

3.14 Why can't a pendulum swing forever?

A pendulum loses a little energy each time it swings because of friction and air resistance. As the ball and string of the pendulum swing, the air slows their motion. Friction also uses up some energy at the place the pendulum's string is suspended. If you could design a pendulum that had no friction and then put it in a perfect vacuum, it *would* swing forever. And *you* would also be the first person in history to do it!

3.15   I've seen movies in which some of the Bedouins (people who live and travel across the desert) wear black clothing. Doesn't wearing black clothing make them feel hot?

No, it doesn't. How cool you feel depends more on your body's ability to lose heat than on the particular color of the clothes you wear. If you wear a fabric that's tightly woven, the heat your body is trying to lose will be trapped in the air right above your skin. For your body to lose heat and cool down, the sweat on your skin must easily evaporate, move away, and be replaced by drier air. Since black clothing absorbs the sun's infrared energy a little faster than white clothing, it may heat the air next to the skin faster. This will speed up evaporation, causing the hot, humid air next to the skin to travel through the fabric and into the air. Since Bedouins' robes are usually worn loose around the body, drier air can enter through the bottom of the robe and move up, over the skin and out of the fabric. This also helps people stay cooler. So does color matter at all? It's true that white fabric reflects more light rays than dark fabric. Even so, how tightly the fabric is woven and how loosely the garment fits are probably more important than what color it is.

3.16   How do refrigerators make and keep things cold?

This may surprise you, but there really isn't any such thing as cold. You can't put cold in or take it out of an object because cold doesn't exist. What *does* exist is heat energy. A refrigerator takes some of the heat energy out of the air that's *inside* it and moves that energy into the air that's *outside* it. Running through the walls of the refrigerator are pipes containing a liquid that can evaporate. Heat energy from the food and air in the refrigerator enters the pipes. The liquid in the pipes gets heated by this energy and evaporates. The heated gas stays in the pipes but moves to a set of coils in the back of the refrigerator. There, the heat energy leaves the pipes and enters the air. When it does, the gas condenses back to a liquid and continues through the pipes back into the refrigerator, where the process happens again and again.

3.17   Do the oceans ever freeze?

Definitely, but it has to be very cold. In fact, if you'd like to see some frozen ocean water, you'll have to take a long trip! Some of the water in the Arctic and Antarctic Oceans *does* get cold enough to freeze. The fact that ocean water has such strong waves and currents usually slows down its freezing. And of course, the salt in ocean water lowers the temperature at which it freezes.

3.18   If I'm traveling through a tunnel, why can I tune in FM radio stations but not AM?

Think of radio waves like waves of water on a lake or pond: Some are fast and close together, and some are slow and far apart. High-frequency FM radio waves, which are fast and close together, tend to bounce around and scatter more than low-frequency AM waves, which are slower and further apart. This means that the AM waves that reach the tunnel opening will travel through it more easily than the FM waves. Many other things also affect how far radio waves of different frequencies will travel through a tunnel, including the materials used to construct the tunnel and whether the tunnel is straight or curvy. So keep all this in mind, and if you like to listen to the music from FM radio stations, try to stay out of tunnels!

3.19   Why does cereal make noise when you pour milk on it?

The surface of cereal has many tiny hollows, like caves. You can see them with a powerful magnifying glass or microscope. When milk flows into these hollows, the air that was in them gets forced out between the milk and the cereal. The escaping air causes vibrations that produce sound waves, which make the pops and crackles you hear.

3.20   How could baseball players stay cool on hot days?

They could sit next to their fans.

3.21   Wool is a great insulator, but wool sweaters are expensive. How many sheep does it take to make a warm wool sweater?

It takes a large number of sheep because most of them don't knit very well.

Chapter 4
Plants

 Activities

    Supermarket Seeds   [LS 2]

    Jungle Room   [LS 3]

    Do You Eat Drupes and Pomes?   [LS 4]

    Do You Eat Tubers?   [LS 4]

    Flower Power   [LS 5]

 Word Play

    Interview a Plant!   [LS 4]

    Word Wonders   [LS 4]

 Magnificent Math

    Tree Chart   [LS 3]

    Plants in a Square   [LS 7]

 Art Connections

    The Plant Picture Challenge   [LS 1]

    Printing with Plants   [LS 1]

 Amazing but True!
Brainstretchers   [LS 1–7]

Part II Creepers and Peepers

Life Sciences

Activities

Supermarket Seeds

Where would you shop to get seeds for a garden? Oh, sure, you could just buy them at a store, but where's the fun in that? There's a much more interesting way of getting seeds. You can remove them from fresh fruits! In this activity, you'll grow a small indoor garden from fruit seeds.

1▶ Get Ready

Collection of at least 10 fresh fruits that includes some of the following: apple, peach, pear, orange, lemon, lime, cherry, and watermelon (Hint: Try to get fruits that are very ripe.)

Small bag of potting soil

20 washed pebbles

10 waxed paper cups

10 saucers or small plastic-coated paper dishes

Marking pen

Sharpened pencil

Paper towels

2▶ Do and Wonder

Use the pencil to poke a few holes in the bottom of each cup. Add a few pebbles to each cup, and then fill it with potting soil.

Put each cup on a saucer or paper dish. Add water to each cup until a little flows out the holes in the bottom.

Remove the pit or seeds from each fruit. If the fruit has many seeds, remove 3 or 4. Rinse the pits and seeds, and remove any plant material attached to them. Then spread them out on a paper towel, and cover them with another paper towel. Let them dry overnight.

Use a different cup for each type of seed. For each one, remove about 1 inch (2.5 centimeters) of potting soil, and put it aside. For a fruit that has one pit, gently press the pit into the soil. For a fruit that has many seeds, sprinkle 3 or 4 on the soil, leaving some space between them. Then cover the seeds with the same soil you removed from the cup. Use your fingers to gently pat down the soil. The surface should stay soft, not hard.

Use the marking pen to label the outside of each cup with the name of the seeds planted in it.

Put the cups in a warm, sunny place. Moisten the soil in each cup every few days, but don't water the seeds too much. If you can see water coming out the bottom of the cup, you're overwatering!

Make a chart that lists each type of seed and when you planted it. Also record your predictions about when the young plants will sprout. Then write down the date each new plant appears.

Your small plants will need a lot of sunlight to grow well. If you're doing this project in the spring or summer, you might want to replant your garden outdoors.

3▶ Think and Write

You might have some seeds that don't sprout. What might explain this?

Here's a problem for you to think about: The seeds of fruits that fall to the ground near the base of a parent plant will compete with the parent for sunlight and soil nutrients. Will they be able to grow successfully? In a paragraph, give your ideas about how nature takes care of this possible problem.

Explanation

Sweet-tasting fruits are as attractive to birds and other animals as they are to humans. Even less sweet vegetables are tasty to animals and humans. In addition, they provide good nutrition for all that eat them. The seeds in some of the fruits and vegetables we buy can be used to grow new plants.

Activity 4.2

Jungle Room

Is your classroom, well, boring? Wouldn't it be fun to add some plants and turn part of your room into a tropical jungle? This activity will let you do just that!

1▶ Get Ready

Collection of fruits grown in warm locations, such as avocado, papaya, kumquat, dates, and ginger (a rootlike stem)
Small flower pots at least 6 inches (15 centimeters) across
Potting soil
Clear plastic wrap

2▶ Do and Wonder

To begin, fill each of the flower pots with potting soil.

Choose one or more plants from below, and follow the directions given for it.

Ginger

Place a piece of ginger on top of the soil. Any thin, brown roots left on the ginger should be facing downward, and any buds should be pointing up.

Moisten the ginger and soil. Then cover the top of the pot with clear plastic wrap. Put the pot in a warm place, and remove the plastic wrap every few days to add a little water.

You should see shoots growing out of the soil in 2 or 3 months.

Dates

Select 4 or 5 dates and remove their pits. Soak them in water for 3 days.

Push the pits into the soil of one pot. Moisten the soil, and keep it in a warm place.

In 3 or 4 months, you'll see small date palm trees growing.

Avocado

Remove the pit from an avocado.

Push it into the potting soil, with the thick end down. About one-third of the pit should be above the soil.

Moisten the pit and soil. Then put the pot in a warm place. Be sure to keep the soil moist.

You should see green shoots coming from the top of the pit in 4 to 6 weeks.

Papaya

Remove 10 or 20 seeds from a ripe papaya, and soak them in water for a few minutes.

Place the seeds on top of the soil in one of the pots. Then sprinkle a little more soil on the seeds.

Moisten the soil, and cover the top of the pot with plastic wrap. Every few days, remove the plastic wrap and remoisten the soil. Keep the pot in a warm area.

Remove the plastic wrap when you see the seeds sprouting. Seedlings should develop in 3 to 5 weeks.

Kumquat

Remove 5 or 10 seeds from an assortment of kumquats, and then wash them.

Plant all the seeds about 1 inch (2.5 centimeters) below the soil. Moisten the soil, and place the pot in a warm place. Be sure to keep the soil moist.

Seedlings should develop in 2 to 3 weeks.

3▶ Think and Write

Keep a diary that records when you planted each type of seed and the changes you observe as you watch it grow.

Did some of your seeds never sprout? If not, why? In a short paragraph, write down a few reasons that may explain why some of your seeds never sprouted.

Explanation

In order to grow, plants from tropical environments usually need plenty of warmth, light, and moisture. If you can re-create much of that tropical environment indoors, you'll be able to get many tropical plants to grow.

Activity 4.3

Do You Eat Drupes and Pomes?

Have you ever eaten a drupe? Believe it or not, you probably have but just didn't know it. In fact, you've also likely eaten pomes! In this activity, you'll discover some interesting things about these very strange-sounding foods.

1▶ Get Ready

Three paper dishes
Plastic knife
One of each of these fruits:
   apple, pear, plum, peach,
   tomato, and grapefruit

Hand lens (magnifying glass)
Pencil

2▶ Do and Wonder

By studying many fruits, scientists have found characteristics we can use to place fruits into groups. You're going to cut apart six different fruits, make some observations about them, and then put each fruit in one of the groups.

Using your plastic knife, slice each fruit in half. (If you bump into a large, hard pit, just cut around it.) Then separate the halves of the fruit.

Now study this list of characteristics for three types of fruits:

Pome: Has many seeds that are surrounded by a fleshy part

Drupe: Has one or two seeds, which are in a hard covering
          Also has two layers: a soft, outer layer and a hard, inner layer that covers a seed

Berry: Has many seeds in the fleshy part

Label the three plates "Pome," "Drupe," and "Berry."

Using the list of characteristics, study each piece of fruit that you cut apart earlier. Based on what you observe, place each fruit on the plate that correctly identifies its type.

Write down the number of seeds you found in each fruit. Draw one of the seeds from each of the fruits you observed.

3▶ Think and Write   Use what you learned in this activity to classify even more fruits into these groups: pome, drupe, and berry. Make a chart showing which group each of the following fruits belongs to:

Apple
Orange
Cucumber
Pear
Plum
Apricot
Cherry
Tomato
Grape
Watermelon
Lemon
Peach
Strawberry

Explanation   Fruits protect and nourish the seeds within them until those seeds grow into plants. Fruits that contain seeds can be classified into three groups: pomes, drupes, and berries.

Activity 4.4

Do You Eat Tubers?

If you like french fries, you're definitely a tuber eater! Most people think that a potato is a root, but it isn't. It's a tuber. You'll learn how to grow your own tubers in this activity.

1▶ Get Ready

Small, white potato with many eyes
Four toothpicks
Jar that's larger than the potato
Water

2▶ Do and Wonder

Study the potato carefully, especially the eyes. They are actually the buds for new plants. Make a drawing of your potato, showing the locations of the eyes.

Stand the potato on one end, and hold it in that position. About one-third of the way down from the top of the potato, stick a toothpick into it. (At least one-third of the toothpick should be stuck into the potato.)

Now turn the potato halfway around and stick another toothpick into it, the same distance from the top of the potato as the first toothpick. You should have two toothpicks sticking out opposite sides of the potato.

Stick the third and fourth toothpicks into the sides of the potato, halfway between the first two toothpicks (and again, the same distance from the top). Now you should have four toothpicks sticking out the four sides of the potato.

Lower the potato over the jar so it's held up by the toothpicks, which should rest on the edge of the jar. Be sure the potato is about two-thirds in the jar and one-third out of the jar. (Adjust the toothpicks if the potato is too far in or out of the jar.)

Remove the potato, and fill the jar about halfway with water. Position the potato back on top of the jar, and add a little more water so most of the potato is underwater.

Put the jar containing the potato in a warm, dark place for a few days. Watch for small roots forming on the potato. When you see them, move the jar into the sunlight.

Keep adding water to the jar, as needed.

In a week or two, you'll see some changes in your potato. Write down your observations.

3▶ Think and Write   In a short paragraph, answer these questions: If the potato really isn't a root, then how does it grow? If you wanted to start a garden, which of the following ways of planting potatoes would make the most sense: (1) getting potato seeds from the store and planting them or (2) cutting up some potatoes and planting the eyes?

Explanation   The common white potato is a bulging structure that grows at the end of an underground stem. It's called a *tuber* (too-bur). The food produced by the plant is stored in the tuber. What people call the eyes of the potato are actually tiny buds that will grow into new stems.

Activity 4.5

Flower Power

When you think of the word *flower,* do you think of a beautiful blossom and maybe a pleasant smell? Well, you should know that there's *much more* than that to flowers. In this activity, you'll learn about parts of a flower that are needed to create new plants.

1▶ Get Ready

Large, simple flower (such as a tulip, hibiscus, lily, or poppy)
White paper towel
Tweezers
Hand lens (magnifying glass)
Microscope (optional)
Plastic knife
Assortment of colored pencils or thin, water-based markers
Sheet of white paper

2▶ Do and Wonder

Look carefully at your flower, observing all its different parts.

Now draw the flower, using the colored pencils or markers. Label the "Petals" and look under them for green parts, which should be labeled "Sepals." Count the numbers of petals and sepals. What do you think the sepals do for the flower?

Place the flower on the paper towel. Look inside the blossom, and draw what you see. Label these parts of the flower:

The "Pistil" is the large part at the center of the flower. It's the female part of the flower.

The "Ovary" is the bulb-shaped part at the bottom of the pistil.

The "Stigma" is the top of the pistil.

The "Style" is the part between the ovary and the stigma.

Gently touch the stigma. Is it sticky?

Using the plastic knife or your fingernail, carefully open the ovary. What do you observe inside? Are there any developing seeds?

Notice the parts sticking up around the pistil. They are the "Stamens" (stay-mins), the male flower parts. At the top of a stamen is the "Anther." The "Filament" supports the anther. Label these parts.

Carefully remove one stamen. Then touch its anther to the stigma on the pistil.

Now use your hand lens to carefully observe the stigma. You may be able to see tiny yellow grains on it. They are pollen. If you have a microscope, examine the pollen grains and draw what you see.

3▶ Think and Write   As you likely found out, the stigma is covered with a sticky, sweet-tasting liquid. Make a hypothesis about the purpose of this liquid. (Hint: Think about insects!)

Explanation   New seeds are produced when the pollen from a male flower part (stamen) falls on the top of the female flower part (pistil). The pollen that sticks to the stigma grows a tube that travels through the style to the ovary. Part of the pollen grain goes down this tube and fertilizes an egg nucleus in the ovary. The fertilized egg cell becomes a seed in the fruit, which will later grow into a new plant.

Word Play 4.1

Interview a Plant!

Plants usually don't say very much, even when they're the special guests on talk shows! That's really too bad, since they lead rather interesting lives. But suppose you *could* interview a plant! In this activity, you'll get just that chance.

1▶ Get Ready

A plant to interview (You can select an indoor or an outdoor plant—or even a tree!)
Paper and pencil

2▶ Do and Wonder

Create the script for an interview with a plant, as if you were a television newsreporter or a talk show host or hostess. Write out the questions you want to ask along with the plant's answers to those questions. Here are a few ideas for questions and answers:

Reporter: How do you feel about those insects buzzing around you and those green things crawling up your stem?

Plant: They're not so bad, once you get to know them. I try to keep in mind that they have an important job to do, carrying the pollen and all.

Reporter: I see some rather large human footprints on the path that runs along you. Don't you find living around humans a bit dangerous?

Plant: Tell me about it! If they're not spraying me with some kind of chemical then they're stepping on me or getting too close with the lawnmower. It's always something!

3▶ Think and Write

Find someone to play the part of the reporter or the plant (whichever part you're *not* playing). Make two copies of your script, and rehearse until you're ready to perform the interview in front of others. You might want to wear costumes or use props to add to the performance.

Perform the interview in front of others, and see if they enjoy it. Also consider asking your audience to call out other questions they would like the plant to answer.

After your performance, revise your script, using some of the questions the audience asked.

Explanation

It sure would be amazing if plants could really talk! No doubt, they would have some very interesting things to tell us. In this interview, you had a chance to use some of what you know about plants to invent a conversation between a reporter and a talking plant.

Word Play 4.2

Word Wonders

Have you ever created your own private signals or code, perhaps with a friend? In this activity, you'll have fun inventing science words, but you'll be the only person who will know what they really mean. You'll test these words to see if they could really fit science definitions, and you'll also learn what seven new science words mean.

1▶ Get Ready

28 index cards
4 rubber bands
Pen or pencil
Reference books about plants that have names and
    drawings of leaf arrangements on a plant stem

2▶ Do and Wonder

Take 7 index cards, and write one of the following words on each card:

opposite	simple	palmate	pinnate
alternate	compound	whorled	

Gather together these cards, and put a rubber band around them. This is your pack of "Real Science Words."

Use the reference books to find a definition for each word above. Then take 7 more index cards, and write *just the definition* of one word on each card. (Don't write the science words on the cards, too.) Now you also should have a pack of 7 cards with different definitions on them. Put a rubber band around these cards. This is your "Definitions" pack.

Take another 7 cards. On each, make a diagram that illustrates one of the words listed above. Put a rubber band around this pack of "Pictures" cards.

On each of the final 7 index cards, write an invented word for one of the 7 real science words listed on page 95. Keep in mind that your invented word must somehow tie in with the real word. Here's an example: For the real word *opposite,* invent the word *acrosstheway.* This is your "Invented Words" pack of cards; put a rubber band around it.

Now it's challenge time! Find a friend who's willing to take the following challenges. After he or she finishes each challenge, write down your observations of how well he or she did. Here goes:

> *Challenge 1:* Use the "Pictures" and the "Real Science Words" packs of cards. Spread out the picture cards, and have your friend try to match each to the correct science word.
>
> *Challenge 2:* Use the "Pictures" and "Invented Words" packs of cards. Spread out the picture cards, and have your friend try to match each with the correct invented word. (Hint: Don't reveal the correct choices yet!)
>
> *Challenge 3:* Use the "Pictures" and "Definitions" packs of cards. Spread out the picture cards, and have your friend try to match each with the correct definition card.

Now you can reveal the correct answers to your friend!

3▶ Think and Write

Look over the observations you made after each challenge. In a short paragraph, tell how well your friend did with each challenge. Be sure to mention those scientific words and definitions that gave him or her the most trouble.

Explanation

Scientists use their own special words to describe things. In this activity, you learned some of the scientific words that describe how leaves may be arranged on a plant stem. You also invented some words to fit the leaf arrangements and challenged a friend to match real scientific words to your invented words and drawings of leaf arrangements.

Magnificent Math 4.1

Tree Chart

Unless you got invited to its birthday party, how could you find out how old a tree is? Are the tallest trees necessarily the oldest? You'll learn how to figure out a tree's age in this activity, while also practicing your measuring and data-gathering skills.

1▶ Get Ready

Part of a sawed-off tree trunk on which rings are visible
Hand lens (or magnifying glass)
Ruler
Paper and pencil

2▶ Do and Wonder

Using the hand lens and ruler, gather data that answers each of the following questions (Hint: Each tree ring equals 1 year of growth.):

How old was the tree when it was cut down?

How old was the tree in the year it grew the most?

How old was the tree in the year it grew the least?

How much more did the tree grow in its best year than in its worst year?

3▶ Think and Write

Prepare a chart of all the information you collected.

In a few sentences, explain why you think the rings of a tree aren't the same thickness each year.

Explanation

Trees grow the *most* in years when the environment provides a lot of sunshine, water, and other nutrients, and they grow the *least* in years when the environment doesn't provide what they need. You can see these differences in growth if you study the distances between the tree rings.

Magnificent Math 4.2

Plants in a Square

When you look at a lawn, doesn't it seem like one large, green
blanket of grass? In this activity, you'll discover that other plants
are hidden in this sea of green.

1▶ Get Ready

Four pieces of string, each 1 yard (1 meter) long
Access to a lawn or grass-covered ballfield
Rubber ball
Paper and pencil

2▶ Do and Wonder

You need to pick one area of the lawn to study. To do so randomly,
turn your back to the lawn and toss the ball over your head.

Go to the spot the ball lands. This is your study area. Use the
four pieces of string to create a box around the ball.

Look at the square yard or meter of lawn carefully, and observe
the type and number of plants in the square. (Remove the ball
so you can see everything in the square.)

Write down the different kinds of plants you see, including how
many of each.

Make a graph to show your data. Label the vertical axis "Number
of Plants" and the horizontal axis "Types of Plants."

3▶ Think and Write

You've just used a technique biologists use to study how well
various plants are surviving in a general location. Since they
can't possibly count *every* plant in that location, they count the
plants living in a small area within it. By doing this many times
using different areas, biologists collect data that will help them
estimate the number of plants that are surviving.

Could you use this technique to estimate the number of animals
in an area? Here's a challenge: Describe in a few sentences how
you could use this technique to estimate the number of pigeons
living in a city.

Explanation

You've learned an easy way to estimate the number of living
things in a certain location. As you use this method, however,
remember that you must take many samples in many different
smaller areas before you can make an estimate for the larger
area.

Art Connections

Art Connections 4.1

The Plant Picture Challenge

Do you think your friends are careful observers? Well, this activity will give them a chance to prove it. You're going to ask your friends to find all the objects in your drawing that are made of plant material—which won't be easy!

1 ▶ Get Ready

Paper and pencil
Water-based markers in assorted colors

2 ▶ Do and Wonder

Draw a picture of this indoor scene: two friends in a room, sitting on the floor playing video games.

Make sure to include all of the following details in the picture you create:

Wooden boards in the floor

Wooden chair and table

Fancy linen tablecloth on the table (linen comes from a plant)

Wooden bookcase

Books in the bookcase (pages are made from wood)

Magazines on the floor (pages are made from wood)

Newspaper on the floor (pages are made from wood)

Friends each eating a piece of cake (flour comes from wheat)

Wooden door

Pad of paper and pencil near the friends (paper and pencil are both made from wood)

Wooden picture frames with photos inside (photos printed on paper, which is made from wood)

3 ▶ Think and Write

Give your picture to one or more friends, and challenge them to find all the objects made of plant material. Write down each friend's results. Who found the most things?

Explanation Wood and wood products, such as paper, are examples of things we use that come from a renewable resource. This means that with good planning, new trees can be planted to replace those that are cut down and used to make wood products. Timber companies need to plant a lot of new trees, since it takes a long time for trees to grow large enough to be used.

Art Connections 4.2

Printing with Plants

No doubt, you've collected leaves at some time, probably on a sunny, fall day. Well, you don't have to wait until fall to collect leaves! In this activity, you'll use all kinds of leaves to create interesting pictures by coating them with paint and printing images.

1▶ Get Ready Handful of leaves and stems of various shapes and sizes
Two or three small jars of tempera paint
Two or three paint rollers with 3 inch (about 8 centimeter) rollers
Two plastic trays to hold paint
Three sheets of white paper

2▶ Do and Wonder Select one leaf or stem, and lay it on a flat work surface.

Roll a thin layer of paint over the leaf or stem. Then press it flat on the white paper. Carefully peel the leaf or stem off the paper, leaving a print.

Repeat these steps again, using other leaves and stems and other colors of paint. Prepare at least three different prints using various combinations of leaves, stems, and colors.

Let your prints dry.

3▶ Think and Write Write a note that explains how you created each plant print, and attach it to the print.

Explanation Throughout history, artists have used the patterns and textures of natural objects—such as leaves and flowers—in their work. Some artists have produced prints and paintings, and others have created sculptures using natural objects as their models. In this activity, you used the objects themselves to create a painting!

Amazing but True!
BRAINSTRETCHERS

4.1 Is there really a flower that smells like rotting meat?

4.2 What's the tallest tree in the world?

4.3 If you have hay fever, does that mean that if you go near hay, you'll get a fever?

4.4 Why do flowers smell so good?

4.5 What are bees doing when they're just buzzing around flowers?

4.6 How can plants that grow in places that don't get much wind spread their seeds?

4.7 What's that blue stuff you sometimes see growing on cheese?

4.8 Some people like to put all kinds of spices on their food before they eat it, while others hate the taste of anything too spicy. What are spices made of?

4.9 Someone told me that if you remove a strip of bark from all around a tree trunk, the tree will die. Is that true?

4.10 Is it possible to grow an apple tree that has all different kinds of apples on its branches?

4.11 Are there really meat-eating plants?

4.12 What are those blue/green patches I see on rocks and on the branches of dead or dying trees?

4.13 What is catnip?

4.14 What is a fungus?

4.15 Is there really seaweed in ice cream?

4.16 Is there really a tree that has more than one trunk?

4.17 One time, when my dad was cutting up onions while making dinner, he started to cry. Why?

4.18 Why are people so upset about destroying the rainforest? Won't it just grow back?

4.19 What's worse than finding a worm in the apple you're eating?

4.20 Where's the best place to find books about trees?

4.1 Is there really a flower that smells like rotting meat?

Actually, there are a few. One is the carrion flower, which grows in Africa. It not only *smells* like rotting meat, but the whole plant *looks* like a chunk of rotting meat, too. Insects that usually lay their eggs in rotting meat are tricked into laying their eggs in this flower. When they do, the pollen from the flower sticks to the insects' bodies and is moved to other flowers. So by tricking the insects in this way, carrion flowers are able to produce seeds. The carrion flower also has another very interesting name: the stinking corpse plant!

4.2 What's the tallest tree in the world?

This is a tricky question because the answer can change from year to year as the tops break off the tallest trees. Overall, the tallest trees are the coast redwoods, which grow in the western United States. The very tallest is the Mendocino Tree growing in the Montgomery Redwoods State Reserve near Uikah, California. It's 367.8 feet tall (112.1 meters).

4.3 If you have hay fever, does that mean that if you go near hay, you'll get a fever?

No, hay doesn't give people hay fever. In fact, people who have hay fever don't even get a fever. Instead, they sneeze a lot and their eyes may water and itch when they're outdoors in the spring, summer, or fall. These symptoms are caused by pollen from trees and other flowering plants. When pollen grains reach the nose and the sinuses, they can make someone who has hay fever sniffle or sneeze. It's a lot like having a cold.

4.4 Why do flowers smell so good?

Flowers that smell good to us contain cells that make good-smelling chemicals. The cells that make the smells are in the petals and other parts of the flower. Insects that are attracted to these good smells usually drink the sweet nectar that's there. And while they're inside the flower, pollen sticks to their bodies. When these insects land on other flowers, some of the pollen may fall off. If the pollen lands on the female flower parts, seeds will be formed.

4.5 What are bees doing when they're just buzzing around flowers?

These buzzing bees are trying to find ways into the flowers so they can get a taste of pollen or a drink of *nectar,* a sweet liquid. The buzzing you hear comes from the high speed with which the insects' wings move through the air.

4.6   How can plants that grow in places that don't get much wind spread their seeds?

Plants have many ways to spread seeds. Wind is just one of them. For some plants, water carries seeds away from the parent plant. Other plants' seeds have tiny hooks growing from them that stick to the coats of animals that brush against them and then carry them away. And the seeds in sweet-tasting fruits are eaten by birds and other animals. The seeds eventually go through the animal's digestive track and return to the ground far from the parent plant.

4.7   What's that blue stuff you sometimes see growing on cheese?

Believe it or not, that blue stuff is *supposed* to be there if the cheese is Roquefort (roak-fort), Gorgonzola (gore-gan-zo-la), or blue cheese. It's a plant called *mold*. You're normally not supposed to eat food with mold growing on or in it, but it's different with blue cheese. People have been eating that mold for hundreds of years, and isn't dangerous. It gives the cheese a very strong flavor.

4.8   Some people like to put all kinds of spices on their food before they eat it, while others hate the taste of anything too spicy. What are spices made of?

When people add spices to food, they're actually adding plant parts! For example, dried mustard is made by grinding up the seeds of mustard plants. Basil, oregano, rosemary, and sage are all dried-up leaves. Ginger comes from a plant root, and pepper comes from a dried berry. Oh, and if you've ever tasted cinnamon, you've eaten tree bark!

4.9   Someone told me that if you remove a strip of bark from all around a tree trunk, the tree will die. Is that true?

Yes. There's a name for doing this terrible thing to a tree: *ringbarking*. But why does it kill the tree? The cells that carry food from the leaves to the rest of a tree are only found in the bark. These food-carrying cells are called *phloem* (flow-em). When you remove a complete ring of bark from a tree, you're cutting its food supply. Any cells below the cut will die because they can no longer get food. This includes the tree's roots, whose cells will no longer get the energy they need to take in water for the tree. In nature, ringbarking can be caused by rabbits that may nibble off tree bark close to the ground or by deer that scrape off bark when they rub their antlers against trees.

4.10   Is it possible to grow an apple tree that has all different kinds of apples on its branches?

Yes! In fact, it's been done for many, many years. Long ago, fruit growers discovered that if they cut fresh buds from the branches of different apple trees, they could put those buds under the bark of one tree and get branches that produce fruit. This is called *grafting*. Unfortunately, you can't graft a bud from an orange tree onto an apple tree. The trees have to be related to one another. So don't expect to see a "fruit salad" tree with apples, peaches, and oranges growing on it! So far, it can't be done.

4.11   Are there really meat-eating plants?

Absolutely! There are over 450 different kinds of meat-eating plants. All of them have some way of trapping and digesting insects. One of these plants is the Venus flytrap. Its insect-trapping leaf is made of two parts that quickly close together when an insect bumps into the trigger hairs on the leaf's surface. When the trapped insect has died, the leaf absorbs nutrients from the insect's decomposing body. Other types of meat eaters trap insects when they come in contact with sticky fluids on the plants' surfaces or drown the insects in the plants' liquids.

4.12   What are those blue/green patches I see on rocks and on the branches of dead or dying trees?

You've been looking at one of the strangest plants on Earth, which is called a *lichen* (lie-kin). It's really two plants that grow together and depend on each other. The part of the plant you can easily see is a *fungus*. It anchors the lichen to the rock or branch and absorbs minerals from the surface. The other part of the lichen plant is a single-celled green *algae* (al-gee) that grows on the fungus. The algae cells make food through photosynthesis. The fungus gets its food from the algae, and the algae lives on the fungus structure. Some lichens look like stains on trees and rocks. Others grow to be very thick, and some grow hanging from trees' branches. So whenever you see a lichen, you're really seeing two plants that depend on each other.

4.13   What is catnip?

Catnip is an herb that's part of the mint family. All cats—even big ones, such as mountain lions and tigers—twist and turn their bodies and start rolling around whenever they smell the odor of catnip. If you have a cat or kitten that you want to keep busy, just toss it a catnip toy.

4.14   **What is a fungus?**

A *fungus* is a plant that doesn't make its own food from sunlight and air. It can't make food because it doesn't contain chlorophyll. Fungi (which is plural for *fungus*) get their food from dead wood and rotting, green plants. Some fungi are so small that they're difficult to see. For instance, yeast is a tiny fungus used in baking. There are even fungi that grow on people's skin. Athletes foot, which is an itchiness of the skin, is caused by a fungus.

4.15   **Is there really seaweed in ice cream?**

Are you hoping for a brand-new flavor? Sorry! Many kinds of ice cream already have seaweed in them—you just can't taste it. Would you like to know whether there's seaweed in your favorite ice cream? Find the list of ingredients on the container, and look for the word *algin*. Actually, algin is a chemical substance that comes from a common seaweed called *kelp*. Why would anyone put seaweed in ice cream? It makes the ice cream thicker.

4.16   **Is there really a tree that has more than one trunk?**

Every now and then, you'll notice a tree in the forest that seems to be growing from more than one trunk. However, there's a particular kind of tree, called the *banyan tree,* that can have hundreds of trunks. After one has been growing for awhile, it sends shoots down from its branches that reach the soil and grow thick to support the branches from which they grew. A banyan tree can spread out over quite an area, since its great weight is supported by all the extra trunks growing from its branches.

4.17   **One time, when my dad was cutting up onions while making dinner, he started to cry. Why?**

Well, he might have been crying because he didn't like making dinner! Or it might have been the onions. When your dad sliced the onions, a chemical from the onions entered the air. It reacted with the moisture in your dad's eyes to make a very weak acid, which irritated his eyes. Tears are the body's way of diluting the acid and carrying it away. You may be wondering, Why does an onion have that chemical in the first place? It discourages insects and small animals from eating the onion while it's in the ground.

4.18   Why are people so upset about destroying the rainforest? Won't it just grow back?

Yes, it will—if we leave it alone for a few hundred million years! But that's not likely to happen. As the rainforest is chopped down, civilization starts to spread out on the newly available land, so the old rainforest has no chance to grow back. Unless people stop destroying the rainforest, it will disappear completely, along with the millions of species of plants and animals within it.

4.19   What's worse than finding a worm in the apple you're eating?

Finding *half* a worm.

4.20   Where's the best place to find books about trees?

A branch library.

Chapter 5

Critters Small, Monsters Tall

Activities

It's Alive! Or Is It?   [LS 1, S&T 3]

Magnificent Mealworms   [LS 2, S&T 3]

Glorious Guppies   [LS 2 & 7]

Deer Here, Deer There   [LS 3 & 7]

The Most Beautiful of the Butterflies   [LS 2–5]

Who? What? Jane Goodall
and Ernest Just   [HNS 2]

Word Play

Lost Words   [LS 1–8]

Life Cycle Scramblers   [LS 1–8]

Two Strange Mammals   [LS 8]

Magnificent Math

Speedy Species!   [LS 8]

How Tall?   [LS 8]

Art Connections

Plaster Tracks   [LS 1]

Mixed-Up Creature Collage   [LS 1]

Amazing but True!
Brainstretchers   [LS 1–7]

Activities

Activity 5.1

It's Alive! Or Is It?

If you've ever watched an old Frankenstein-type movie, you probably remember the part when the creature starts to move and someone screams, "It's alive!" In this activity, you'll make a few of your own creatures that will make your friends wonder whether they're observing living or nonliving things. You'll make these creations right before their eyes, but they'll still be puzzled!

1▶ Get Ready

Small, flat-bottomed, clear glass baking dish
Four small pieces of shirt cardboard, each 8½ × 11 inches
   (about 22 × 28 centimeters)

Pepper shaker	Access to water
Liquid soap or detergent	Overhead projector
Eyedropper	Movie projection screen
Masking tape	Scissors

2▶ Do and Wonder

You'll be projecting moving shadows on a screen, and it's important that others not be able to see how you're doing it. To make sure they can't, build a sort of shield to put around the projector. Tape the pieces of cardboard together, forming a three-sided U on the surface of the projector. Place the shield so your audience won't be able to see what your hands are doing.

Project 1

Thoroughly rinse out the baking dish. Then pour in enough water so the dish is about one-fourth full.

Now do this out of the sight of your observers: Sprinkle pepper on the water surface. Add a lot of pepper so it's pretty well covered.

Carefully place the dish on top of the projector. Turn on the projector so the pepper is being projected on the screen. Then place a drop of liquid soap or detergent on the surface of the water. Your observers should see the shadows of the pepper flakes immediately spread to the sides of the dish.

Project 2

Again, thoroughly rinse out the dish and pour in enough water so it's about one-quarter full.

Cut two or three small boats out of a piece of heavy paper or thin cardboard. Each boat should be about 1 inch wide (2.5 centimeters) and 2 inches (5 centimeters) long. Cut a circular slot into the back end of the boat, so that it looks like the one shown here.

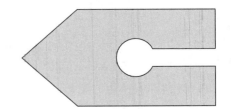

Place the pan of water on the projector and turn it on. Float one of the boats on the water and project its shadow.

Now place a drop of liquid soap or detergent in the circular slot. Your observers should see the boat move quickly across the water.

To repeat the activity, thoroughly rinse out the bowl to remove the soapy water. You'll also need to use a different boat.

3▶ Think and Write   Just because you see an object move, does that mean that you're looking at something that's alive? Write a paragraph about what sort of proof is needed to tell whether something is alive.

Explanation

Adding soap reduces the surface tension of the water. In Project 1, when the drop of soap touches the pepper-covered surface of the water, the pull of water molecules for each other breaks down at that spot. In addition, the surface tension on the rest of the water pulls the pepper toward the edges of the container. In Project 2, the surface tension of the water in the slot of the boat is broken when the soap hits it. The skin of water around the boat keeps its tension and pulls the boat along.

In these projects, you made two different objects move. Does that mean they're alive? Of course not. After all, you *made* these objects! So, movement isn't the only characteristic you should use to classify something as being alive. A more helpful characteristic is whether the object can reproduce by making more of its own kind.

Safety Hints

Be sure to rinse the glass dish thoroughly between activities, removing all traces of soap.

Avoid getting soap in your eyes or mouth.

Be careful not to spill any water on or around the projector.

Magnificent Mealworms

Even if you don't like worms, you'll like this project. Why? Because a mealworm really isn't a worm. In fact, it's an animal that happens to look a little (very little) like a worm at one particular stage in its life cycle. Now, don't you feel better?

▶ Get Ready

5 to 10 mealworms from petstore (See how to grow and keep them in the section Do and Wonder.)
2 cups bran cereal or oatmeal
½ apple and ½ potato, sliced
Small quantities (less than ½ handful) of each of the following: rice, crushed cornflakes, sugar, flour, and salt
1 tablespoon peanut butter
Hand lens (magnifying glass)
Small flashlight
Plastic spoon
Clear, plastic rectangular container, with volume of 2 quarts (about 2 liters)
Sheet of cardboard big enough to make lid for container
White paper plate
Scissors
Paper and pencil
Reference books and/or access to the World Wide Web

▶ Do and Wonder

Getting and Raising Mealworms

First you need to have a way to keep and grow mealworms. You can get them at a petstore, since they're used as live food for fish and other animals.

To keep mealworms at home or school, you'll need a clean, clear, plastic rectangular container. You can keep 10 or 20 mealworms in a 2 quart (2 liter) container.

Before you put in the mealworms, put 1 or 2 cups of bran or oatmeal cereal and 2 or 3 slices of apple or potato in the container. Then add the mealworms.

Prepare a cardboard lid for the container, and punch holes in it. Tape the lid to the top of the container.

Your mealworms will stay healthy for a month or so. If you clean out the container from time to time and add new food and apple and potato slices, your mealworms will stay healthy for a longer time.

Body Parts and Functions

Using your hand lens to look at a mealworm, try to discover answers to these questions:

> How many legs does it have?
>
> How many body segments does it have?
>
> Does it have a head?
>
> How is its head different from its tail?

Make a drawing of your mealworm that shows its head, thorax, abdomen, legs, antennae, and segments. Label each body part, and write a note about what it does. Use reference books and/or information on the World Wide Web to check your work.

Life Cycle

Carefully observe the contents of the mealworms' container to find clues about their life cycle.

Do some research in reference books and/or on the World Wide Web to discover the stages of the mealworm's life cycle.

Behavior

Arrange the various food materials (flour, sugar, peanut butter, etc.) on the paper plate in a circle along its outer edge. Leave plenty of room at the center.

Place 2 or 3 mealworms at the center of the paper plate. Now, using the pencil, trace the paths of the mealworms on the plate.

Is one food more popular than the others? What do the mealworms do when they get to a food they like? For instance, do they stay on top of it? Do they burrow into it?

Use your flashlight and a sheet of paper to make shadows on the plate on or near the mealworms. How do they react to light and darkness?

Ecology

Use reference books and/or information on the World Wide Web to answer these questions:

> What are the mealworm's natural predators?
>
> Does the mealworm prey on other animals?
>
> Does it eat vegetable matter?

What things might a mealworm, an adult grain beetle, and a grain beetle egg all need from their surrounding environments?

Adaptations

What did you notice about the mealworm's body parts that would probably help it survive in its environment?

Relationship to Humans

Use reference books and/or information on the World Wide Web to answer these questions:

> How do beetles, such as the grain beetle, affect the human food supply?
>
> How do humans use mealworms?

3▶ Think and Write

Think back over your experiments and research, and then answer the following questions in two short paragraphs: What characteristics of mealworms help them survive in their natural environment? What dangers do mealworms face in their environment?

Explanation

Mealworms are not worms! Rather, they're insects. In fact, the mealworm is just one stage of the life cycle of the black grain beetle. The grain beetle has a four-stage life cycle: egg, larva (the mealworm), pupa, and adult. The mealworm (or larva) stage lasts 4 to 5 months. As the mealworm grows, it continually sheds its outer covering, replacing its skin 10 to 20 times.

Safety Hint

Throughout this project, you'll be working with living creatures. Treat them as gently as possible, and try not to injure them. Always handle them with care and respect.

Activity 5.3

Glorious Guppies

Have you ever seen a large aquarium filled with beautifully colored fish? Chances are, some of those fish were guppies, which are common tropical fish. In this activity, you'll discover if *you* can successfully raise guppies. To do so, you'll need an aquarium, but it doesn't have to be large, fancy, or expensive.

1▶ Get Ready

3 or 4 guppies (including at least 1 male and 2–3 females)
Small tropical fish aquarium with heater, filter, gravel,
    plants, and so on
Tropical fish food
Small flashlight
Paper and pencil
Assortment of colored markers
Reference books and/or access to the World Wide Web

2▶ Do and Wonder

Getting and Raising Guppies

Check with a petstore to get specific information about how to care for and feed guppies. Also ask the people at the store to help you find booklets about raising tropical fish.

What did you learn about how much food to give the fish and how often? Would feeding the guppies too much or too often cause any problems?

Body Parts and Functions

Female guppies are larger than males, but males tend to be more colorful.

The male guppy has a long, pointed organ that is part of its tail. Sperm go from this organ into the female.

Select a male and a female guppy. Make a labeled drawing of each, showing major body parts.

Life Cycle

A female guppy keeps her fertilized eggs in her body until they hatch, which takes about 4 weeks. You can actually see the eggs inside the female guppy's stomach! The number of guppies born may be as few as 10 or as many as 200.

After they're born, the young guppies hide in clumps of plants to keep from being eaten by other fish, including adult guppies. People at the petstore may recommend you add what's known as a *fish trap* to your aquarium to keep young guppies safe from predators.

When one of the females gives birth, estimate how many guppies are born and how many actually survive.

Behavior

Fish sense what's going on in their environment in many ways. The pupils of their eyes move forward and backward to keep objects in focus. Fish don't have ears, but they do have organs in their heads and along the sides of their bodies that sense vibrations.

Gently tap your finger on the side of the aquarium. How do the guppies react?

Shine a light into the aquarium. Do the guppies swim toward it or away from it?

Ecology

Guppies are usually found in tropical waters, where they feed on algae, crustaceans, and worms. They also stay near underwater plants, which provide hiding places when they are threatened by larger fish.

What might guppies have in their natural environment that they don't have in the aquarium? List both living and nonliving things.

Adaptations

The dull coloring of female guppies lets them blend easily into their environment, which is an important defense mechanism. Like all fish, guppies have bodies that fit their watery environment perfectly.

Use the colored markers to make a drawing that shows the colors of the guppies in your aquarium. Each female may have a dark spot toward the rear of her body. Don't forget to include it in your drawings.

Make some hypotheses about these questions:

> How does the guppies' shape help them move through water?
>
> What is the purpose of the large tail fin and the other fins?

Relationship to Humans

Humans have actually used guppies to control the mosquito populations in tropical countries. How do you think guppies could do this? (Hint: Mosquito larvae are often found in water.)

3▶ Think and Write

Think back over your experiments and research, and answer the following questions in two short paragraphs: What dangers do guppies have in their natural environment? What characteristics of guppies help them survive?

Explanation

In nature, guppies can survive in freshwater as well as saltwater. They originally lived north of Brazil in the warm waters off the Guyanas, Venezuela, and Barbados. Now they live in many different parts of the world. Depending on where they live, their size, color, and body shape can be very different. Males are usually about 1½ inches (4 centimeters) long. Their bodies have an olive green or brownish color, but their tales are bright and colorful. Females are much larger—up to 2½ inches (6 centimeters) long—and have a gray/brown color with some white areas. In the wild, guppies eat algae, insect larvae, small shelled animals, and fish eggs.

Safety Hint

Throughout this project, you'll be working with living creatures. Treat them as gently as possible, and try not to injure them. Always handle them with care and respect.

Deer Here, Deer There*

Have you ever seen deer outdoors? They're fast, graceful animals. In this activity, you'll learn many things about deer and their behavior. Best of all, you'll learn all these things as you play a game. So get a group of friends together and play!

1▶ Get Ready

At least 12 friends to play various roles
Pencil
Graph paper
Masking tape
Chalk
Reference books and/or access to the World Wide Web
Open space or large room

2▶ Do and Wonder

To prepare for the game, use reference books and the World Wide Web to gather information about deer and what they need from their environment to survive.

Divide your friends into two groups: half to play deer and half to play things in the deer's environment (such as food, water, and shelter).

If you're indoors, use the masking tape to make a line on the floor, dividing the room in two. If you're outdoors, use the chalk to make a line on a parking lot surface or use a stick to draw a line through the dirt. Make one side of the line the "deer" side and the other side the "environment" side. Ask your friends to go to their correct sides.

Each person on the environment side must secretly choose to be food, water, or shelter. Each person on the deer side must each choose what he or she needs from the environment. Each deer can only choose *one thing* from the environment each season. And each environment member can be chosen as a resource *only once*.

*This activity is based on the game Oh, Deer, developed by Project Wild. You can get materials with other environmental activities from the Project Wild National Office, Bethesda, MD 20814.

The deer and the environment members should send messages using these signs, or gestures:

Food—Rubbing their stomachs

Water—Raising imaginary glasses to their mouths

Shelter—Holding arms over their heads with hands together to make a roof

Everyone should practice all the signs.

Have members of both groups line up on opposite sides of the line, *with their backs to one another.* Each deer has to decide what he or she needs (choosing only one need), and each environment member has to decide what he or she is going to be (only one resource). No one should show his or her sign yet.

At the count of 3, members from both sides must turn to face one another and show their signs. Each deer should show what he or she needs, and each environmental resource should show what he or she is. No one is allowed to change signs!

Each deer who sees the environmental resource he or she needs should walk across the line, get the resource, and bring it to the deer side. That resource then becomes a deer. The deer who don't see their signs don't survive because they don't satisfy their needs from the environment. These deer die (but don't have to fall down), move across the line, and become resources in the environment for the next round.

Make a graph showing the changes that happened in the first round. (Each round is a season.) Label the horizontal axis "Season" and the vertical axis "Number of Deer." Play the game for a few seasons, and record the results for each round. What pattern of changes do you see in the deer population?

After you've played a few rounds, start the game over again, but this time make a few changes. For a few seasons, whisper to the environment members that they can't be food. Continue the game as before, and whisper to any deer that become part of the environment that they can't be food, either. Graph the results.

Now start the game again. This time, whisper to the environmental resources that they can't be food or shelter. As you play, also whisper to any deer that become part of the environment that they can't be food or shelter, either. Play the game for a few seasons. Graph the results.

Next you should play the part of a predator who eats two deer each season. How does that affect the deer population after a few seasons? Then play the part of a hunter who kills one deer a year. Graph the results.

Finally, organize the game so that you demonstrate what happens when a small number of deer move into an area with a lot of food, water, and shelter and no predators, such as a small town or suburb.

Major Hint: Be absolutely sure that no one shows his or her sign before turning around for each season.

3▶ Think and Write   Think back over your experiments and research, and answer the following questions in two short paragraphs: What dangers do deer face in their natural environment? What characteristics of deer help them survive in their environment?

Explanation   Deer are vegetarian mammals that feed on moss, bark, buds, and leaves. There are about 50 different kinds of deer living all over the world. The Virginia white-tailed deer, the Colombian black-tailed deer, and the mule deer are common in parts of North America. Deer have excellent senses of vision, hearing, and smell. Their predators include cougars, wild dogs, and wolves. And although male deer with antlers can defend themselves, their most important defenses are having keen senses and great speed.

Activity 5.5

The Most Beautiful of the Butterflies

Butterflies are some of nature's most beautiful creatures. The bright colors and patterns of their wings make them quite a sight as they fly from flower to flower on summer days. In this activity, you'll study one of the most amazing butterflies around: the Monarch.

1▶ Get Ready

Pupa (chrysalis) of a Monarch butterfly or caterpillar
Aquarium or rectangular plastic container
Screen to use as a lid for the container
1 pound (454 grams) of potting soil (You can buy a bag
    of soil this size at a supermarket or garden store.)
Scissors
Paper and pencil
Reference books and/or access to the World Wide Web

2▶ Do and Wonder

Getting and Raising Butterflies

Depending on what part of the country you live in, you may be able to find a Monarch chrysalis by searching outdoors. If there are Monarchs in your area, they will likely be attached to the branches of a milkweed plant. If you can't find a Monarch chrysalis, you can order a chrysalis of another butterfly that will go through the same life stages as a Monarch.*

If you find a chrysalis, remove the entire stem to which it's attached. If you see a caterpillar eating milkweed leaves, it's probably the larva stage of a Monarch butterfly. Carefully capture it and bring it indoors with the milkweed leaves and twigs.

Dump all of the potting soil into the container, and spread it out evenly across the bottom. Moisten the soil slightly.

*The Painted Lady is another butterfly you can easily raise at home or school. You can purchase a Butterfly Garden Kit, containing a coupon that can be used to receive a chrysalis, from a number of sources, including Museum Products Company, 84 Route 27, Mystic, CT 06355, 1-800-395-5400.

Next put the twigs and milkweed leaves and either the chrysalis and its stem or the caterpillar in the container.

If you have a caterpillar, you'll need to add milkweed plant leaves every day or so, as the caterpillar will quickly eat them.

If you have a chrysalis, you'll also need to keep the air in the container moist. To do so, lightly wet the soil every day or two (or however often is needed to keep the soil slightly moist). This will keep the air above it moist and prevent the chrysalis from drying out.

Cover the top of the container with the screen.

Body Parts and Functions

Prepare drawings of the caterpillar and butterfly, labeling their major body parts. Pick two body parts of each animal, and explain how they help it survive.

Life Cycle

Use drawings to make a chart that shows the butterfly at each of the four stages of its life cycle.

Behavior

Using reference books and/or information on the World Wide Web, solve this mystery of a Monarch butterfly's behavior: How does a completely new generation of butterflies in the north know what route they must take during their migration south?

Ecology

Based on your research and observations of Monarch butterflies, what animals or plants depend on them? If the Monarch were to become extinct, how would the other animals and plants in its environment be affected?

Adaptations

The Monarch butterfly seems to taste bitter to many birds. How does this affect the survival of the Monarch species?

Relationship to Humans

If the Monarch butterfly were to become extinct, would humans be affected in any way? Why or why not?

3▶ Think and Write   Think about your research and observations, and answer the following questions in two short paragraphs: What dangers do Monarch butterflies face in their natural environment? What characteristics of Monarchs help them survive in their environment?

Explanation   All butterflies have a four-stage life cycle: egg, larva, pupa, and adult. You can raise a Monarch butterfly at home or school from its pupa stage. The chrysalis (cocoonlike) container for the Monarch can be found attached to a milkweed plant in late summer and early fall. The leaves of this plant are the major food source for Monarch caterpillars (larvae). The Monarch butterfly migrates north from California or Mexico each year. While in the north, it lays eggs that become caterpillars. Each caterpillar then becomes a pupa in its chrysalis stage and emerges as an adult butterfly. Then a new generation of butterflies fly south to spend the winter in California or Mexico.

Safety Hints   Throughout this project, you'll be working with living creatures. Treat them as gently as possible, and try not to injure them. Always handle them with care and respect.

Milkweed plants contain a sticky, milky substance that's poisonous. Don't touch or taste it.

Activity 5.6

Who? What? Jane Goodall and Ernest Just

Scientists are very curious about the world around them. In this activity, you'll do some research to discover what one scientist was curious about. See what interesting things you can find out about the life and work of Jane Goodall or Ernest Just, and then share what you learn with your friends.

1▶ Get Ready

Paper and pencil   Two sheets of poster paper
Ruler   Felt-tipped markers in assorted colors
Resource books and/or
   access to the World Wide Web

2▶ Do and Wonder

In this activity, you'll do two things: (1) Gather a lot of information about the life and discoveries of a scientist, and (2) create two posters that will show what you learned.

Pick one of these scientists for your research: Jane Goodall or Ernest Just.

To begin, read the brief biography of this scientist in the Explanation section at the end of this activity.

Use resource books and/or the World Wide Web to find more information about your scientist. Take as many notes as you can about the individual and his or her discoveries.

Now you're ready to create your posters.

Poster 1

Write the scientist's name at the top of the poster, and draw a picture of him or her below it.

Write down when and where the scientist lived.

List important facts about his or her life.

Poster 2

At the top of the poster, write the problem or question the scientist worked on.

Draw the kinds of equipment he or she used to make his or her discoveries.

If you could ask the scientist two questions about his or her life and discoveries, what would they be? Write them down.

3▸ Think and Write

Imagine that the scientist you selected was going to visit your classroom. What would you like him or her to bring to show you and your classmates? What science questions do you think you and your classmates might ask the scientist? What are two things the scientist might tell about his or her life and work?

Write one or two paragraphs about the scientist's visit to your classroom, describing what he or she would show and tell you and your classmates.

Explanation

Jane Goodall

Jane Goodall was a British anthropologist and conservationist who studied the behavior of chimpanzees at the Gombe Game Reserve in Africa for over 35 years. She was born in 1934 and as a young girl read books about animals and nature. As an adult, she traveled to Africa and began studying chimpanzee behavior. She received her Ph.D. in 1965 from Cambridge University. Dr. Goodall's research has led to many important discoveries about chimpanzee behavior—for example, that chimps make and use simple tools and eat meat. Her research has also taught people the importance of understanding how all creatures are affected by each other and their environment.

Ernest Just

Ernest Just, a famous cell biologist (a person who studies the cells of plants and animals), was born in Charleston, South Carolina, in 1883. He started working at a very young age to help support his family. He was such an excellent student that he attended a preparatory school in New Hampshire, where he could get ready for college work. He was accepted at Dartmouth College, where he majored in biology. Dr. Just eventually became the head of the biology department of Howard University. In the summers, he did experiments at Woods Hole, Massachusetts, and became famous for his interesting ideas about how cells function. Many of his ideas came from experiments with living things that he gathered from the ocean. Ernest Just died in 1941.

Word Play

Word Play 5.1

Lost Words

Are you interested in animals? Well, you should be because you are a *human* animal. In this activity, you'll discover how much you know about your relatives in the animal world! To do so, you'll have to think of the lost words that will make the paragraphs below make sense.

1▶ Get Ready

Paper and pencil
Resource books and/or access to the World Wide Web

2▶ Do and Wonder

As you can see, the paragraphs that follow are missing some key words. Do your best to fill in each blank with the word that completes the sentence. (Letter hints have been added for some of the words.)

If you have trouble finding the correct word for any of the blanks, look through the list of words in the Explanation section of this activity. Also keep in mind that some words may be used more than once. Good luck!

Animals are different from p_____ in many ways. One way is that animals _____ produce food in their bodies. To live, animals must _____ _____ or animals. Another difference is that animals can _____ from place to place during all or some of their _____ .

Humans, cats, and birds are all examples of animals called vertebrates. All vertebrates have b_____s. Insects, clams, and worms are all examples of animals called i_____ . None of them have b_____s.

Insects and crabs have a _____d outer covering called
an exoskeleton. It supports their _____ and also helps
_____ them from predators. Fish, frogs, and camels each
have a bundle of _____ passing through their backbones.
That bundle is called the _____.

Food provides animals with the e_____ they need to do
all that it takes to stay alive. Herbivores are animals that just
eat _____. Carnivores are animals that just eat _____.
Omnivores are animals that eat any other living _____.

Hunting animals that kill and eat other animals are
called p_____. An animal that is hunted, killed, and eaten
by another animal is called p_____. Animals that eat the
remains of dead animals are called s_____s.

The bat is an interesting p_____r. Did you know that
even though bats fly, they aren't b_____s? Bats nurse
their young, which means they belong to a group of animals
called m_____. Some bats eat fruit, while some draw
blood from other animals and feed on it. Some bats catch
and eat i_____ in the dark. They do this by sending out
_____. The bounce of the s_____ off the p_____ gives
bats a lot of information. The returning sound tells the
_____ where the i_____ is.

3▶ Think and Write   Check your work using the list in the Explanation section.

Explanation   The following list contains all the words you'll need to fill in
the blanks in the paragraphs above—in order!

plants	backbones	animals	insects
don't	hard	thing	sounds
eat	bodies	predators	sounds
plants	protect	prey	prey
move	nerves	scavengers	bat
lives	spinal cord	predator	insect
backbones	energy	birds	
invertebrates	plants	mammals	

Word Play 5.2

Life Cycle Scramblers

Do you look the same now as you did when you were born?
Certainly not! You've grown and changed in many ways. *All* animals
and plants go through times or stages in their lives when they're
growing and changing. All together, these stages make up what's
called the animal's *life cycle.* In this activity, you'll discover whether
you know the key words used to describe the life cycles of a
grasshopper, a butterfly, and a frog.

1▶ Get Ready   Paper and pencil
                          Resource books and/or access to the World Wide Web

2▶ Do and Wonder   Using the hint provided, unscramble each of the following
                          words. Write your answer on the line after each scrambled
                          word.

Grasshopper Scramble

The first stage in the grasshopper's life cycle.	GEG	_____
This looks like the adult but has now wings.	PHYMN	_____
The egg-producing stage.	LUTAD	_____

Butterfly Scramble

The female produces many of these.	GESG	_____
A butterfly in the larva stage.	PLIATERCARL	_____
A chrysalis is made during this stage.	APPU	_____
During this stage, the butterfly has wings.	DATUL	_____

Frog Scramble

Where a frog's eggs are
most likely found.   RETAW   _____

A frog is in this stage
when it has a tail and
gills.   DOPTALE   _____

Where adult frogs live
most of their lives.   NALD   _____

3▶ Think and Write

Choose one of the three animals from above: grasshopper,
butterfly, or frog. Write a short paragraph using the puzzle
answer words to describe the life cycle of that animal.

Check your answers in each word scramble using the lists
in the Explanation section.

Explanation

Here are the answers to the scrambles:

Grasshopper Scramble
EGG
NYMPH
ADULT

Butterfly Scramble
EGGS
CATERPILLAR
PUPA
ADULT

Frog Scramble
WATER
TADPOLE
LAND

Word Play 5.3

Two Strange Mammals

What do the following have in common: a grizzly bear, a giraffe, a human, a whale, a cow, an echidna, and a duck-billed platypus? Wait a minute: What are an *echidna* and a *duck-billed platypus?* Believe it or not, they're mammals, as are all the animals just listed. In this activity, you'll learn some very surprising things about these two mammals, which you'll share by writing a letter to a friend.

1▶ Get Ready

Paper and pencil
Resource books and/or access to the World Wide Web

2▶ Do and Wonder

First use resource books and/or the World Wide Web to discover all the major characteristics of mammals. Make a list of the characteristics.

Next use resource books and/or the World Wide Web to find out what makes the duck-billed platypus and echidna so very different from other mammals. Be sure to include information about the environment in which each animal lives.

Make a drawing of each animal in its environment.

3▶ Think and Write

Write a letter, telling a friend about these two strange mammals. Be sure to include these things about each animal: where it's found, what it eats, how it gets its food, and what characteristics make it different from most mammals

Include your drawing with the letter, so your friend can see what each animal looks like.

Explanation

The group of animals called *mammals* are warm blooded, usually covered with fur or hair, give birth to live offspring, and then nurse those offspring. But there are a few mammals that are very different from the rest, such as the duck-billed platypus and the echidna. These species are both members of a group of animals called *monotremes* (mono-treams).

Magnificent Math

Magnificent Math 5.1

Speedy Species!

Animals have many tools for survival. For instance, some have protective coloring that helps them blend in with their surroundings. Others have chemicals that they can use to poison or kill either a predator or prey. Some species survive because of their amazing ability to *sprint,* which means they can run really fast for a short distance from a standing stop. In this activity, you'll discover the fastest sprinters in the animal world.

1▶ Get Ready   Graph paper   Pencil

Table 1   Top Speeds for Short Distances (Sprints)

Species	Miles/Hour	Kilometers/Hour
Land Mammals		
Roe deer	38	61
Racehorse	41	66
Human	29	46
Greyhound (dog)	39	63
Saluki (dog)	38	61
Afghan hound (dog)	29	47
Cheetah	62	100
Ocean Mammals		
California sea lion	24	39
Common dolphin	34	55
Killer whale	38	61
Fish		
Swordfish	55	89
Bluefin tuna	63	101
Sailfish	66	106

2▶ Do and Wonder

You'll use the data in Table 1 to make a bar graph that shows the fastest sprinters in the animal world. Prepare the graph by labeling the vertical axis "Speed in Miles/Hour (or Kilometers/Hour)" and labeling the horizontal axis "Animal Species."

Record the information in Table 1 on the graph (using either Miles/Hour or Kilometers/Hour).

3▶ Think and Write

Study your graph and figure out which is the fastest land mammal, the fastest ocean mammal, and the fastest fish.

Write a hypothesis that explains how the speed of each of these fastest animals helps it survive.

Explanation

The ability to sprint gives some animals many advantages, but it doesn't guarantee their survival. Prey animals that can't run long distances without tiring will easily be caught by predators, such as packs of wild dogs or wolves. Predators such as these *can* run long distances without getting tired.

Magnificent Math 5.2

How Tall?

Although we humans are probably the *smartest* land creatures on Earth, we're certainly not the *tallest*. Many animals are much taller than we are. To see just how much taller, you'll make some scale drawings in this activity that will let you compare the height of the average human with the heights of giraffes, gorillas, bears, and elephants.

1▶ Get Ready

One or two sheets of graph paper   Pencil
Ruler   Scissors

2▶ Do and Wonder

The data in Table 2 show the heights of various animals, including human beings. Use this information to make a scale drawing of each animal on graph paper, using any scale you would like. (Hint: Try 1 square = 6 inches [about 15 centimeters] or 1 square = 4 inches [about 10 centimeters].)

Cut out your scale drawings, and lay them on a flat surface. Line them up in order from tallest to shortest.

Table 2   Heights of Animals

Animal	Height in Feet and Inches	Height in Meters
Human male	5'9"	1.75
Human female	5'5"	1.65
Gorilla	5'6"	1.7
Giraffe	19'	5.79
Grizzly bear (on hind legs)	10'	3
African elephant	10'	3

3▶ Think and Write   Write a short paragraph that answers these questions: When you compared the heights of the animals to the heights of the average man and woman, were you surprised by any? If so, which ones? What advantages do tall animals have for survival? What disadvantages do tall animals have for survival?

Explanation   An animal's survival depends on many things, including physical characteristics such as height. Being tall may permit some animals to see things in their environment that shorter animals cannot. On the other hand, shorter animals may have certain advantages over taller ones. For instance, humans are shorter than many species, but we have ability to think, solve problems, and make tools. These qualities give us many advantages over other animals.

 # Art Connections

Art Connections 5.1

Plaster Tracks

While on a hike or even walking to school, you've probably noticed animal tracks on a dirt path or along a streambank. But the next time you returned to this place, the tracks were likely gone. Animal tracks disappear quickly as people walk over them or rain washes them away. In this activity, you'll discover a way to preserve tracks in plaster.

1▶ Get Ready

Outdoor Materials

Premixed plaster of paris compound (You can get this at any hardware store. It's used to repair walls.)

Piece of very thin cardboard about 6 × 8 inches (15 × 20 centimeters)

Plastic sandwich bag   Vegetable oil cooking spray

Disposable plastic spoon   Tape

Indoor Materials

Small square of fabric about 5 inches (13 centimeters) on each edge

Pencil   Tempera paints in assorted colors

White glue   Scissors

2▶ Do and Wonder

Outdoors

To begin, go exploring for animal tracks! The best time to look is after a light rainstorm. Look for a place on a path that's just slightly muddy. Try to find a deep track.

Cut the cardboard in half the long way, creating two strips about 3 inches wide × 8 inches long (8 × 20 centimeters). Take one strip and bring its ends together to form a ring. Tape the ends together. (Keep in mind that the ring must be big enough to fit over the animal track.)

Spray the track with the vegetable spray. Then place the cardboard ring over the track, and press it into the soil.

Using a plastic spoon, gently put some of the plaster of paris on the track. Add enough until the plaster is about 2 inches deep inside the ring (about 5 centimeters).

Lay the plastic sandwich bag over the cardboard ring, and place a few pebbles on it to hold it in place. This will protect the ring while the plaster dries.

Make sure the plaster is dry and hard before you remove it. (It normally takes about 24 hours.) When it's ready, carefully remove the ring and plaster from the track. Then peel away the ring, and brush off any loose soil sticking to the plaster.

Indoors

Lay the plaster on the fabric with the track side up. Use a pencil to trace around the plaster on the fabric. Remove the plaster, and cut out the piece of fabric you traced. Glue it to the side of the plaster without the track.

Paint the track so it will be more easily visible.

You can use your plaster track as a paperweight, doorstop, or bookend.

3▶ Think and Write   What can you learn about an animal by just studying its tracks? Write three hypotheses that answer this question.

Explanation   An animal leaves a lot of information behind when it makes a track. Predators can sniff tracks to easily follow the trail of their prey. Trained human trackers can even tell when an animal track was made the track by observing if its edges have been worn down by wind or rain.

Art Connections 5.2

Mixed-Up Creature Collage

Do you like horses or lions or birds or fish? In this activity, you'll use your favorite animal as the starting place for an art project that will make people smile. Better yet, it will also make people think about why animals look like they do.

1▶ Get Ready

Ruler	White glue
Pencil with eraser	Scissors
Three sheets of white paper	

One sheet of oak tag paper or very thin cardboard
Ten sheets of construction paper in various colors
Three or four watercolor markers of assorted colors
Reference books with animal pictures

2 Do and Wonder

To begin, look through the reference books to find pictures of three of your favorite animals. Use a pencil to draw these favorite animals, one on each sheet of white paper. Make all three drawings about the same size.

Next use your ruler to measure each drawing. Figure out where to divide it into thirds, and draw lines through each drawing at those two points (that is, at one-third and two-thirds down). Cut along the lines to make three equal-sized pieces from each drawing.

Select one piece from each drawing, and combine them to form an imaginary animal. Adjust the pieces so they fit together better by erasing and redrawing some of edges.

Glue each of your newly created animals to the oak tag or cardboard.

Now you're ready to make the collage. Tear each sheet of construction paper into tiny pieces the size of the end of your thumb or smaller. Make one pile of pieces for each different color of paper.

Use the pieces of paper to "paint" your collage! Glue pieces of different colors to the animal shapes. Do the same to form a scene around the animals on the oak tag or cardboard. Overlap pieces to create a three-dimensional look for the collage.

Finally, use the markers to add details to your collage.

3 Think and Write

In a short paragraph, answer these questions about your imaginary creatures: Do you think each could survive in nature? What parts of each animal would help it survive? What parts of each animal would make it difficult to survive?

Explanation

Different parts of animals' bodies help them survive. But the parts that are helpful to one creature would probably not be helpful to another creature. For instance, a feather-covered fish and a bird with hooves would probably both have trouble surviving in their natural environments.

Amazing but True!
BRAINSTRETCHERS

5.1	What kind of dinosaurs did the early cave people kill and eat?
5.2	Why don't spiders get stuck in their own webs?
5.3	Do chameleons really change color?
5.4	Do hummingbirds really hum?
5.5	Are unicorns real?
5.6	Are butterflies and moths different animals?
5.7	How long is the longest snake?
5.8	How is a rainforest like an apartment house?
5.9	What was the largest dinosaur that ever lived?
5.10	How big was the smallest dinosaur that ever lived?
5.11	How can you tell the difference between a crocodile and an alligator?
5.12	How can you tell the difference between a frog and a toad?
5.13	Are dragons real?
5.14	How do fireflies make those flashes of light?
5.15	Why do fireflies make those flashes of light?
5.16	Is it true that a shark will sink if it stops moving?
5.17	What do killer whales eat?
5.18	How do killer whales get their prey?
5.19	Do camels really store water in their humps?
5.20	Is the abominable snowman real?
5.21	What is the Loch Ness Monster?
5.22	Are vampires real?
5.23	Do some animals really shoot their own food?
5.24	Do penguins ever feel lonely?
5.25	What game do sharks like to play?
5.26	What do you call a young deer that eats grass?
5.27	What's the difference between a fish and a piano?

5.1   What kind of dinosaurs did the early cave people kill and eat?

This is a trick question! Although many individuals think the cave people lived during the same time as the dinosaurs, they're wrong. Dinosaurs appeared on the earth about 225 million years ago and became extinct about 65 million years ago. But the first humanlike creatures didn't begin roaming the earth until about 3 million years ago. This means that the dinosaurs had been gone for about 62 million years before humans even existed. So humans never ate dinosaurs—or were eaten by dinosaurs!

5.2   Why don't spiders get stuck in their own webs?

Spiders don't get stuck because they're very talented and careful walkers! When a spider builds a web, it spins some strands that are sticky and some that are not. After it's finished building the web, the spider goes to one part of it and stays very still. When the spider feels vibrations on strands of the web, it knows it's trapped an insect. The spider then races out to get the insect, keeping its feet and legs on the nonsticky strands. Of course, this is more complicated than it sounds, since the spider has to know which strands aren't sticky *plus* keep track of where its eight legs are at all times. It helps that the ends of spiders' legs have an oily substance on them, which lets spiders move around their webs without sticking to them.

5.3   Do chameleons really change color?

Yes, chameleons really do change color, taking on the colors of the things around them. They can do this because all the colors exist in their skin at the same time. By opening and closing tiny openings (called *pores*) in its skin, the chameleon allows just certain colors to show through at one time. If the chameleon happens to be on a green leaf, for instance, the pores that expose its red and yellow colors close, which makes the skin looks green.

5.4   Do hummingbirds really hum?

Hummingbirds *do* make a humming sound, but they don't hum the way you do. Their humming sound comes from the sound waves they produce by beating their wings really quickly—50 or 60 times a second—and in a figure-eight pattern. As you can imagine, hummingbirds' wings move so quickly that we really can't see them at all. The movement is just a blur to our eyes. What we notice instead is the sound they make—the humming.

5.5 Are unicorns real?

There is an animal called a *unicorn,* but it doesn't look at all like the unicorns you may have read about in stories and myths. The real unicorn is the unicorn of the ocean, which is a whale called the *narwhal* with the scientific name Monodon monoceros (moan-oh-don mahn-oh-ser-us). The narwhal has just one tusk that can be 9 feet (about 3 meters) long. This type of whale is related to the white whale and feeds on squid, cod, and crustaceans.

5.6 Are butterflies and moths different animals?

Actually, both butterflies and moths are part of the same group of insects called *Lepidoptera* (leh-peh-dop-tera), which means "scaly wings." Moths and butterflies also have other things in common. For instance, both pass through egg, larva, pupa, and adult stages, and both have six legs, four wings, and sucking mouth parts. Butterflies and moths are also different in many ways. For example, most moths are active at night, while most butterflies are active during the day. Also, moths have feathery or straight antennae, while butterflies have straight, smooth antennae with knobs at the tips. Finally, moths have short, stout bodies, and butterflies have slender bodies.

5.7 How long is the longest snake?

Actually, there are *two* snakes that could be considered the longest: the reticulated python and the anaconda. The python—which lives in Southeast Asia, Indonesia, and the Philippines—can grow to a length of about 32 feet (10 meters). The Brazilian anaconda can reach a length of about 37 feet (a little more than 11 meters).

5.8 How is a rainforest like an apartment house?

In an apartment house, some people live on the top level, some live on the middle levels, and some live on the ground level. The same is true of the creatures that live in the rainforest. Monkeys, birds, and tree frogs live in the top level of the rainforest. At the next level down, there are plenty of insects but few large animals. This level contains plants that don't grow to full size because the branches and leaves of the top level block out so much sunlight. The bottom level, or floor, of the rainforest is home to many insects, small mammals, and in some places, large mammals, such as jaguars or gorillas.

5.9   What was the largest dinosaur that ever lived?

It depends on what you mean by *largest*. Do you mean "longest," "heaviest," or "tallest"? This is a question that scientists are always arguing about. One reason scientists can't agree on a definition of *largest* is that every few years, someone finds the fossils of a dinosaur that are bigger than any found before. Another problem is that scientists have to base their size estimates on the small number of fossils they discover. And they very rarely find a complete dinosaur! Now back to the question: The *longest* dinosaur, for which scientists have plenty of fossils, is a Diplodocus (deh-plah-duh-kiss). It was at least 87 feet (about 27 meters) long. Scientists have found a few fossils of even longer dinosaurs, but they're still working on figuring out the true sizes of these creatures. The future record holder for dinosaur length may be an Ultrasaurus, which was probably over 100 feet (30.5 meters) long.

5.10   How big was the smallest dinosaur that ever lived?

The smallest dinosaur was Compsognathus (com-so-nah-this), and it was about the size of a chicken. It had two front "arms," and each arm had three clawed hands. This dinosaur also had very sharp teeth. Despite its small size, Compsognathus could take care of itself. A *real* chicken would be chicken salad if a Compsognathus ever got hold of it!

5.11   How can you tell the difference between a crocodile and an alligator?

Luckily, you don't need to get close to either a crocodile or an alligator to tell them apart! An alligator has a wide head and a rounded snout. A crocodile is thinner and has a pointed snout. You can also tell which is which by looking at the animal's teeth (in case you accidentally get close to either one). When an alligator's mouth is closed, you can't see its teeth. But when a crocodile's mouth is closed, you can see a large tooth on its lower jaw that points upward.

5.12   How can you tell the difference between a frog and a toad?

This is an easy one: If you kiss a toad, you'll turn into a prince! Not really, but if you *did* kiss a toad (which you shouldn't do), you would discover that its skin is dry and has little bumps on it. A frog's skin is much smoother. Another difference is that frogs are active during the daytime, and toads are usually active at night.

5.13   Are dragons real?

The answer is no—and yes. If you mean the fire-breathing kind
that's found in stories and myths, the answer is definitely no. But
there is a creature that looks a lot like the dragons you've read about
and is even called a *dragon.* Scientists discovered this animal in 1912,
living on a few small islands in Indonesia. It's the Komodo dragon,
the biggest lizard in the world! It can reach a length of 10 feet
(about 3 meters) from head to tail and has dark gray, scaly skin. It
can easily kill pigs, deer, and small water buffalo. And oddly enough,
the Komodo dragon has a pink tongue that it flicks in and out of its
mouth. Maybe that's why people think dragons blow fire out of their
mouths.

5.14   How do fireflies make those flashes of light?

The firefly has a special organ on the underside of its body that
contains light-producing chemicals. The light fireflies produce is a
greenish color.

5.15   Why do fireflies make those flashes of light?

Fireflies make flashes of light to attract mates. Male fireflies fly
close to the ground and flash a pattern of light. Female fireflies of
the same species, which sit in bushes or on the ground, are on the
lookout for the pattern made by males of their own species. When the
females see the right pattern, they flash back. The male fireflies then
fly over to the females.

5.16   Is it true that a shark will sink if it stops moving?

Yes. Unlike other fish, sharks don't have a body part called a *gas
bladder,* which gives fish the ability to float easily in water. This
means that sharks must constantly swim through the water. If they
stop, they will begin to sink.

5.17   What do killer whales eat?

Just about anything they want to! The killer whales that live in the
Antarctic Ocean feed on leopard seals and penguins. Those that live
in the northern waters of the Pacific Ocean feed on fish, harbor seals,
and California sea lions. Killer whales also eat fish, squid, seals, and
even other whales.

5.18   How do killer whales get their prey?

Killer whales often hunt as a small group. They surround their prey, which might be a school of fish or group of seals, and then they attack. They use their sharp teeth to grab their prey, but they don't chew. Instead, they swallow their food whole or in large chunks. Killer whales will also cruise just offshore if they see seals on land. And when a seal comes into the water to feed, it discovers that it's become prey for killer whales. In some places, killer whales will even attack seals that are *on* the beach near the water line. The whales will actually throw their bodies on the beach to get to seals near the edge of the water. Wouldn't that be a sight to see?

5.19   Do camels really store water in their humps?

No. Camels store *fat* in their humps. And even though the fat doesn't help with a camel's thirst, it does provide the camel's cells with the fuel to make energy. So next time you're on a long trip with your camel, remember that it gets just as thirsty as you do!

5.20   Is the abominable snowman real?

The *abominable* snowman (sometimes called the *abdominal* snowman by mistake) is supposed to be a huge, wild creature (from 7 to 15 feet tall, or 2.1 to 4.6 meters) that's a cross between a human and an ape. People from many parts of the world claim to have seen such a creature, but there's no real scientific evidence of its existence. If you do research on the abominable snowman, you'll find that people in the northwest United States and the western portions of Canada call this creature *Bigfoot* or *Sasquatch*. In the Himalayan Mountains of Asia, the native people call it *Yeti,* or "the abominable snowman." (Look up the word *abominable* in the dictionary, and you'll understand why!) So far, no abominable snowman has ever been captured, photographed by a news organization, or interviewed on television.

5.21   What is the Loch Ness Monster?

First of all, Loch Ness is a deep lake in Scotland. It contains very cold water and is connected to the ocean at each end. People claim to have seen some strange creatures in the lake, which have become known as the *Loch Ness Monster.* There are as many descriptions of the monster as there are people who say they have seen it. Some say the creature is about 20 feet (about 6 meters) in length and has a long neck and a small head. A few people have even managed to take pictures of what they think is the monster, both above and under the water. But the pictures are blurry and could very well be shots of floating logs, large fish called *sturgeon,* or eels. So far, no Loch Ness Monster has been captured, photographed by a news organization, or interviewed on television.

5.22   Are vampires real?

Absolutely! But only if you use the word *vampire* to mean a creature that sucks blood from another creature without the victim knowing about it. There are worms, leeches, and insects that do it all the time. And there's also a larger blood-sucking animal—the vampire bat. Although there are almost 900 species of bats in the world, only 3 are blood thirsty. The most common vampire bat leaves its roost in the evening and gently lands on a cow or a horse to get an evening meal. The bat doesn't actually suck the blood from its victims. Instead, it makes a cut in the animal's flesh and licks the blood that comes out. The animal's wound heals slowly because of an anticlotting substance in the bat's saliva. The bat returns night after night to continue its feast. There's no reason *you* should worry about being the feast for a vampire!

5.23   Do some animals really shoot their own food?

Definitely, but they don't use guns or bows and arrows. In fact, they have much better equipment. For instance, the archer fish locates insects that are sitting on leaves or very low branches above the water and fires bursts of water at them. If an insect is hit, it falls into the water, where the archer fish is waiting to gobble it up. Another animal, the bola spider, weaves one thread with a sticky glob at its end. The spider aims and shoots the sticky end at a passing insect, and if it sticks, the spider just pulls in the thread and the insect along with it. Ummm, lunch!

5.24   Do penguins ever feel lonely?

No, but sometimes they feel ice-olated.

5.25   What game do sharks like to play?

Swallow the Leader.

5.26   What do you call a young deer that eats grass?

A fawn mower.

5.27   What's the difference between a fish and a piano?

You can't tuna fish.

Chapter 6
Amazing You

Activities

Sugar Checking   [SPSP 1]

Fat Finding   [SPSP 1]

Your Body Guards   [LS 6 & SPSP 1]

Weak Bones, Strong Bones   [SPSP 1 & LS 6]

Think Fast!   [LS 6]

Who? What? Charles Richard Drew and Daniel Hale Williams   [HNS 2]

Word Play

Food's Fantastic Voyage   [LS 4]

System Check   [LS 6]

Magnificent Math

Fast-Food Figures   [SPSP 6]

Exercise and Calorie Survey   [SPSP 6]

Art Connections

Faces, Please!   [LS 4]

Body Proportions   [LS 4]

Amazing but True!
Brainstretchers   [LS 1–4 & SPSP 1]

Activities

Sugar Checking

Foods that contain sugar and fat are high in calories. When we eat more of them than our bodies can use, both sugar and fat are stored as fat. In this activity, you'll learn one way to check foods to discover whether they contain a simple sugar called *glucose.*

1▶ Get Ready

Water

Package of TES-Tape or Clinistix (These products are used to test for the presence of glucose in urine. You can get them at a pharmacy. Shop carefully, as some brands are much more expensive than others.)

1 tablespoon of each of the following:

Lemon juice	Sugar
Orange juice	Crushed, overripe banana
Chopped, crushed pieces of onion	Honey
Small piece of hard candy	Crushed Saltine cracker
Crushed cornflakes	Salt
Any unsweetened cereal	Cookie

Three small, clean jars with tops

Tablespoon

Pencil and paper

2▶ Do and Wonder

You'll be putting substances in jars and testing them to see if they contain glucose. Test the substances in groups of three.

144

Choose three substances from the list on page 144, and put each in one of the jars. Add 1 tablespoon of water to each jar, put the cover on, and shake it vigorously.

Remove the cover of the jar, and insert a glucose test strip. Remove the strip after a few seconds. Compare your result to the information about results that came with the product. Write down your observations.

After you're done testing the first group of samples, dump them out of the jars. Rinse and dry each jar to prepare for the next group.

Test the rest of the substances in groups, three at a time, following the same steps. Be sure to write down your observations for each group.

▶ Think and Write

In one paragraph, summarize the results of your tests. Were you surprised by any of the results? If so, explain why.

Explanation

Simple sugars (including glucose) are made by the cells of green plants. These sugars contain a lot of energy. The amount of energy in a substance is measured in calories. If you want to reduce the number of calories you take in, you must eat less food containing sugar. (Of course, you must also eat less fatty food, since 1 gram of fat has almost twice the calories as 1 gram of sugar.) Also note that the testing strips you used in this experiment are normally used to measure how well a person's body is changing sugars to starches. To do this, the strips determine whether the simple sugar glucose is in a person's urine. The tapes don't tell whether common table sugar is present, since it's a complex sugar.

Safety Hints

Be sure to rinse out the jars thoroughly between groups of substances.

Wash the jars thoroughly when you're done.

Activity 6.2

Fat Finding

In this activity, you'll test some foods to see if they contain fat.
Those that do contain fat provide your body with a lot of energy.
But if you eat more fat than your body can use, you'll gain weight
and have other health problems, too.

1▶ Get Ready

Small sample of each of the following:

Pepperoni	Hard cheese
Bologna	Mayonnaise
Peanuts	Butter or margarine
Lettuce or spinach	Bread
Celery	

Large, clean, brown paper bag
Scissors
Thin-tipped marker
Lamp or sunlit window

2▶ Do and Wonder

You'll be testing each food on a sheet of brown paper. So to
begin, take the paper bag and pull apart the seams at the bottom.
Then cut the bag lengthwise, creating a large sheet of paper.

Next select one of the foods and rub it on a square spot on the
paper that's about 2 inches (5 centimeters) per side. Use the
marker to draw a square around the test spot. Label it with
the name of the food.

Test each food the same way. Be sure to label each test spot.

After you've tested all the foods, wave the paper through the
air to dry off any moisture from the test spots.

When the paper is dry, hold it up to a lamp or sunlit window.
You'll be able to see light coming through some of the spots.
Place a checkmark next to each of those spots. They are foods
that contain fat.

Make a chart that shows which foods contain fat.

3▶ Think and Write

In one paragraph, summarize the results of your tests. Were
you surprised by any of the results? If so, explain why.

Explanation

Many foods contain fat or oil, which is just liquid fat. If you eat
more fat than your body needs, you'll store it. Having too much
fat in your diet can make you overweight. It can also cause
problems for your digestive and circulatory systems.

Activity 6.5

Your Body Guards

As you probably know from experience, it's not fun to be sick or hurt. Fortunately, your body has many ways to help keep you healthy. It will protect you the *best* if you eat healthy foods, get regular exercise, and stay away from alcohol and illegal drugs. In this activity, you'll learn how your body defends itself from injury and disease.

1▶ Get Ready

Resource books and/or access to the World Wide Web
Paper and pencil

2▶ Do and Wonder

Use resource books and/or the World Wide Web to research how each of the following protects your body:

Tears	Excellent vision
A scab on a wound	Excellent hearing
Blinking	White blood cells
Sweating	Blood clotting
Leg muscles	(cells sticking together)
Skin	

Write a sentence that summarizes what you learned about each.

3▶ Think and Write

Pick two of the body's defenses you studied. Write a paragraph about each that tells the dangers someone would face if that body defense wasn't working.

Explanation

The bodies of humans and other living things are constantly trying to fight off injuries and diseases by using *defense mechanisms*. These defense mechanisms include some parts of the body, such as skin, and also certain activities, such as blinking and sweating. You can keep your body's defenses strong by eating clean, healthy food, by exercising on a regular basis, and by staying away from illegal drugs and alcohol.

Activity 6.4

Weak Bones, Strong Bones

Have you ever watched a large building under construction? If so, you probably noticed beams of wood or steel being used to give the building shape and support. Your bones do the same things for you. If your bones are strong, you'll be strong, too. But if they're weak, you'll collapse like a building made of straws. In this activity, you'll discover what keeps your bones strong.

1▶ Get Ready

Two cooked chicken bones that are about the
    same size and shape
Water
Two narrow jars with caps
Scrubbing brush
Hot water
Soap
Vinegar

2▶ Do and Wonder

First clean the cooked bones by scrubbing them with hot, soapy water. Then rinse them thoroughly.

Put one bone in each jar. Fill one jar with enough vinegar to completely cover the bone. Fill the other jar with enough water to completely cover the bone. Put the cap on each jar.

You're going to leave the bones in the jars for five days. On the first day, predict and write down the changes you expect to see.

After five days, open the jars and take out the bones. Rinse the bones thoroughly.

Carefully observe each bone. Then gently try to bend each. Which bone bent more easily, the one stored in vinegar or the one stored in water?

3▶ Think and Write

Think about what you observed in this activity, and then write a paragraph that answers these questions: What hypothesis can you make about how the bones changed? What were you trying to show by putting one bone in water and the other in vinegar?

Explanation   Minerals are substances that your body needs to work properly. Some minerals, such as potassium, keep your muscles strong. Others, such as calcium and phosphorous, form and maintain the hard parts of your bones and teeth. Dairy products, such as milk and cheese, contain a lot of calcium. So do eggs. Excellent sources of phosphorus include nuts, peas, whole-grain cereals, leafy green vegetables, and dairy products. If you don't get enough of these minerals, your bones and teeth will get as weak as the chicken bone that was kept in vinegar. That bone became weak because the vinegar removed minerals from it.

Safety Hints   Be sure to wash and rinse the bones thoroughly before beginning the activity.

If a bone breaks when you try to bend it, be careful with the sharp edges.

Activity 6.5

Think Fast!

Have you ever had to duck to miss being hit in the head by a flying ball? Or have you ever had to quickly step on the brakes to avoid hitting something with your bicycle? In this activity, you'll measure how fast your body reacts in situations like these.

1▶ Get Ready

Reaction Time Strip   Tape
Ruler   Paper and pencil
Scissors   Partner

2▶ Do and Wonder

You're going to test how much time it takes you to react and catch a dropped object. To do so, you'll use the Reaction Time Strip found along the edge of page 151. Note that the strip is divided into parts of a second.

Keep in mind that *all* objects speed up at the same rate when they fall. That means you can tell how far an object falls in 1 second. The Reaction Time Strip changes the *distance* the object dropped into the *time* it took to fall that far. So by using the strip to measure how far an object has dropped when you catch it, you can determine how long it took for your body to react.

Cut the strip off the edge of the page, and tape it to the ruler.

Hold out your hand with your thumb and forefinger open, forming a V. Have your partner hold the ruler so the bottom end is right above your open thumb and forefinger. (They should be just below the bottom edge of the Reaction Time Strip, which is taped to the ruler.)

Without warning you, your partner should drop the ruler straight down. Close your thumb and forefinger as quickly as you can, trying to catch the ruler.

Once you catch the ruler, hold it in place with your closed thumb and forefinger. Then look at where along the Reaction Time Strip your closed fingers are. The number right above them tells how long it took you to react and catch the falling ruler. Write down this number.

Repeat the experiment two or three times. Also try it using different hands. Record your results.

Do some exercise, such as running in place for a few minutes. Then try the experiment again. Record your results.

Switch places with your partner, and measure his or her reaction times in the same types of experiments. Record his or her results in a column next to your results.

3 ▶ Think and Write

Do some thinking about what could affect a person's reaction time. For instance: Does reaction time seem to get faster with practice? Does reaction time seem to depend on which hand someone uses? Does exercise seem to make reaction time faster or slower? What else might make reaction time faster or slower?

Write a paragraph that gives your opinion about how being tired, drinking alcohol, or taking illegal drugs might affect an automobile driver's reaction time. Which of his or her reactions might slow down?

Explanation

The time between your observing something happen and reacting to it is called *reaction time*. Being tired, drinking alcohol, and taking illegal drugs can all slow down a person's reaction time. When automobile drivers are affected by any of these things, they become dangerous to other people in the car, to other drivers, to pedestrians, and to themselves.

Time (seconds)

Reaction Time Chart

.22

.21

.20

.19

.18

.17

.16

.15

.14

.13

.12

.11

.10

.08

.06

.04

Activity 6.6

Who? What? Charles Richard Drew and Daniel Hale Williams

How curious are you about how your body really works? In this activity, you'll learn about a scientist who was *very* curious and used what he discovered to help people who were sick or injured. Charles Richard Drew and Daniel Hale Williams were both medical doctors who worked hard not only to help their own patients but to help other doctors, too.

1▶ Get Ready

Paper and pencil
Ruler
Resource books and/or
    access to the World Wide Web

Two sheets of poster paper
Felt-tipped markers of assorted colors

2▶ Do and Wonder

In this activity, you'll do two things: (1) Gather a lot of information about the life and discoveries of a scientist, and (2) create two posters that will show what you learned.

Pick one of these scientists for your research: Charles Richard Drew or Daniel Hale Williams.

To begin, read the brief biography of this scientist in the Explanation section at the end of this activity.

Use resource books and/or the World Wide Web to find more information about your scientist. Take as many notes as you can about the individual and his discoveries.

Now you're ready to create your posters.

Poster 1
Write the scientist's name at the top of the poster, and draw a picture of him below it.

Write down when and where the scientist lived.

List important facts about his life.

Poster 2
At the top of the poster, write the problem or question the scientist worked on.

Draw the kinds of equipment he used to make his discoveries.

If you could ask the scientist two questions about his life and discoveries, what would they be? Write them down.

3▶ Think and Write

Imagine that the scientist you selected was going to visit your classroom. What would you like him to bring to show you and your classmates? What science questions do you think you and your classmates might ask the scientist? What are two things the scientist might tell about his life and work?

Write one or two paragraphs about the scientist's visit to your classroom, describing what he would show and tell you and your classmates.

Explanation

Charles Richard Drew

Charles Richard Drew was an American physician who was born in Washington, D.C., in 1904. As a young man, he attended Amherst College in Massachusetts, where he was an outstanding student and athlete. After graduating, he went on to McGill University Medical School in Montreal, Canada, where he graduated in 1933. As a physician, Dr. Drew struggled with a problem: How could donated human blood be kept long enough for it to be used by patients in surgery and others who needed blood transfusions? Over many years, he developed techniques for preserving blood that were eventually used by doctors all over England and the United States. Dr. Drew's knowledge was the starting place for future discoveries that have saved the lives of people all over the world. Dr. Drew died in 1950 at the young age of 46.

Daniel Hale Williams

Daniel Hale Williams was born in 1858 in Hollidaysburg, Pennsylvania, but spent much of his life in Chicago. He received his M.D. degree from Chicago Medical College, Northwestern Medical School, and later helped establish Provident Hospital in Chicago. Dr. Williams is perhaps most well known for being one of the first surgeons to perform open heart surgery. He also was the only African American included among the 100 members of American College of Surgeons in 1913. In addition, he helped set up training for African Americans who wanted to become interns and nurses. Dr. Williams died in 1931, but he was remembered long after that. In 1970, the U.S. Congress honored him by having the U.S. Post Office issue a stamp celebrating his work in the field of medicine.

Word Play

Food's Fantastic Voyage

If you were going to take a fantastic voyage, would it be a journey to another planet? Or maybe a boat cruise down a jungle river? In this activity, you'll use some information plus your imagination to describe a fantastic voyage that will be interesting as anything you could dream up. And you won't have to travel very far—just through your own body!

1▶ Get Ready   Paper and pencil
Resource books and/or access to the World Wide Web

2▶ Do and Wonder   In this activity, you'll describe the journey that food takes through the human body. To begin, study the body's organs to review what you already know about digestion:

Mouth: The opening in your head where food enters. Your teeth break up food into smaller chunks. Saliva begins digestion by starting to act on starches in foods.

Esophagus (ee-sof-a-gus):   The tube that connects your mouth and stomach.

Stomach: A container-type organ that receives and holds the food you've chewed in your mouth. Acid and other chemicals in your stomach break down the food. The acid also kills some of the harmful bacteria and other living things in your food.

Small Intestine: Food from your stomach enters this long, coiled tube. This organ is many yards (meters) long. As food moves through the small intestine, nutrients and water are absorbed into its walls. They then enter your bloodstream and are carried to cells all through your body.

Large Intestine: This tube is wider (has a larger diameter) than the small intestine. It receives undigested food material from the small intestine and absorbs the water from it.

Next use reference books and/or the World Wide Web to get more information about the parts of the digestive system. Take notes to record what you find.

3▶ Think and Write

Imagine that you are a molecule of starch in a piece of pizza crust. Think about the journey that you'll take from the time you're eaten and enter a person's mouth to the time you become a cell on that person's skin. (Hint: The starch will have become a sugar molecule by the time it's absorbed into the walls of the small intestine.)

Describe your journey by writing a three- or four-paragraph story that begins this way:

> There I was, just sitting around, minding my own business in the crust of a medium-sized pepperoni pizza. I was with friends. There were starch molecules all around. We were all peacefully chatting about the places we might visit. All of a sudden, the crust started to shake and break apart as these teeth with braces (which must have belonged to a teenager) started chomping through the crust. Fortunately, I wasn't hurt, but I sure got scared when the lights suddenly went out. Those teeth continued to break up the crust into smaller and smaller pieces. Then . . .

Explanation

The human body needs energy to do all the things it does. That energy enters your body as starches, sugars, fats, and other substances that are contained in the food you eat each day. Your digestive system takes what it needs from the food and gets rid of what it doesn't need.

Word Play 6.2

System Check

Do you think you know a lot or a little about the human body? You'll find out in this activity, which is about the body systems that keep you healthy and strong.

1▶ Get Ready

Paper and pencil

2▶ Do and Wonder   Draw a line that connects each body system in the lefthand column with the item in the righthand column that best describes it.

Body System

1. Muscular
2. Digestive
3. Skeletal
4. Respiratory
5. Circulatory
6. Excretory
7. Immune
8. Sensory (includes the eyes)
9. Reproductive
10. Nervous (includes the brain)
11. Endocrine (includes the gland that makes adrenaline [a-dren-a-lin])

Description

a. Produces young
b. Gathers information about the world using the senses
c. Supports the body
d. Moves the body
e. Takes in oxygen and gets rid of carbon dioxide and water vapor
f. Sends chemical instructions through the body
g. Analyzes information from the senses and sends instructions
h. Main job is to protect the body from diseases caused by bacteria, viruses, fungi, and so on
i. Gets rid of body wastes
j. Moves blood through the body
k. Main job is to take in and digest food

3▶ Think and Write   People sometimes confuse two of the systems listed above—the sensory system and the nervous system—because they seem a lot alike. Think about how these systems are different from one another using these hints: The sensory system includes the eyes, ears, nose, tongue, and skin. The nervous system includes the nerves, spinal cord, and brain.

Write a paragraph about how these two systems are different.

Explanation   Check your answers to the puzzle:

1. d	7. h
2. k	8. b
3. c	9. a
4. e	10. g
5. j	11. f
6. i	

Magnificent Math 6.1

Fast-Food Figures

Do you like to eat at fast-food restaurants? Some people worry that the food at these restaurants contains a lot more fat than the food you eat at home. In this activity, you'll learn about the nutrients in fast foods and make a graph showing the amounts of fat, protein, fiber, and sugar in some popular fast foods. You might just be surprised!

1▶ Get Ready

Graph paper
Paper and pencil

2▶ Do and Wonder

Using just the foods in Table 1 (page 158), list the items you would choose for a fast-food meal. Then find out the total grams of fat and the total number of calories for this meal.

Now use the table to make a list of the foods you would pick for a healthy, lowfat meal. Figure out the total number of calories and fat grams for this meal.

Suppose that you were going to start your own fast-food restaurant called "(Your Name)'s Healthy Speed Food." Look again at the foods listed in the table, and choose five that you would include on your menu. Explain why you picked each.

Create a graph showing the nutrients found in the five foods you selected for your restaurant. Divide the horizontal axis into four equal-sized units, and label them "Fat," "Protein," "Fiber," and "Sugar." Label the vertical axis "Grams," and make a scale that goes from 0 to 35. Record the data for the five foods.

Table 1   Foods and Their Nutrients

Food	Portion Size	Calories	Fat (g)	Protein (g)	Fiber (g)	Sugar (g)
Regular-size hamburger	106 g	250	9	12	2	1
Regular-size cheeseburger	119 g	300	13	15	2	1
Quarter-pound hamburger	116 g	400	20	23	2	2
Fish sandwich	141 g	370	18	14	2	0
Chicken sandwich (grilled)	240 g	400	12	31	1	2
French fries:						
Small	68 g	220	12	3	2	0
Medium	97 g	320	17	4	3	0
Large	122 g	400	22	6	4	1
Salad (without dressing)	265 g	170	9	17	2	4
Salad dressing:						
Blue cheese	1 pkg.	240	21	3	3	3
Light vinaigrette	1 pkg.	50	2	0	0	6
Orange juice	6 oz.	80	0	0	0	18
Milk (1% fat)	8 oz.	100	2.5	8	0	13
Cola soda	Medium	210	0	0	0	50

▶ Think and Write   Look at the foods in the table and the amounts of fat, protein, fiber, and sugar each contains. Also compare how many calories they have. How much of this information surprised you? Explain what you learned about the calories and nutrients in some of these foods.

Explanation   Eating fast food has become a regular part of many people's busy lives. Most modern fast-food restaurants offer enough choices so you can pick out foods for a healthy, lowfat, and low-sugar meal that is still tasty—and fast! The next time you go to a fast-food restaurant, ask the restaurant manager for a list of the foods served and the nutrients and calories found in each. Having this information will help you make wise food choices.

Magnificent Math 6.2

Exercise and Calorie Survey

Everyone should exercise on a regular basis, whether to get in shape, keep in shape, or lose weight. Whatever kind of exercise *you* decide to do, you'll be burning calories. Scientists can figure out how many calories different kinds of exercise actually use up. In this activity, you'll interview some adults to see how many calories they *think* they use up when they exercise. They may be surprised when you give them the correct answers!

1▸ Get Ready

Graph paper
Pencil

2▸ Do and Wonder

Table 2 (page 160) tells how many calories a 150 pound person uses up while doing different kinds of exercise. Although you probably weigh much less than 150 pounds, the table will give you an idea of which exercises burn the most calories.

Select 10 of the activities listed in the table. Then interview a teacher, a parent, or another relative, asking him or her to predict how many calories are burned by doing each activity for 1 hour. Write down his or her predictions.

Make a graph showing how many calories are burned by doing each of the 10 activities for 1 hour. Divide the horizontal axis into 10 equal-sized units, and label them with the names of the activities. Label the vertical axis "Calories Burned per Hour," and show units 0, 50, 100, 150, 200, and so on up to 800. On the graph, mark the adult's predictions with O's and the actual amounts with X's.

3▸ Think and Write

Show your graph to the adult you interviewed, and explain what it means. Ask whether he or she is surprised by any of the differences between his or her predictions and the actual calories burned.

Write three or four sentences about what most surprised the adult you interviewed. Include your ideas about why some of his or her predictions were incorrect.

Table 2   Calories Used during Exercise

Type of Exercise	Calories Used per Hour
Basketball	500
Bicycling (5½ miles/hour, about 9 kilometers/hour)	210
Gardening	200
House cleaning	180
Jogging (5 to 10 miles/hour, about 8 to 16 kilometers/hour)	500–800
Sitting	100
Cross-country skiing	600–660
Downhill skiing	420–480
Raking leaves	300–360
Square dancing	350
Standing	140
Swimming (moderate)	500–700
Volleyball	350
Walking (2 miles/hour, a little more than 3 kilometers/hour)	150–240
Walking (4 miles/hour, about 6½ kilometers/hour)	300–400

Explanation

A *calorie* is a measurement that tells how much energy is in food. It is also a measurement of how much energy is used by doing various exercises. If you take in *less* calories than you burn up through exercise, you'll lose weight. But if you take in *more* calories than you burn up, you'll gain weight.

Art Connections

Faces, Please!

When you see someone, how can you tell whether you *know* him or her? It's simple: You recognize people by their faces. But are people's faces really all that different? Some things about them are pretty much the same. This activity will bring out the artist in you by showing what information you need to accurately draw a face—your face!

1 Get Ready   Paper and pencil   Ruler
                     Mirror

2 Do and Wonder Hold the mirror in front of you so you can see your entire face. Study it for a minute or two.

Begin by drawing the basic shape of your head. To do this, think of your head as being pretty much egg shaped when viewed from the front. Draw an egg shape, with the widest part of the egg toward the top of your picture.

Next draw a faint line from left to right across the middle of the head. (Later, you'll draw the middle of your eyes on this line.)

Draw another light line from left to right across the head halfway between the middle line and the bottom of the head. (This is where the tip of your nose will go.)

Now draw another light line between the second line and the bottom of the head. (This is where the bottom of your mouth will go.)

Draw in your eyes, your nose, and your mouth.

Next add eyebrows to your drawing.

Add ears, positioning them between your eyebrows and the tip of your nose.

Finally, add your hair.

161

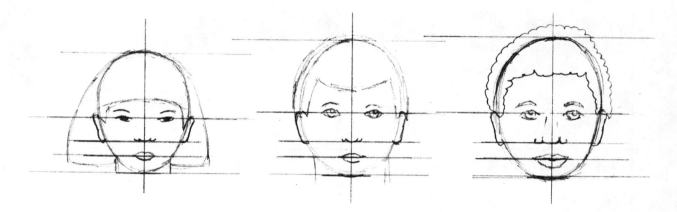

3▶ Think and Write   Take a good look at your drawing. Does it really look like you? Are your eyes about the right distance apart? Are they the right shape? How about your mouth? Your nose? Your ears? Your eyebrows? Your hair? Write a paragraph about what you've noticed about your face by making this drawing.

Suppose you want to draw a lion's face. How could you figure out where the guiding lines should be placed? Briefly explain your ideas in writing.

Explanation   People are very different from one another but also alike in many ways. This is especially true of people's faces. It will be easy for you to draw any human face using what you learned in this activity.

Art Connections 6.2

Body Proportions

How good are you at drawing people? Most artists admit that people are one of the toughest subjects to draw. It helps to think about what you're going to draw *before* you draw it. Great artists know some tricks that help them draw people that look real. You'll learn some of those tricks in this activity, which will help make *your* drawings of people look real, too.

1▶ Get Ready   Paper and pencil
Ruler
Pastels or water-based markers in assorted colors
Child and adult models (1 of each)

Do and Wonder

Here are some of the artists' tricks that will help you with your drawings:

If you draw a young child or baby, make the size of the head (from top to bottom) one-fourth the length of the body.

If you draw an older child, make the head about one-sixth the length of the body.

If you draw an adult, make the head about one-seventh the length of the body.

The legs begin about halfway down the body.

The knees are halfway down the legs.

When the arms are at the sides, the fingertips should be halfway between the hips and the knees.

The elbows start halfway down the arms.

Drawing an Adult

To start your drawing of an adult, lightly draw eight equal-spaced lines across your paper. (This will give you seven equal-sized spaces between the lines.) Draw a vertical line down the center of your paper through all eight lines.

Draw the head in the first (top-most) space on the paper. Center it on the vertical line.

Then use the artists' tricks listed above to finish drawing the adult.

When you've finished drawing the adult's body, add more details. Use the pastels or markers to color in the person's features and clothing.

Drawing a Child

To start your drawing, lightly draw seven equal-spaced lines across your paper. (This will give you six equal-sized spaces between the lines.) Draw a vertical line down the center of your paper through all seven lines.

Draw the head in the first (top-most) space on the paper. Center it on the vertical line.

Then use the artists' tricks listed above to finish drawing the child.

Finally, add details and color in the drawing.

Adult   Child

3▶ Think and Write   Look carefully at both of your drawings, and think about the artists' tricks you followed to make them. Write a paragraph about how having this information made it easier to draw people.

Suppose you want to draw a horse or a dog. How could you figure out where the guiding lines should be placed for one of these animal pictures? Briefly explain your ideas in writing.

Explanation   People are very different from one another but also alike in many ways. This is especially true of people's bodies. The guidelines that artists use to draw bodies were developed by studying the many ways in which people are alike. By following these guidelines, you'll find it easier to make good drawings of people.

Amazing but True!
BRAINSTRETCHERS

6.1   What is a belly button?

6.2   What are those strange sounds my stomach makes?

6.3   Do animals' hearts beat faster or slower than mine?

6.4   Why does my heart beat faster when I exercise?

6.5   Why is blood red?

6.6   Why do some people start crying when they laugh really hard?

6.7   Why does my nose run when I have a cold?

6.8   What makes me hiccup?

6.9   What are fingernails made of?

6.10   Why do young children's teeth fall out?

6.11   What are those squiggles and dots I sometimes see when there really isn't anything there?

6.12   I've seen commercials on TV for pills that get rid of stomach acid. If I don't take these pills, will the acid in my stomach someday burn a hole right through it?

6.13   If bacteria live all over our skin, how come we aren't always sick?

6.14   Are there any creatures besides bacteria that live on or in us?

6.15   When people get head lice, does it mean they haven't kept their hair clean?

6.16   Why do feet smell?

6.17   If you were out on the ocean in a boat and ran out of drinking water, why couldn't you just drink seawater?

6.18   Why does my mouth sometimes water when I open a carton of ice cream or reach for a big slice of chocolate cake?

6.19   What's the difference between an artery and a vein?

6.20   What does it mean when a cut gets infected?

6.21   What are bruises, or black-and-blue marks?

6.22   How can you prevent diseases caused by biting insects?

6.23   What did one eye say to the other?

6.24   What did the silly dentist call his x-rays?

6.1 What is a belly button?

Your belly button is the place where you were connected to your mom while you were in her uterus. A tube containing blood vessels ran between you and your mom. That's how nutrients passed from her body to yours. When you were born, the tube was cut and the end was tied off. That end of the tube is your belly button.

6.2 What are those strange sounds my stomach makes?

The rumbling and gurgling sounds your stomach makes come from the muscles in your digestive system working to push liquids and solid foods through your body. Those muscles are always busy, since food usually enters and leaves your body within a single day. Your body also makes *another* sound when air and gas bubbles from your stomach and intestines are finally pushed out by your muscles. Unfortunately, there's nothing you can do when this happens (except maybe point to the person next to you).

6.3 Do animals' hearts beat faster or slower than mine?

The hearts of different animals pump at different rates. For instance, an elephant's heart rate is about 30 beats per minute, a crocodile's heart rate is between 30 and 70 beats per minute, and a cat's heart rate is about 200 beats a minute. Of course, if the cat is being chased by the crocodile, both will have much higher heart rates! Also keep in mind that *your* heart rate won't be the same your entire life. It depends on your age. The heart rate of a young child is usually between 90 and 100 beats per minute. When that child is an adult, his or her heart rate will have slowed down to about 70 to 80 beats a minute.

6.4 Why does my heart beat faster when I exercise?

Think of your heart as a pump that works harder when the machine it's running—your body—needs more fuel. That's what happens when you exercise. Your muscles need more energy than they do when you're resting. That energy comes from the cells, which combine oxygen with sugar (glucose) in chemical reactions. When you exercise, your lungs work harder to take in air containing oxygen and to release the carbon dioxide produced by the cells. Your heart pumps faster to carry the oxygen-rich blood to the cells and the carbon dioxide–rich blood away from them.

6.5 Why is blood red?

Blood is the color it is because the substance in a red blood cell that picks up oxygen also happens to be a red pigment called *hemoglobin* (he-mo-glow-bin). When blood that's rich in oxygen releases some of that oxygen to cells in the body, the blood changes color. Some people think the blood returning to the lungs through the veins is blue. Actually, it's more maroon or dark purple.

6.6   Why do some people start crying when they laugh really hard?

When you laugh or cry, the muscles of your face tend to push everything together. This usually means your mouth is open and your eyes are squeezed shut. When your face is in this position, your tear glands get pressed and tears are squeezed out. You actually make yourself cry!

6.7   Why does my nose run when I have a cold?

Your nose is just protecting your body by getting rid of whatever is bothering it—maybe the bacteria from a cold, dirt from the air, or pollen from flowers. Your nose does this by producing a thick liquid called *mucus* (mew-kiss), which flows out, carrying out whatever is causing the irritation. It's not pretty, but it works!

6.8   What makes me hiccup?

Toward the bottom of your rib cage, going right across your body, is a large muscle called the *diaphragm* (dye-a-fram). When it pulls downward, your lungs inflate a little and air enters your windpipe. If you eat too fast or upset your stomach by drinking very cold soda, your diaphragm might start quickly contracting and relaxing. When it twitches like this, your diaphragm lets a little air into your windpipe, which makes the "hic" sound. To prevent too much air from entering your lungs, a little flap at the top of your windpipe snaps shut, which makes the "cup" sound.

6.9   What are fingernails made of?

Have you ever seen a horse's hoof, a bird's feather, or a lion's claw? If so, you have seen some other things made of the same substance as your fingernails. That substance is a protein called *keratin* (keh-rah-tin). Like all proteins, keratin is made of large molecules that are strong and difficult to break apart.

6.10   Why do young children's teeth fall out?

"Baby teeth" fall out because they're *supposed* to fall out. As you get older, your entire body gets larger—that is, everything but your teeth. And since teeth don't grow, they have to fall out to make room for larger teeth. Those larger teeth are needed for chewing the kind and amount of food an adult has to eat to fuel his or her larger body.

6.11   What are those squiggles and dots I sometimes see when there really isn't anything there?

Those squiggles and dots are called *floaters*. They're small pieces of leftover blood vessels that were needed when your eyeballs were developing before you were even born. After each eyeball reached its full size, the job of the blood vessel was done, so it fell apart. But since the eyeball developed around those pieces, they had nowhere to go. You still have them today.

6.12   I've seen commercials on TV for pills that reduce stomach acid. If I don't take these pills, will the acid in my stomach someday burn a hole right through it?

Your stomach definitely has acid in it—hydrochloric (high-dro-klor-ik) acid. It's there to break up the foods you eat and get them ready to be used by your body. This acid won't burn a hole through your stomach because your stomach walls are covered by a thick, slimelike material called *mucus*. Stomach acid isn't powerful enough to get through the mucus and eat away your stomach lining. The pills people take make the stomach acid weaker.

6.13   If bacteria live all over our skin, how come we aren't always sick?

You may be surprised to learn that not all bacteria are bad. In fact, most of the bacteria that live on your skin don't harm you at all. Some may even destroy harmful types of bacteria that end up on your skin. Also, bacteria can't get through your skin unless you accidentally cut or scrape it.

6.14   Are there any creatures besides bacteria that live on us or in us?

You're walking around with *many* different creatures on you and in you! You probably have amoebae (simple, one-celled animals) living in your mouth. You may also have fungus growing over the skin in parts of your body that are moist and dark, and you may have tiny creatures called *mites* (with the scientific name Demodex) living in your eyelashes. Aren't you glad you asked?

6.15   When people get head lice, does it mean they haven't kept their hair clean?

No, definitely not. Head lice are happy to live in anyone's hair, whether it's clean or dirty. If you have head lice, you'll probably notice that your scalp is more itchy than usual. And if you run a very fine-toothed comb through your hair, you may even find the tiny shells (or *nits*) of the lice. Head lice can be easily removed by washing your hair with a special shampoo that's sold at all drugstores.

6.16   Why do feet smell?

Feet smell because of sweat. All of your skin contains tiny organs that release the moisture we call *sweat* or *perspiration*. That moisture contains water, salt, and the chemical *urea* (you-ree-ah). The odor of perspiration is caused by urea. In most parts of your body, evaporation carries the moisture away. Your feet are a different matter completely. Think about them for a moment. Most of the time, they're stuck inside shoes and socks. That means the moisture from your perspiration has nowhere to go except those shoes and socks. The combination of urea and whatever bacteria choose your shoes and socks as a happy place to live and reproduce is what causes smelly feet. The best thing you can do to avoid having smelly feet is to wash them—often!

6.17   If you were out on the ocean in a boat and ran out of drinking water, why couldn't you just drink seawater?

Your body actually does need a little salt, but not as much as you'd get by drinking seawater. The amount of salt found in seawater would quickly overpower your body's excretory system. Your body would eventually get poisoned by the salt. The only way to get rid of the salt would be to drink freshwater.

6.18   Why does my mouth sometimes water when I open a carton of ice cream or reach for a big slice of chocolate cake?

This isn't going to sound very nice, but your mouth isn't really *watering*, it's *salivating*. That means that extra saliva is coming from the saliva-producing glands in your mouth. You're producing extra saliva because your eyes have sent messages to your brain, telling it that yummy food is on the way. Saliva contains chemical substances called *enzymes* (en-zimes) that begin the process of breaking large food molecules into smaller ones. So your mouth waters because your body is getting ready to start digestion.

6.19   What's the difference between an artery and a vein?

Actually, arteries and veins are both *blood vessels*. Arteries are blood vessels that carry blood *from* your heart to other parts of the body. Veins are blood vessels that carry blood from other parts of your body *to* your heart.

6.20   What does it mean when a cut gets infected?

If you cut or scrape yourself, you've made a doorway that harmful bacteria can use to get into your bloodstream. If the bacteria do get in, special cells in your bloodstream—called *white blood cells*—go on the attack. These cells surround the bacteria and try to kill them. When this happens, your body starts producing extra white blood cells to send to the location of the battle. The remains of the bacteria, the remains of the white blood cells, and any of your own body's cells that have been destroyed form a whitish-yellow liquid called *pus.* This is a major sign of infection. Another sign is that the area of the battle turns red and may feel tender. For most simple infections, the body is able to kill off the bacteria and heal itself. For more serious infections, special drugs called *antibiotics* (which a doctor prescribes) are needed to help kill off the bacteria.

6.21   What are bruises, or black-and-blue marks?

If you fall on a hard surface, the force of the fall can break the small blood vessels under your skin. These vessels, which are called *capillaries,* will bleed for awhile and then stop when a blood clot forms. If you didn't fall hard enough to break open your skin, the blood will stay under the skin and form a dark spot. What you see as a black-and-blue mark, or bruise, is the blood trapped under your skin. Over a period of time, your body will carry away this blood and the spot will disappear.

6.22   How can you prevent diseases caused by biting insects?

Don't bite any.

6.23   What did one eye say to the other?

Between you and me, something smells.

6.24   What did the silly dentist call his x-rays?

Tooth-pics.

Chapter 7

Rocks and Continents

 Activities

Find It, Size It, Name It!   [ESS 1]
Rock Breaker   [ESS 1]
Soil Detective   [ESS 1]
The Layer Cake Rock   [ESS 1]
Puff Goes the Volcano!   [ESS 4]
Mountain Maker   [ESS 5]
Shape the Land   [ESS 5]

 Word Play

Create a Puzzle   [ESS 4]
The Rock Reporter's Notebook   [ESS 4]

 Magnificent Math

How Thick?   [ESS 4]
The Global Grid   [ESS 4]

 Art Connections

Stone Sculptures   [ESS 1]
Sand Painting   [ESS 1]

 Amazing but True!
Brainstretchers   [ESS 1–5]

Part III Rocks to Rockets

Earth/Space Sciences

Activities

Find It, Size It, Name It!

Have you ever seen a *cobble*? Actually, you've probably seen many of them. So what are they? A cobble is a fairly large-sized rock. You'll learn the scientific names for many different-sized rocks in this activity.

1▶ Get Ready

Ruler
Hand lens
1 teaspoon powdered cleanser (such as Ajax or Comet)
Paper and pencil
Clipboard
Outdoor area that has rocks on its surface

2▶ Do and Wonder

Before you head outdoors, make a three-column chart to record information about the rocks you find. List all the types of rock sizes in the first (lefthand) column (see types in Table 1). In the second (middle) column, leave some space to write down how many rocks of each size you find. And in the third (righthand) column, leave some space to write down the total number of rocks you find of each type.

Gather the materials listed above, the chart you just made, and Table 1 on rock size information. Then go outside to look for rocks.

Table 1   Rock Size Information

Type of Rock Size	Size in Inches (in.)	Size in Centimeters (cm) or Millimeters (mm)
Boulder	More than 10 in. across	25 cm
Cobble	$2\frac{1}{2}$ to 10 in. across	6 to 25 cm
Pebble	$\frac{1}{8}$ to $2\frac{1}{2}$ in. across	30 mm to 6 cm
Granule	$\frac{1}{16}$ to $\frac{1}{8}$ in. across	15 to 30 mm
Sand	$\frac{1}{64}$ to $\frac{1}{16}$ in. across	5 to 15 mm
Silt	Size of cleanser particles	Size of cleanser particles
Clay	Particles can only be seen with microscope	Particles can only be seen with microscope

Walk around outside looking for rocks that are examples of each size. On the chart you made, put one checkmark in the space in the middle column for each type of rock you find. For particles that are too tiny and numerous to count, write T for "too many to count."

To find silt, scoop up some soil from the bottom of a mud puddle. You may or may not be able to find examples of clay.

When you've finished looking for rocks, add up how many of each type you found. Use these words to describe how many of each you find: Few (1–4), Many (5 or more), and T (too many to count). Write down the correct word or letter for each rock type in the third (righthand) column on your chart.

3 Think and Write   Write a few sentences that tell about the sizes of the rocks you found. What type of rock did you find the most of? The least of? Also be sure to mention the smallest and largest rocks.

Explanation   Rocks can be classified in many different ways, including size. That's what you did in this activity. And in doing so, you also learned the scientific names that geologists use to classify rocks.

Rock Breaker

It's hard to believe, but the soil on the earth's surface was made by breaking down huge rocks into tiny particles. Of course, it took millions of years for this to happen. In this activity, you'll discover one way nature changes rocks to soil.

1▶ Get Ready

Empty plastic 35 mm film container with cap
Small foil or metal pie pan
Water
Small tray
Access to a freezer

2▶ Do and Wonder

Fill the pan with water until it almost overflows. Place it on the tray, and then put both in the freezer. What do you think will happen to the water level when the water freezes?

Hold the film container over a sink, and fill it with water until it overflows. Then put the cap on the container. Try not to trap an air bubble under the cap (but it's OK if there's a small bubble). Place the container in the freezer. What do you think will happen to the cap when the water inside the container freezes?

Observe the water levels in the pie plate and the container after the water in each has frozen.

3▶ Think and Write

Write a short paragraph about what you observed. What happens to water when it freezes? Sidewalks usually have a few cracks in them. If water gets into these cracks and freezes, the small cracks become large cracks and eventually break the sidewalk apart. This is a real problem in cold climates. What could you do to prevent it?

Explanation

Liquid water expands as it freezes. When water gets inside rocks and freezes, it can easily break them up. As time passes, large rocks gradually break into smaller and smaller pieces. This is called *weathering*. Other things can cause weathering, too, including wind and rain.

Activity 7.3

Soil Detective

If you look at soil from a distance, it looks as though it's all made of the same thing. But if you take a very close look at soil, you'll see that's not the case. That's what you're going to do in this activity, and you may discover some things that will really surprise you.

1▶ Get Ready

1 tablespoon of soil from each of three different places near your school or home (Try to get at least one sample from a moist area.)

1 tablespoon of potting soil (You can buy this in any large supermarket.)

Four sheets of white paper

Hand lens (magnifying glass)

Pencil

2▶ Do and Wonder

Take each soil sample and the potting soil, and spread it out on a sheet of paper. On the paper, write where the soil came from. (You should have four samples of soil on four different sheets of paper.)

Before using the hand lens to look more closely at each type of soil, make some predictions about what you'll find.

Now spread each sample out into a very thin layer, and carefully observe it using the hand lens.

3▶ Think and Write

Compare what you observed about the four different types of soil. Be sure to include observations about which soil had the most pieces of sand and rock, plant materials, and living creatures.

Explanation

Soil is made of very small pieces of weathered rock. Some of the pieces are so small that they have become sand or clay particles. Soil near the surface of the ground usually contains a lot of material from living things, which is called *organic matter*. The potting soil you bought at the store holds moisture very well because it contains a lot of organic matter.

Activity 7.4

The Layer Cake Rock

Do you have recycling containers at your school? As you probably know, their job is to collect materials that can be used again. The *best* recycler is nature. Nature recycles everything—even rocks! As rocks are broken down, the small pieces that are left are carried away and deposited in layers of material that will eventually form new rocks. You'll make these multilayer rocks in this activity.

1▸ Get Ready

3 cups plaster of paris
3 cups aquarium sand
2–3 cups water
Plastic bucket
Stirring stick
Empty 2 liter plastic soda bottle with the top, narrow portion removed (Have an adult remove this part of the bottle.)
Three small seashells
Petroleum jelly (such as Vaseline)
Spray cooking oil
Food coloring in three colors

2▸ Do and Wonder

Mix 1 cup of sand and 1 cup of plaster of paris together in the bucket. Add just enough water to create a dough. Then add a few drops of food coloring. Mix well using the stirring stick.

Smear the inside of the plastic bottle with petroleum jelly. Then press the dough into the bottom of the bottle, forming a layer.

Coat one of the shells with petroleum jelly, and gently press it into the top of the dough. Then very lightly spray the top of the layer of dough with cooking oil.

Mix another batch of dough by following the same directions, but make this batch a different color from the first. Press this dough on top of the first layer already in the bottle. Coat a second shell with petroleum jelly, and gently press it into the top of the second layer of dough. Then lightly spray this layer with cooking oil.

Make a third batch of dough in yet another color. Again, press it on top of the previous layer, add a seashell, and spray with cooking oil.

Let the plastic bottle containing your "layer cake" rock sit for at least two days. (It should be hard before you remove it from the bottle.) When it's ready, try to slide the rock out of the plastic bottle. If this doesn't work, have an adult carefully cut apart the plastic bottle to remove the rock.

Break apart the layers to locate your shells and any imprints that remain when you remove them. (Even the imprints of shells, leaves, and bones are considered fossils by geologists.)

3▶ Think and Write

Look closely at your layer cake rock. Which layer is the oldest? The youngest? Do the positions of the layers give clues about the ages of any fossils they contain?

Write a short paragraph telling what you observed.

Explanation

Sediment is made up of small pieces of broken rock that are carried away by water and deposited in lakes and oceans. The sediment settles to the bottom to form rock layers, or *strata*. Parts of fish, animals, and plants can also become part of the rock material in these layers. Rocks that are formed this way are called *sedimentary rocks*.

Safety Hints

Wash your hands after working with the plaster of paris.

Be sure to have an adult remove the top portion of the plastic bottle for you.

Also ask an adult to cut apart the plastic bottle to remove the layer cake rock.

Puff Goes the Volcano!

Have you ever seen pictures of an erupting volcano? It really is spectacular but also a little scary. In this activity, you'll make your own erupting volcano. But instead of sending rocks and ash into the air, your volcano will toss out rice cereal and crushed rice cereal. Everything near your volcano—walls, ceilings, windows, and humans—will be completely safe.

1▶ Get Ready

6 cups flour
3 cups salt
3–4 cups water
Piece of plastic tubing 20 inches (about 50 centimeters) long
    (You can get this at a petstore, as it's used with aquariums.)
Large pot, at least 6 quarts (about 6 liters) in size
Stirring stick or large spoon
1 cup puffed rice cereal
1 cup puffed rice cereal that has been ground to a powder
Red, brown, and black tempera paint
Foil or metal pie plate
Pencil and paper
Brushes
Water
Reference books and/or access to the World Wide Web

2▶ Do and Wonder

Before you begin making your volcano, find out what one looks like using reference books and/or the World Wide Web. Make a sketch of what your volcano is going to look like.

Now make the dough. Put the flour and salt in the pot, and mix them together. Keep mixing as you add water, a little at a time, to make a stiff dough.

Use the dough to build a volcano in the pie plate. In the top of the volcano, create a cone-shaped hole that reaches down almost to the bottom.

Insert the tubing through the bottom of the volcano, and run it just into the bottom of the hole. Check to be sure that you can blow air through the tube into the hole. The tubing should fit tightly at the place it enters the hole.

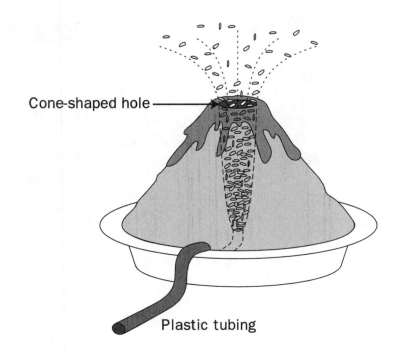

Cone-shaped hole ——

Plastic tubing

Your volcano will probably take two or three days to dry. When it's ready, it should feel hard to the touch.

Paint some reddish lava flowing down the sides of the volcano. Paint the rest of the volcano in various shades of brown and black.

Mix the rice puffs and crushed rice puffs together, and put them in the cone-shaped hole.

Blow through the tubing to make your volcano erupt.

3▶ Think and Write   In a few sentences, describe how well your model of an erupting volcano worked. What changes could you make to improve your volcano?

Explanation   In your model, your blowing into the tube produced the force needed to push the material inside the volcano out the top. In nature, hot gases push lava and rocks up and out of the volcano with an explosive force.

Activity 7.6

Mountain Maker

Do you live near any mountains or valleys, or is the land around you mostly flat? The shape of the land depends on invisible forces that push and pull apart the earth's crust. In this activity, you'll use modeling clay to show how the land surface changes because of these forces.

1▶ Get Ready

6 sticks of modeling clay (3 different colors, 2 of each)
Roll of wax paper
Ruler
Spray cooking oil
Reference books and/or access to the World Wide Web

2▶ Do and Wonder

Mix together two sticks of the same color of clay, and knead them until they're soft.

Place the clump of clay on a sheet of wax paper, and spread it out to form a rectangular shape. The finished rectangle should be about 3 to 4 inches (about 8 to 12 centimeters) wide and 6 to 8 inches (about 18 to 24 centimeters) long. Use the ruler to make sure your rectangle is the right size.

Repeat these steps with the other two colors of clay, so you end up with three separate layers (each on separate sheets of wax paper).

Now take the second layer of clay and lay it on top of the first, clay sides together. Peel away the wax paper from the second layer. Do the same with the third layer of clay, laying it on top of the second layer and peeling away the wax paper. Press the layers together.

These layers show what a piece of the earth's crust looks like. Flattened out like this, the layers create a land form called a *flatland*.

Now hold the layers at each end, and lift them in the air. The dip in the center is another land form: a *valley*.

The flatter parts at the ends of the layers create another land form called *block mountains* on each side of the valley.

To make the next land form, spray another sheet of wax paper with cooking oil. Move the stack of layers onto this oiled sheet. Grip each end of the stack of layers, and push toward the center, so the middle of the stack moves up. Now you've made a *folded mountain*.

3 ▶ **Think and Write**   Your models show how the Himalayan Mountains (a folded range of mountains) and the great rift valley in eastern Africa were formed. Use reference books and/or the World Wide Web to gather information about each place.

In two or three sentences, summarize what you've learned about each place. Be sure to tell when the crust was shaped to create the land form, and include directions that would help someone find each place on a map.

Explanation   The pieces of the earth's crust called *plates* are slowly moving. They grind against one another as they move. Sometimes they pull apart, and sometimes they push together. Both movements cause layers of rock to change shape. Many mountains and valleys have been created by movement of the plates.

Activity 7.7

Shape the Land

Geologists don't spend *all* their time outside, studying rocks and rock layers. They use some of the information they gather to create models. Then they experiment with their models to discover how changes in wind and water might affect *real* rocks, rock layers, and land formations. In this activity, you'll construct your own model to use in studying those kinds of changes.

1 ▶ Get Ready

4 cups flour   Five pie plates
2 cups salt   Stirring stick or spoon
2–3 cups water   Tempera paint in various colors
¼ cup sand   Collection of twigs and pebbles
Reference books and/or
    access to the World Wide Web

2 ▶ Do and Wonder

To begin, use reference books and/or the World Wide Web to find information on land forms, such as plateaus, canyons, and mountains. Look for good pictures that will help you create your own land forms.

To make the dough, mix together the flour and salt. Then add the water a little at a time to form a stiff dough.

Use the dough to make a model of each of the following: a plateau, a valley, a mountain, a coastline, and a canyon.

Add twigs, pebbles, and sand to your models to make them as realistic as possible.

Allow the models to dry, which will take 12 to 24 hours.

Paint the models when you're done.

3 ▶ Think and Write

Write a paragraph that describes each model. Also tell how you could change the model to show how a flood, windstorm, or hurricane might affect it.

Explanation

Geologists sometimes make models of the land and rock layers they're studying. They then conduct experiments with the models to learn how wind, heat, and running water can change the surface of the land.

Word Play

Word Play 7.1

Create a Puzzle

Geologists use many special words in their work. In this activity, you'll make a crossword puzzle using 10 different words that geologists use to discuss the earth's crust and rocks.

1▶ Get Ready

Two sheets of graph paper
Pencil and paper

2▶ Do and Wonder

Use one sheet of graph paper to make the crossword puzzle. (Hint: Begin by writing the longest word near the center of the graph paper, one letter per square—for instance, SEISMOGRAPH, which is an "Across" word. Then, find a word from the "Down" list that contains one of the same letters as your original word, and write it on the paper—for instance, MINERALS, connecting the two words at the letter S. Remember that all the words in the puzzle have to connect at their shared letters.)

Use these as the definitions for the "Across" words:

(1) An instrument that measures the sizes of earthquakes. (SEISMOGRAPH)

(2) A black mineral. (COAL)

(3) A hot spring that sends steam and hot water in the air. (GEYSER)

(4) The outer layer of the earth. (CRUST)

(5) A place where rock layers have cracked. (FAULT)

183

Use these as the definitions for the "Down" words:

(1) The hot, liquid center of the earth. (CORE)

(2) Rocks are made of these. (MINERALS)

(3) Evidence of ancient plants and animals found in rocks. (FOSSIL)

(4) A mineral that is shiny and yellowish in color. (GOLD)

(5) A rock found near an old volcano may be made of this. (LAVA)

3▶ Think and Write

In making the crossword puzzle, you actually created the answer key. Use the second sheet of graph paper to prepare a blank copy of the puzzle that someone else can complete. Trace around those boxes that will contain words in the puzzle, copying the layout of the original puzzle exactly. In the box for the first letter of each word, write in the number of the clue for that word. Finally, write the word clues below the puzzle, listing the "Across" words in one column and the "Down" words in another.

Give your puzzle to a friend, and ask him or her to complete it. Then use the answer key to check how well he or she did.

Explanation

One way to learn new science words is to use them in making crossword puzzles. By making the puzzle in this activity, you not only had the chance to practice spelling some words from the science of geology but also learned their meanings.

Word Play 7.2

The Rock Reporter's Notebook

In this activity, you're going to be a newspaper reporter and write an article about something you've probably never seen—an erupting volcano! Just like a reporter, you'll have to gather interesting and important information and then share it with others by writing an article.

 **Get Ready**

Paper and pencil
Reference books and/or access to the World Wide Web

2▶ Do and Wonder

Use reference books and/or the World Wide Web to gather a lot of information about what happens during the eruption of a volcano. Here are some hints to help you get started:

Find out what happened during eruptions at these places: Pompeii (Italy), Mount St. Helens (U.S./Washington), Mount Pinatubo (Philippines), Kilauea (U.S./Hawaii).

Find out how magma travels through the earth's crust.

Find out how lava flows out of a volcano and how rocks, ash, and gases are thrown into the air.

Be sure to take good notes during your research, keeping track of what you want to say in your article.

3▶ Think and Write

Imagine that you're a newspaper reporter at the scene of an eruption. Use the information you've gathered to write an article about that. Be sure your article contains the correct information and is interesting to read.

Explanation

Volcanoes form when melted rocks under the earth's surface move up and through layers of rock and then break through the crust. When a volcano erupts, it's certainly an amazing thing to see. And for the people who live nearby, it's both dangerous and exciting. This activity gave you a chance to find out what it's like to be near an erupting volcano.

Magnificent Math 7.1

How Thick?

Look down at a spot on the ground. Suppose you started digging a hole right there and kept on digging until you reached the center of the earth. What do you think you'd discover along the way? Rock, rock, and more rock? You might surprised at what you learn in this activity about the planet that's right under your feet!

1▶ Get Ready

Four different colors of modeling clay or modeling dough
Ruler
Piece of dental floss 2 feet (about 60 centimeters) long

2▶ Do and Wonder

Since you don't have enough clay to make a full-sized Earth, you'll have to make a scale model. Study the data below, and create a scale that will show how thick each of the following layers is compared to the other layers: Crust, Mantle, Outer Core, and Inner Core.

Layer	Thickness
Crust	30 miles (about 48 kilometers) at thickest point
Mantle	1,800 miles (about 2,900 kilometers)
Outer core	1,350 miles (2,160 kilometers)
Inner core	800 miles (1,280 kilometers)

Here's an example to get you started: You can see from the data that the outer core is 1,350 miles thick and the inner core is 800 miles thick. To compare the thicknesses of the two, divide the outer core by the inner core: $1,350 \div 800 = 1.7$. This means the outer core is 1.7 times thicker than the inner core. So in your model, if the inner core is 1 inch (about 2.5 centimeters) thick, the outer core should be 1.7 inches thick.

Now construct your model by making a ball of clay that includes all four layers of the earth. Use the scale you created to figure out the thickness of each layer. (Hint: It will be a bit tricky making the crust, since it's so thin. Try rolling the clay into a thin sheet before you add it to the earth.)

After you've finished creating your Earth, you're going to cut it in half to show its layers. To do so, hold one end of the dental floss in each hand, roll it up a bit so it's tight, and then firmly pull it down, straight through your model.

3▶ Think and Write   Take a close look at your model of the earth, especially the layers you can see inside it. Write a short paragraph about the model. Tell about any surprises you got when you sliced your model in half and saw the interior.

Explanation   It's hard for scientists to think and talk about things they can't see. For example, geologists have a hard time trying to understand how layers of rock beneath the surface move and change. One way they can study the movements of the layers is by making a model and looking at how it changes.

Magnificent Math 7.2

The Global Grid

If you carefully look at a globe, you'll notice a pattern of lines going up, down, and around it. That pattern is called a *grid*. This activity will challenge you to locate some of the most important lines on the grid.

1▶ Get Ready   Globe
Paper and pencil

2▶ Do and Wonder   Draw a large circle on your paper to make a map of the earth.

Find each of the following items on the globe. Then draw and label it on your own map.

Meridians (meh-rid-ee-uns):   The lines that run from north to south and connect the North and South Poles.

A great circle: If you follow a meridian from north to south, around the bottom of the globe, and back up to north on the other side, you'll take a circular path called a *great circle*. Note that there are many great circles.

Prime meridian: A great circle with the value 0 degrees longitude.

Longitude: A measurement of how far a certain place is east or west of the prime meridian.

Latitude lines: Lines drawn from east to west on the globe; also called *parallels*.

Equator: The parallel halfway between the North and South Poles; has the value 0 degrees latitude.

Latitude: A measurement of how far a certain place is north or south of the equator.

90 degrees N latitude: The North Pole's latitude.

90 degrees S latitude: The South Pole's latitude.

3▶ Think and Write   Use the globe to find the latitude and longitude of the city or town you live in. For example, if you live in New Orleans, Louisiana, the latitude is about 30 degrees North and the longitude is about 90 degrees West.

Explanation   Lines of latitude and longitude help us locate where we are on the surface of our planet. They also make it possible to find some place on a globe or map and then figure out the easiest way to get there.

Art Connections

Art Connections 7.1

Stone Sculptures

Nature is filled with objects that have beautiful and interesting shapes, colors, and sizes. In fact, you could say that nature is quite an artist! You're going to borrow some of nature's art in this activity to make your own stone sculpture from a collection of stones and pebbles.

1▶ Get Ready
Washed stones and pebbles of different colors, shapes, and sizes
White glue
Water
Assorted colors of permanent markers
Small jar
Paintbrush

2▶ Do and Wonder
Decide what you're going to create with your sculpture. Consider making an animal or a person.

Look through your collection of stones and pebbles, and think about how you can use the different pieces. For instance, maybe one will make a good head or a good tail (depending on what you're going to create, of course).

After you're done planning, arrange the stones and pebbles to make the shape you decided on. Glue them together, piece by piece.

Use the markers to add any needed details, such as eyes, ears, feathers, or scales.

Make a mixture of 1 part glue and 4 parts water in the jar. Paint the glue/water mixture over the sculpture to give it a shiny look.

3 Think and Write   Attach a note to your sculpture that explains how you created it and where the stones and pebbles came from. Use the sculpture as a paperweight, or give it to someone as a gift.

Explanation   The stones and pebbles around us can be used for many different purposes. Sometimes, they're added to create materials like cement, which is used to construct roads, buildings, and dams. And sometimes, stones and pebbles are used to create art projects like yours, bringing pieces of nature's outdoor beauty indoors.

Art Connections 7.2

Sand Painting

For thousands of years, people all over the world have used sand of different colors to create beautiful paintings. In this activity, you'll make your own sand painting, using sand you find outdoors or aquarium sand you get from a petstore.

1 Get Ready   Three different colors of food coloring
White glue
Water
3 cups clean, washed sand
Four baby food jars
Three plastic spoons
Paintbrush
Two or three white paper plates
Pencil

2 Do and Wonder   Decide what you want to make in your paintings. Then use your pencil to create a design or drawing on each plate.

In one jar, prepare a glue/water mixture that is half glue and half warm water.

Fill each of the other three jars about halfway with sand. Then add just enough water to each jar so all the sand is moistened. Next add a few drops of food coloring to each jar (a different color in each). Use a plastic spoon to stir the sand well (a different spoon for each jar), and let it sit for 15 minutes. Then spread out each color of sand on a paper towel to dry (about 20 minutes).

Follow these steps to create your sand paintings:

(1) Select one jar of sand, and think about all the places on each painting (plate) where you want to use that color. Brush a layer of the glue mixture on each of those places.

(2) Sprinkle the first color of sand over the places painted with glue. Gently wiggle each plate around so all the places receive a good coating of sand. Dump any loose sand off the plate.

(3) Put the plates away to let the first color of sand dry in place.

(4) Repeat steps 1–3 using the other two colors of sand. Be sure to let the second color dry before adding the third.

3▶ Think and Write   Write a note about how you made each painting, and tape it to the bottom of the plate. Then display your paintings or give them as gifts.

Explanation   Sand is a mixture of tiny particles of rock, so the color of the sand depends on the color of the rock. If you look at the sand along a shoreline, you'll see that the tiny rock particles are usually mixed with tiny pieces of shell and coral. You can find sand deposited by wind in sand dunes, by water on beaches, and below the ground in layers that were once shorelines.

Amazing but True!
BRAINSTRETCHERS

7.1   Why does it look like the continent of South America would fit perfectly into the big curve on the west side of Africa?

7.2   Do the continents touch anywhere?

7.3   What's at the center of the earth?

7.4   How old is the earth?

7.5   Why is the earth round like a ball?

7.6   About how long would it take to walk around the earth?

7.7   What's the tallest mountain that's ever been discovered?

7.8   How did Death Valley in California get its name?

7.9   Is it possible for a river to fall *up* a waterfall?

7.10   Can rocks float?

7.11   Are the dinosaur fossil bones in museums *really* bones?

7.12   What is a petrified forest?

7.13   Did scientists really discover a man trapped in a glacier?

7.14   I've seen pictures of people using metal pans to scoop gold out of streams. Do people really find gold this way?

7.15   What is a fossil fuel?

7.16   I saw the word *spelunker* in a book about caves. What is it?

7.17   I read that the continents are moving. What is powerful enough to push or pull a continent?

7.18   What is a volcano?

7.19   What is a geyser?

7.1 Why does it look like the continent of South America would fit perfectly into the big curve on the west side of Africa?

South America and Africa look like puzzle pieces that will fit together because they really used to be stuck together. The continents you see on a map today haven't always been in these same places. In fact, a long time ago, they were *all* part of one large land mass. Scientists named this early giant continent *Pangaea* (pan-jee-ah). About 100 million years ago, Pangaea started to break up. The continents were formed when pieces slowly moved away from one another. Those pieces are top sections of the earth's crust called *tectonic plates*. And they're still moving!

7.2   Do the continents touch anywhere?

No, but there are places where the continents *almost* touch. For instance, Europe and Africa are only about 8 miles (13 kilometers) apart at the Strait of Gibraltar, which connects the Mediterranean Sea with the Atlantic Ocean. (A *strait* is a narrow body of water that connects two larger bodies of water.) Asia and North America are just 56 miles (93 kilometers) apart at the Bering Strait. And Europe and Asia are only ½ mile (about 0.8 kilometers) apart at the Bosporus, which is a strait between the Black Sea and the Sea of Marmara. North and South America are, of course, actually connected.

7.3   What's at the center of the earth?

No one really knows for sure, but scientists have some pretty good ideas about what's at the center of the earth. By using several methods—such as tracking the vibrations caused by earthquakes and studying the earth's magnetic field—scientists are pretty sure of two things: (1) The center of the earth, or the *core,* is a ball of hot liquid made up of melted nickel and iron, and (2) there might also be solid nickel and iron at the center of the core.

7.4   How old is the earth?

To answer this question, you need to ask *another* question: How old are the oldest rocks on the earth? This is an important question because the earth must be *at least* as old as the oldest rocks. Well, the oldest rocks are about 4.8 billion years old, so the earth must be at least that old.

7.5   Why is the earth round like a ball?

Actually, the earth isn't *exactly* round. It's sort of flattened out at the top and bottom. Even so, we can certainly say the earth is ball shaped. It has that shape because of how it formed. The earth was first a gas and then a liquid. As a liquid, it took on the shape of a *sphere,* or ball. That happened because liquids that aren't touching other surfaces tend to form a shape that contains the most possible liquid while having the smallest possible surface. That shape is a sphere. Well, eventually the earth changed from a liquid to a solid, but it kept the ball shape.

7.6   About how long would it take to walk around the earth?

If you walked along the equator (which would mean getting your feet wet in the oceans) *and* could cover about 23 miles (37 kilometers) a day, it would take you about three years. Of course, if you wanted to eat or sleep or stop to take photos, it would take a lot longer!

7.7 What's the tallest mountain that's ever been discovered?

This is a great question to stump your friends with! The highest mountain that's ever been discovered isn't even on Earth. It's on Mars! This giant mountain, Olympus Mons, is 95,000 feet (about 29,000 meters) high. What's the tallest mountain on Earth? Not counting the Hawaiian Islands (which are actually the tops of mountains that begin on the seafloor), Mount Everest is the tallest mountain on Earth. It's 29,028 feet (about 8,839 meters) high, which is less than one-third the size of Olympus Mons!

7.8 How did Death Valley in California get its name?

Death Valley earned its name because in the 1800s, many of the pioneers who tried to travel through it died. Why? Because Death Valley is the hottest place in North America. It's a desert that cuts through California and Nevada and is 282 feet (about 86 meters) below sea level. Any pioneer who tried to cross this deep, hot, dry desert without taking safety precautions was doing something very dangerous.

7.9 Is it possible for a river to fall *up* a waterfall?

Well, there is a river that travels in the wrong direction over a waterfall: the St. John River in eastern Canada. For most of the day, this river goes over a waterfall and runs into the Bay of Fundy. But at high tide, a strange thing happens. The water level in the river below the falls rises and eventually gets higher than the waterfall. At that point, the river starts flowing *across* the waterfall. (Of course, the river doesn't actually flow *up* the falls.) When the tide goes down again, the water begins to move back over the falls in the normal direction.

7.10 Can rocks float?

One kind of rock can certainly float. It's called *pumice* (puh-miss) and is formed during a volcanic eruption. Hot gases are sometimes trapped in magma (melted rock), which gets pushed out of an erupting volcano as lava. When the lava cools and forms a hard rock, the gases escape, leaving holes all through the rock. Pumice has so many holes in it that it's less dense than water.

7.11 Are the dinosaur fossil bones in museums *really* bones?

No. Many of the bones on display in museums are made of plaster or some other substance that was poured into a mold made from a fossil bone. And even if a museum puts real dinosaur bones on display, they're actually fossils, not bones. The real bones disappeared millions of years ago. Fossils are rocks that are made when minerals replace the calcium in the actual bones. The rocks that are formed keep the exact shapes and sizes of the original bones.

7.12   What is a petrified forest?

A petrified forest is a place where you can see ancient tree fossils. One example is the Petrified Forest National Park in Arizona. Millions of years ago, trees were swept into a swampy area, where they were eventually buried by soil and ash from volcanoes. Over time, the cells in the logs were replaced by the mineral silica (sil-eh-kah) along with other minerals and iron. This is what made the fossils various colors.

7.13   Did scientists really discover a man trapped in a glacier?

Scientists didn't actually find a man trapped in a glacier, but some hikers did. (They didn't bother using first aid, since the man had been dead for 5,000 years!) The hikers found the very well-preserved body of the Ice Man, as he's known, in 1991 while on a trek in the Alps near the border of Italy and Austria. Evidence on and around the body included a bronze ax, a wooden backpack, a stone knife, and a small net for carrying things.

7.14   I've seen pictures of people using metal pans to scoop gold out of streams. Do people really find gold this way?

Gold is only found in streams that travel over or near rocks that have gold in them. The gold in those rocks was once deep in the earth but eventually moved closer to the surface. Sometimes, flakes and nuggets of gold from rocks get washed into streams. When people pan for gold, they catch a little water and gravel and swirl it around in the pan, looking for tiny flakes of gold to settle to the bottom. In the great California Gold Rush of 1848, about 40,000 people headed west, thinking they were going to strike it rich. Only a few really did. So don't rush out and buy a gold-mining pan!

7.15   What is a fossil fuel?

You might think it sounds strange to use the word *fossil* when talking about fuel. But actually, any fuel that's produced by the decaying of plant and animal materials in the earth's crust is a *fossil fuel*. Coal, petroleum, and natural gas are all examples of fossil fuels.

7.16   I saw the word *spelunker* in a book about caves. What is it?

Isn't *spelunker* a great-sounding word? You can use it to talk about a person who explores caves for fun. Of course, it isn't much fun when a spelunker gets lost in an underground cave. That's why spelunkers use safe procedures, such as always exploring with at least one other person, spooling out a line of string as they move through connected caves so they can follow it back to the entrance, and most important of all, telling friends or relatives exactly where they'll be spelunking.

7.17   I read that the continents are moving. What is powerful enough to push or pull a continent?

This is an excellent question! There's a tremendous amount of heat energy below the earth's surface, which comes from the melted rock and minerals near the center of the earth. That energy moves upward, causing the rock layers above it either to melt or move. Some of the energy actually forces apart sections of the rock layer on which the continents ride, which are called *plates*. In some places in the world, the plates are actually pushed into each other by this heat energy that started near the center of the earth.

7.18   What is a volcano?

A mountain blowing its top.

7.19   What is a geyser?

Mother Nature getting all steamed up.

Chapter 8

Oceans and Weather

Activities

Air, Air Everywhere!   [ESS 3]

Air Weighs In   [ESS 3]

Making a Coral Reef   [ESS 4]

Underwater Cracks in the Crust   [ESS 5]

Who? What? Eugenie Clark
and Alfred Wegener   [HNS 2]

Word Play

The Round-Trip of a Drip   [ESS 2]

Solving Weather Mysteries   [ESS 3]

Magnificent Math

The Layer Cake Atmosphere   [ESS 3]

Oceans: How Deep? How Wide?   [ESS 5]

Art Connections

Paper Snowflakes   [ESS 3]

Making a Wave Bottle   [ESS 4]

Amazing but True!
Brainstretchers   [ESS 1–5]

Activities

Air, Air Everywhere!

Air is really strange stuff! You usually can't see, taste it, or feel it—but it's there. In this activity, you'll discover how to show that air really is all around you, *even though you can't see it.* That may sound impossible, but it's easy and a lot of fun to do.

1▶ Get Ready

Two short, clear, straight-sided drinking glasses, each about 3 inches (about 9 centimeters) tall and 2 inches (5 centimeters) in diameter
Roll of paper towels
Large pot, at least 3 quart (about 3 liter) size or larger
Food coloring

2▶ Do and Wonder

Tear a sheet of paper towel in half, crumple it, and tightly stuff it into the bottom of one of the glasses. (The paper towel should be tight enough to stay in glass when you turn it over. If it falls out, remove it and use a larger piece of toweling.) While the glass is upside down, press in any parts of the towel that are hanging down. (The surface of the paper towel should be as flat as possible.)

Fill the pot halfway with water, so the water level in the pot is a little higher than the height of the glass. Add a few drops of food coloring to the water in the pot to make it more visible.

Now gently push the upside down glass straight down into the water. Hold it underwater so the actual top of the glass (the open end) is touching the bottom of the pot. Predict whether the paper toweling in the glass is now wet or dry.

Remove the glass by pulling it straight up and out of the water. Observe the towel. Is it wet or dry?

Repeat the experiment, but this time, tilt the glass to one side while it's underwater. What do you observe? If you don't see anything happen, tilt the glass a little further. (Hint: Look for evidence of something leaving the upside-down glass.) Again, predict whether the paper towel is wet or dry.

Remove the glass from the water, and check the paper towel.

❸▶ Think and Write

Imagine that you had two small, clear glasses and a pot of water. Create an experiment that would prove that air takes up space, but don't use a paper towel to do so. (Here are some hints: Use two glasses at the same time. Turn one upside down and push it straight into the water. Turn the other glass to the side, so it fills with water when you push it in. Then turn the same glass upside down, so the mouth is pointing straight down. If you can discover a way to get the air from one glass to the other, you will be able to show that air takes up space.)

Write a paragraph describing your experiment. Then try it.

Explanation

Even though we can't see air, we can prove that it really is all around us. In this activity, the air in the glass was trapped when you pushed the glass into the water. That air bubble kept the water from reaching the paper towel.

Activity 8.2

Air Weighs In

Does air weigh anything? Since we can't see it or feel it, answering that question may seem impossible. Actually, it's easy to show that air has weight. This activity will show you just *how* easy!

1▶ Get Ready

Yardstick (or meterstick)	Access to a wooden doorframe
Spool of string	Scissors
Four round party balloons, all the same size	Two thumbtacks

2▶ Do and Wonder

Activity 1

Cut a length of string about 1 yard (1 meter) long. Tie the string to the center of the yardstick (or meterstick). If you pull up on the string, the stick should balance in a horizontal position.

Find the center of the board that goes across the top of a doorway. Use a thumbtack to attach the free end of the string there, so the measuring stick is hanging in the doorway.

Cut two lengths of string 6 inches (about 15 centimeters) long. Use the strings to tie uninflated balloons to the ends of the measuring stick (one balloon per end). What do you observe?

Carefully remove one balloon. Inflate it and knot the end. Then retie the balloon to the measuring stick. What do you observe?

Activity 2

Remove both balloons from the measuring stick, but leave the stick hanging in the doorway. Keep the strings handy.

Inflate two same-sized balloons and knot their ends. Tie one balloon to each end of the measuring stick. Adjust the measuring stick and balloons so the stick hangs level again.

Take one thumbtack and gently pierce the *neck* of one balloon. (You want the air to escape from the balloon slowly.) Observe what happens to the measuring stick.

3▶ Think and Write

In a short paragraph, summarize your observations and make a hypothesis that explains what you observed.

Explanation

The air in our atmosphere is really a mixture of many gases, and the molecules of those gases all have weights. In this activity, you proved that air had weight because an inflated balloon was pulled down by gravity more than an uninflated balloon.

Making a Coral Reef

In warm oceans, there are places you can find rocks made by animals. That's right—animals! *Coral* is a type of rock that's formed by millions and millions of tiny animals. When a rocky area becomes large enough, we call it a *coral reef.* This activity will have you do some research in the library and/or on the World Wide Web to discover which animals and plants live in, on, and near coral reefs. Then you'll make a collage to show what you learned.

1▶ Get Ready

Construction paper of various colors
Scissors
Glue stick or liquid white glue
Felt-tipped markers of various colors
Old "nature" magazines, resource books, and/or access
    to the World Wide Web

2▶ Do and Wonder

Use magazines, resource books, and/or the World Wide Web to find information about how coral reefs are formed. Try to find color photographs of coral reefs and the animals and plants that live there.

Using the pictures you find to guide you, make some of your own drawings of coral reefs to use in creating a collage. *And if it's allowed,* cut out photographs from magazines to use, too.

Arrange the drawings and photos on a piece of construction paper and glue them in place, creating a collage. It should show a coral reef that's partly underwater and partly above water. Include the plants, fish, and other animals that live near or on the reef.

3▶ Think and Write

Using what you learned through your research, write a paragraph that backs up this idea: *A coral reef within an ocean is like an oasis in a desert.*

Explanation

Corals include many different small sea animals, such as the sea anemone (ah-nem-o-nee). Some corals protect themselves by producing a rocklike substance that forms where the coral is attached to rocks. Then when the coral is threatened, it can retreat into its own rock house. Corals cement their houses to others nearby and on top of houses where other corals once lived. Over many hundreds and thousands of years, these cemented houses form a reef. Coral reefs are found near islands where the ocean water is shallow and warm. Coral reefs eventually become homes for other ocean animals and plants. The small and large openings in them provide safe places for fish and other animals to hide.

Activity 8.4

Underwater Cracks in the Crust

Some of the deepest openings in the earth's crust are hidden from view because they're underwater. Scientists have recently begun exploring these ocean trenches, which are miles and miles deep. In this activity, you'll make a graph to show just how deep some trenches are.

1▸ Get Ready
Globe or world map
Graph paper
Ruler
Pencil

2▸ Do and Wonder
First set up your graph on a sheet of graph paper. Label the vertical axis "Depth in Yards (or Meters)," and label the horizontal axis "Name of Trench."

Create a scale for the "Depth" axis that will give you enough room to fit all the data on your chart. (Hint: Try 1 square on the graph paper = 500 yards or 500 meters. If your paper is large enough, use 1 square = 250 yards or 250 meters.) Then mark and label the vertical axis at each 1,000-yard (or 1,000-meter) interval: 1,000, 2,000, and so on.

Use the data in Table 1 (page 204) to prepare your graph.

3▸ Think and Write
Try to locate the trenches listed in Table 1 on a globe or world map. Then write a brief answer to each of the following questions: Where is the deepest trench? Where is the shallowest trench?

Do some research to find out the height of Mount Everest. Could you hide Mount Everest in the deepest ocean trench? Write a brief answer to this question.

Table 1   Depths of Ocean Trenches

Trench	Depth (in Yards)	Depth (in Meters)
Pacific Ocean		
Aleutian	8,862	8,100
Kurile	11,534	10,542
Japan	9,204	8,412
Mariana (Trench Name: Challenger Deep)	12,139	11,100
Philippine	11,488	10,500
Tonga	11,906	10,882
Kermadec	10,944	10,003
Peru-Chile	8,813	8,055
Atlantic Ocean		
Puerto Rico	9,462	8,648
South Sandwich	9,190	8,400
Indian Ocean		
Java	8,452	7,725

Explanation   Trenches are long, narrow cracks that reach down to the deepest parts of the ocean. The Pacific Ocean has more trenches than any other ocean along with the deepest trench, called *Challenger Deep*.

Activity 8.5

Who? What? Eugenie Clark and Alfred Wegener

Under the sea is a world all its own, filled with unique plants, animals, and land formations. The scientists who study this world have plenty to do. In this activity, you'll learn some interesting things about one of these scientists: Eugenie Clark or Alfred Wegener.

1▶ Get Ready

Paper and pencil	Two sheets of poster paper
Ruler	Felt-tipped markers in assorted colors
Resource books and/or access to the World Wide Web	

2▶ Do and Wonder

In this activity, you'll do two things: (1) Gather a lot of information about the life and discoveries of a scientist, and (2) create two posters that will show what you learned.

Pick one of these scientists for your research: Eugenie Clark or Alfred Wegener.

To begin, read the brief biography of this scientist in the Explanation section at the end of this activity. Then use resource books and/or the World Wide Web to find more information about your scientist. Take as many notes as you can about the individual and his or her discoveries.

Now you're ready to create your posters.

Poster 1

Write the scientist's name at the top of the poster, and draw a picture of him or her below it.

Write down when and where the scientist lived.

List important facts about his or her life.

Poster 2

At the top of the poster, write the problem or question the scientist worked on.

Draw the kinds of equipment he or she used to make his or her discoveries.

If you could ask the scientist two questions about his or her life and discoveries, what would they be? Write them down.

3▶ Think and Write   Imagine that the scientist you selected was going to visit your classroom. What would you like him or her to bring to show you and your classmates? What science questions do you think you and your classmates might ask the scientist? What are two things the scientist might tell about his or her life and work?

Write one or two paragraphs about the scientist's visit to your classroom, describing what he or she would show and tell you and your classmates.

Explanation

Eugenie Clark

Eugenie Clark was born in 1922. She started her career studying some living things you may have in your own home or classroom: aquarium fishes. Later in life, her interests in snorkeling, scuba diving, and exploring the ocean in underwater vehicles helped her study ocean fishes. For awhile, she even carried out projects in which she trained sharks to press targets to get food. Dr. Friday's scientific work about ocean life has been reported in television specials, such as *Sharks* and *Reef Watch,* and in the IMAX film *Search for the Great Sharks.* In addition, she has been awarded many prizes for her studies of ocean life and her projects dealing with saving the environment. Today, she is a senior research scientist at the University of Maryland.

Alfred Wegener

Alfred Wegener was born in Germany in 1880. He was a meteorologist who became famous not for his ideas about weather but for the theory he created to explain how continents were formed and separated by oceans. In his theory of *continental drift,* Dr. Wegener said that long ago, there were only one ocean and one enormous continent called *Pangaea.* Then about 200 million years ago, this supercontinent broke apart. The pieces slowly moved away from each other, forming individual continents separated by oceans. In 1915, Dr. Wegener published a book about these ideas called *The Origin of Continents and Oceans.* More modern research has supported his ideas by showing that the ocean floor is spreading apart and by discovering similar rock layers and fossils on different continents. Dr. Wegener died in 1930.

Word Play

Word Play 8.1

The Round-Trip of a Drip

You've surely written and read enough stories to know that most have a beginning, a middle, and an end. In this activity, you'll write a story that *never* really ends! Your subject will be a drop of water from an ocean or lake that takes a long trip to a faraway place, returns to where it began, and then starts another trip to some other distant place. Name your story "The Round-Trip of a Drip."

1 ▶ Get Ready

Pencil and paper
Resource books and/or access to the World Wide Web

2 ▶ Do and Wonder

Use resource books and/or the World Wide Web to gather information about the stages of the water cycle. Be sure you learn and take notes about each of these steps:

(1) At the ocean's surface, the sun warms the water, causing some of it to evaporate. Liquid water becomes the gas we call *water vapor*.

(2) The water vapor cools as it rises in the atmosphere and becomes *precipitation*—water droplets (rain) or ice crystals (snow).

(3) The precipitation falls on the land or in the oceans, lakes, and rivers.

(4) Some of the precipitation that falls on land will be absorbed into the soil. Some of it will run off the land into streams, rivers, and lakes. Some of this water will then be carried back to the oceans, where the trip will begin again.

3▶ Think and Write   Use the notes from your research to write the story of the trip taken by a drop of water floating along on the ocean's surface. Here's an idea for a beginning sentence: "I was just floating along on a hot summer day." Go on to tell about what happens to the drop as it evaporates, becomes part of a cloud, falls to the earth as rain or snow, and eventually returns to its starting place.

Explanation   The water on the earth is used, recycled, and used again in a never-ending process called the *water cycle*. Liquid water from the oceans and lakes enters the atmosphere as a gas and returns to the earth as a liquid, which eventually enters the lakes and oceans. Even water that enters the soil is eventually released back into the atmosphere.

Word Play 8.2

Solving Weather Mysteries

The meteorologists' job of studying and predicting the weather is a tough one. It seems that no matter how much scientific training or equipment they have, they're still often puzzled by the weather. In this activity, you're going to help out the meteorologists by explaining four weather mysteries.

1▶ Get Ready   Pencil and paper
Resource books and/or access to the World Wide Web

2▶ Do and Wonder   Use resource books and/or the world Wide Web to gather information that will help you explain at least 4 of these 12 weather mysteries:

(1) Why are some summer days called *dog days?*

(2) How can you use a cricket's chirp to tell the temperature?

(3) What is *ball lightning?*

(4) What is *St. Elmo's fire?*

(5) What is the *jet stream?*

(6) How did the *horse latitudes* get their name?

(7) How are these storms different from one another: cyclones, hurricanes, and tornadoes?

(8) How do hurricanes get their names?

(9) What causes dew to form?

(10) Can the ring around the moon be used to predict the weather?

(11) Can groundhogs really predict the weather?

(12) Can the stripes of a woolly bear caterpillar be used to predict the weather?

3▶ Think and Write   Use your notes to write a one-paragraph explanation for each of your four weather mystery questions.

Ask two adults to try to answer your questions. See how they do, and then give them your explanations.

Explanation   Here is a hint that should help you answer each mystery question:

(1) Has to do with the star Sirius

(2) Has to do with counting the chirps in a minute

(3) Is a moving sphere

(4) Are tall, metal objects in a lightning storm

(5) Usually flows west to east

(6) Places with very little wind

(7) Wind speed

(8) Cultures and languages of places

(9) Low temperature

(10) Crystals in the sky

(11) Superstition?

(12) Superstition?

Magnificent Math 8.1

The Layer Cake Atmosphere

When you look up on a clear day, the sky seems to stretch up and away as far as you can see. But actually, the atmosphere isn't exactly the way it looks. Instead, it's made of layers. In this activity, you'll make a scale drawing to show those layers.

1▸ Get Ready

Large sheet of easel or chart paper
Five colored pencils or watercolor markers in light colors
Ruler
Pencil

2▸ Do and Wonder

Use the information in Table 2 to make a scale drawing of the layers of the atmosphere. Be sure to write the scale you use at the bottom of your drawing.

Table 2 Layers of Atmosphere

Layer	Distance above Earth (Miles)	Distance above Earth (Kilometers)	What It's Like
Troposphere	0–10 miles	0–16 km	Contains gas, water vapor, and dust particles.
Stratosphere	10–30 miles	16–50 km	Contains the jet stream. Among its gases is ozone.
Mesosphere	30–50 miles	50–80 km	Temperature drops rapidly.
Thermosphere	50–300 miles	80–480 km	Very thin air. Region of very low air pressure. Very warm layer.
Exosphere	300–600 miles	480–960 km	Very few molecules of gases that make up air. Region where artificial satellites orbit planet.

Experiment a bit to figure out the scale that will let you fit all the layers on the sheet of paper. See whether any of these scales will work: 1 inch = 10 miles (or 1 centimeter = 10 kilometers). This will be a challenge because you have to fit one very thin layer and other very thick layers on just one sheet of paper.

Make your scale drawing, being careful to be as accurate as possible. Then use your colored pencils or markers to label the layers. If possible, color in some parts of each layer.

3▶ Think and Write   Look carefully at your scale drawing, and then answer these questions in a short paragraph: Which layers produce the weather on Earth? Do the space shuttle astronauts orbit in or above the weather-producing layers?

Explanation   The earth is covered by layers of gases that make up the *atmosphere*. One of those layers contains the water vapor that will eventually fall as rain and the oxygen that animals and plants need to survive. It also contains the carbon dioxide needed by plants. Another contains ozone, which protects all life on the earth from harmful rays that enter the atmosphere from outer space.

Magnificent Math 8.2

Oceans: How Deep? How Wide?

The line "Water, water everywhere, and not a drop to drink" could begin a poem or story written by any thirsty sailor out on the ocean. The oceans that cover the earth are truly enormous in size. That's why it's sometimes called *the blue planet*. In this activity, you'll get an idea of how large and deep the oceans really are.

1▶ Get Ready   Globe or world map
Three sheets of graph paper
Pencil

2▶ Do and Wonder

Use the globe or world map to locate the four oceans on Earth: the Pacific, the Atlantic, the Indian, and the Arctic. Then answer these questions: Which seems the largest? Which seems the smallest?

Use the sheets of graph paper to make three graphs. For each graph, label the horizontal axis with the names of the four oceans, all spaced evenly apart. Then label the vertical axes "Area" (graph 1), "Average Depth" (graph 2), and "Deepest Point" (graph 3). For the scales on the vertical axes, use either English or metric units.

Use the data in Table 3 to create the graphs comparing size, average depth, and deepest point.

Look closely at your graphs. Compare your predictions about size with the actual measurements. Also compare the oceans' average depths and deepest points.

3▶ Think and Write

Using just the information recorded on your graphs, make a hypothesis about which ocean actually contains the most water. Explain what information supports your hypothesis (without actually trying to calculate the amount of water).

Explanation

At least 75% of the earth's surface is covered by water. We think of that water as being divided into four oceans: the Pacific, the Atlantic, the Indian, and the Arctic. Although they're different in size and depth, they're all important because they contain so many living things. The oceans are also the starting point of the water cycle.

Table 3   Data about Oceans

Ocean	Area Square Miles	Area Square Kilometers	Average Depth Feet	Average Depth Meters	Deepest Point Feet	Deepest Point Meters
Pacific	64,000,000	165,760,000	13,800	4,280	35,810	11,100
Atlantic	31,815,000	82,400,000	11,730	3,635	31,360	9,720
Indian	25,300,000	65,526,700	12,600	3,905	23,375	7,250
Arctic	5,440,200	14,090,000	3,410	1,055	17,880	5,545

Art Connections

Art Connections 8.1

Paper Snowflakes

Think about the snowflake decorations that people put on their windows during the winter holiday season. If you looked at them closely, you'd notice that most have five sides or pointy ends. Unfortunately, these decorations don't show nature as it really is. Real snowflakes actually have six sides or pointy ends. In this activity, you'll make this type of a snowflake—a real one!

1▶ Get Ready
Sheet of tissue paper (the kind used for art projects and wrapping gifts)
Paper bowl that's smaller than the tissue paper
Protractor (a drawing tool that looks like a half circle; has markings along its edge that go from 0 to 180)
Pencil
Ruler

2▶ Do and Wonder
Using the paper bowl as a guide, draw a circle on the tissue paper. Cut out the circle and fold it in half.

Lay the circle of tissue paper on a table top, with the curved part at the top and the crease at the bottom going from left to right. Using the ruler, find the mid-point of the crease. Mark that spot with a small X.

Align the protractor so its flat bottom side is on the crease. Then move the protractor along the crease until the small X is right under the small hole or cross hairs at the bottom of the protractor.

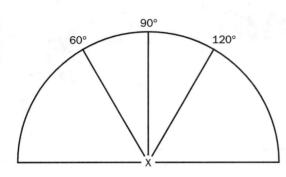

Next locate the marks 60, 90, and 120 on the protractor. (These marks are actually angle measurements in units called *degrees*.) Using the ruler, draw a line from the midpoint of the crease to the edge of the half circle at each of the 60, 90, and 120 marks (three lines in all).

Fold the tissue paper at the lines for 60 and 120, forming a pie wedge shape. Then make one more fold at the 90 line.

Draw a pattern along the thickest fold, and then cut along the edge of the pattern.

Open the tissue paper very carefully. You should have a six-sided snowflake!

3▶ Think and Write   Real snowflakes are formed high above the earth's surface, which means they have to fall a long way. Look at your paper snowflake. If it were real, would it have a good chance of reaching the earth without being broken? Write out your answer, and include a small drawing of your snowflake.

Explanation   Snowflakes begin as tiny six-sided crystals of ice that form in the clouds high above the earth's surface. They grow larger and larger as moist air enters the clouds. Since they begin as six-sided crystals, complete snowflakes have six sides or prongs (pointy parts that stick out). These perfectly formed snowflakes often break apart when they bump into other flakes, so those that reach the earth may have various shapes and sizes. On occasion, scientists have observed huge snowflakes as large as 4 to 6 inches (10 to 15 centimeters) across, which probably formed from smaller flakes sticking together.

Art Connections 8.2

Making a Wave Bottle

Many people find it very peaceful just to sit on a beach, watching the waves roll in. After doing this activity, you'll be able to watch the waves anywhere you happen to be!

1▸ Get Ready

Clear, *plastic* soda bottle with a screw-on top
Clear mineral oil (available at a pharmacy) or very pale
   vegetable cooking oil
Blue food coloring
Access to water

2▸ Do and Wonder

Carefully remove any labels on your bottle. First soak the bottle in warm, soapy water to loosen the glue under the labels.

Fill the bottle one-fourth full of water. Add two or three drops of food coloring, and shake it well. Then add enough oil to the bottle so it's about half full of liquid.

Put the top back on the bottle, and tightly screw it on.

Lay the bottle on its side. Wait a few minutes for any oil and water that have mixed together to separate. What do you observe?

Now tilt the bottle up and down until waves of oil roll across the liquid. What do you observe?

Try tapping one end of the bottle. What do you observe?

See if you can make small waves that move along and eventually get so high that they break (fall over).

3▸ Think and Write

Write a paragraph that answers these questions: Where does the energy come from that moves waves across a lake or ocean? Where does the energy come from that moves the waves in your bottle?

Explanation

The waves on an ocean or lake are usually caused by wind. Sometimes, however, waves are caused by earthquakes on the ocean bottom. These waves can become so large and move so fast across the surface of the ocean that they cause major damage to the cities along the coasts. These big waves are called *tidal waves* or *tsunamis* (tsoo-nam-eees).

Amazing but True!
BRAINSTRETCHERS

8.1   How much rain do rainforests get?

If you placed a big tub in the middle of a rainforest, it would soon be overflowing with rain. Of course, some rainforests get more rain than others, but even the driest rainforests are pretty wet. On average, rainforests receive between 160 and 400 inches (400 to 1,000 centimeters) of rain each year. Now that's *a lot* of rain!

8.2   Are there any rainforests nearby?

Well, it depends on where you live, obviously. There are rainforests in Brazil, Zaire, Indonesia, Hawaii, and some of the Caribbean islands.

216

8.3   Is it true that no two snowflakes are exactly alike?

Probably. A snowflake is a crystal of snow that changes shape as it falls through the air. It might grow larger, get smaller, or evaporate and disappear. *How* the snowflake changes depends on the characteristics of the air it's falling through. Slight differences in air temperature and humidity will affect the snowflake. Even so, the chance of two snowflakes changing in exactly the same way and landing in the same spot, so someone could observe them before they melted, is very slim.

8.4   What are rainbows made of?

A rainbow forms in an area of the sky that's full of tiny rain droplets. When sunlight travels through the atmosphere and hits those water droplets, it can be broken apart into many different colors. (Sunlight is really made up of many of different types or colors of light.) If you're in exactly the right place when this happens, you'll see a rainbow.

8.5   What is fog?

This is an easy one! *Fog* is just a cloud that happens to be at the earth's surface. It forms when air near the ground cools, causing the water vapor in the cloud to condense and form droplets. If you've ever walked in the fog, you've really walked inside a cloud!

8.6   What is a hailstone?

A hailstone starts out as a single drop of water inside a cloud. If the droplet is carried up to a cool part of the cloud, it will turn into a solid piece of ice, or *hailstone*. If the hailstone then falls down to a warm part of the cloud, it will pick up a covering of liquid water, since other droplets will stick to it. If the cloud has very strong up and down air currents, the little hailstone will be carried up and down in the cloud like this many times. Eventually, it will become too heavy to be supported by the air movements in the cloud and will fall to the ground. Hailstones that reach the earth are usually small but can be as big as an egg or a baseball. A few have been found that were the size of a small melon!

8.7   What causes tornadoes?

Tornadoes form when very dense, cold air moving from north to south strikes warm air. This collision causes fast-moving winds to form, spinning counterclockwise. When a funnel-shaped cloud is also produced, that's a *tornado*. The winds of a tornado can reach 300 miles an hour (almost 400 kilometers per hour). Anyone who has seen the damage caused by a tornado will tell you that this fast-moving funnel can move or rip apart anything in its path.

8.8   What's an easy way to tell how far away lightning is?

Use a watch to figure out how much time passes between when you see a flash of lightning and when you hear the thunder it causes. When you see the lightning, you're seeing it at the instant it really happens. But the sound of the thunder is delayed because sound waves move very slowly compared to light waves. In fact, sound takes 5 seconds to travel just 1 mile (about 1.6 kilometers). So if you see a lightning flash and hear the thunder 25 seconds later, you can figure out that the lightning bolt was about 5 miles (8 kilometers) away. (Just divide the number of seconds it took to hear the thunder by 5, since sound travels about 1 mile [about 1.6 kilometers] every 5 seconds.)

8.9   What causes hurricanes?

Hurricanes form over ocean water when there are large temperature and pressure differences between the water and the high clouds above it. Moisture and air from the surface of the water begin to be pulled up toward the clouds. This air column begins to spin slowly in a counterclockwise direction. Over time, it gets faster and faster. If the column becomes wide enough and the spin becomes fast enough, a hurricane will form.

8.10   What are the hottest and coldest temperatures ever recorded on Earth?

The hottest temperature, 136 degrees Fahrenheit (58 degrees Celsius), was recorded in the Libyan desert in Africa. The coldest temperature, –128 degrees Fahrenheit (–89 degrees Celsius), was reached in Antarctica. These temperatures were both *so* extreme that most outdoor thermometers wouldn't even be able to show them.

8.11   How deep is the ocean?

Well, it depends on where you measure. The *average* depth of the ocean is about 13,000 feet (4,800 meters). The *very deepest* part of the ocean is at the Mariana Trench in the Pacific, which is 36,200 feet (11,033 meters) deep. If you wanted to go fishing there, you sure would need a lot of fishing line!

8.12   Is there a place on Earth where you could swim and never sink?

Yes, there are a few such places. The most well known is the Dead Sea, a body of water on the border between Israel and Jordan that has no outlets to an ocean or sea. The water that reaches it from rivers, streams, and underground sources evaporates and leaves salt behind. Over time, the water gets saltier and saltier. Eventually, it's much more dense than the human body, which makes it hard to even get under the surface. But don't think it's perfectly safe to swim there, just because you can't sink. If you took any of that saltwater into your lungs, you'd suffocate.

8.13 Why is ocean water blue?

Ocean water *isn't* blue! It just *looks* that way. The surface of the ocean absorbs all light rays except for blue light. That blue light is reflected from the water's surface and reaches our eyes, making us see blue water. Next time you go to the ocean, hold some water in your hand. You'll be able to see right through it. But then back away from the ocean and get on the beach to look at the water's surface. Then you'll see it as a bluish color.

8.14 How do fish breathe underwater?

You get your oxygen from the air, but fish get their oxygen directly from the water. Water enters their mouths and travels over organs called *gills*. The gills take in oxygen from the water and send it into the bloodstream, which carries it to all the cells in the fish's body. The gills also do another important job: They transfer carbon dioxide produced by cells into water that leaves through openings on the sides of the fish's head. Just think . . . If you had gills, you wouldn't ever have to think about getting breaths of air when you went swimming.

8.15 Who owns the oceans?

Actually, no one owns the oceans. Countries that border the oceans usually require ships from other countries to keep a certain distance away from their shoreline. They call this off-limits section of ocean their *territorial water.* Some countries claim just a few miles or kilometers, but others claim hundreds of miles or kilometers. Even though countries make these claims, most of the oceans aren't controlled by anyone.

8.16 Do some beaches really have green or black or red sand?

Yes, sort of. The color of the sand on a beach depends on the type of quartz that was the source of the sand. Along the eastern part of the United States, the sand is usually a whitish color. On the island of Bermuda, the sand has a slight reddish color. On the Pacific islands, including Hawaii, the sand is actually made of ground-up pieces of volcanic rock, which may be black or red. And a few beaches have sand that's pale green, which comes from the mineral olivine.

8.17   What is El Niño?

El Niño is a current of warm water in the Pacific Ocean located west of Central and South America. Every now and then, this area of water becomes larger and moves closer to the land. When this happens, the air above these warm waters heats up, creating large areas of moist, hot air that produce powerful thunderstorms over Central and South America. If the area of warm water is very wide and deep, it can even cause unusual weather in North America and around the world!

8.18   Where is the ocean the deepest?

On the bottom.

8.19   What did the ocean say to the shore?

Nothing. It just waved.

Chapter 9
Taking Up Space

Activities

Tracking the Moon   [ESS 2]
Piecing Together the Planets   [ESS 6]
Planet Places   [ESS 6]
Who? What? Benjamin Banneker,
Caroline Herschel, and Mae Jemison   [HNS 2]
When? Where? A Taking-Up-Space
Puzzle   [HNS 3]

Word Play

Planet Poetry   [ESS 6]
A Message from the Space Shuttle   [ESS 6]

Magnificent Math

Planet Thermometers   [ESS 6]
Weighing In on the Planets   [ESS 6]

Art Connections

String Star Sculptures   [ESS 2]
Moon Phase Flip Book   [ESS 2]

Amazing but True!
Brainstretchers   [ESS 1–6]

Activities

Tracking the Moon

How often do you notice the moon up in the sky? Well, in this activity, you'll observe the moon every night for two months. You might just be surprised at how much fun you'll have keeping track of the earth's nearest neighbor!

1▶ Get Ready

Binoculars
Calendar that has room for small drawings near each date
Pen or pencil
View of the moon each night for at least two months

2▶ Do and Wonder

About the same time each night, find the moon in the sky. If you can see the moon, draw its shape in the box for that date on the calendar and color in any very dark spots. If the sky is too cloudy to see the moon, write "Cloud covered" for that date. Observe the moon and record what you see for two months. Be sure to draw the moon each time you see it.

After two months, look at your calendar and try to find patterns in the shape of the moon. Find two dates at least three weeks apart when the moon had the same shape. How many days apart are those two dates?

Use the following information to label some of the repeated shapes you observed:

If the moon was completely lit—in other words, if you saw a complete circle in the sky—you saw a *full moon*.

If the lit part looked like half a circle, you saw a *quarter moon*. (Yes, that sounds strange, but if you think about it, you'll understand. Hint: How much of the *entire* moon did you really see?)

If the lit part was shaped like a banana, you saw a *crescent moon*.

If the lit part was about halfway between a crescent moon and a quarter moon, you saw a *gibbous (gib-bus) moon*.

When none of the part of the moon that faces the earth is lit by the sun (so you don't see anything), it's a *new moon*.

3▶ Think and Write

Did the dark spots you saw on the moon ever change position during your two months of observation? If they didn't, could that mean we always see the same part of the moon? Answer these questions in a short paragraph.

Explanation

The moon is a satellite of the earth that rotates on its axis once a month. Actually, the moon rotates once every $29\frac{1}{2}$ days, which also happens to be how long it takes for the moon to make a trip around the earth (the moon's *revolution*). Since the moon rotates once each time it goes around the earth, we see just half of the moon. So even though it looks like the moon changes shape during the month, it really doesn't. What *does* change is the angle from which we view the moon. We're always seeing it from a slightly different angle, so the image we see is always different.

Activity 9.2

Piecing Together the Planets

In this activity, you'll use what you learn about the planets to create your own planet *mosaics:* pictures made using bits and pieces of colored paper. Then you'll challenge a partner to see if he or she can recognize the planets you created!

1 ▶ Get Ready

20 cotton balls
9 sheets of black construction paper
10 sheets of various colors of construction paper
Paper glue or glue stick
2 or 3 pieces of aluminum foil about 8½ × 11 inches in size
Resource books and/or access to the World Wide Web
Partner

2 ▶ Do and Wonder

Gather information about the planets using reference books and/or the World Wide Web. Take careful notes about each planet, including its colors and any interesting features.

Set aside one sheet of black construction paper for each planet. Then tear the sheets of colored paper into pieces less than 1 inch (about 2.54 centimeters) on each edge.

Now "paint" a picture of each planet by gluing pieces of colored paper to the black construction paper. Also use pieces of cotton balls and aluminum foil. Show each planet's important features, including its moons. *Don't* write the planets' names on the mosaics.

Mix up the mosaics. Ask your partner to put the planets in the correct order, from closest to furthest from the sun.

3 ▶ Think and Write

How did your partner do? Were any of the planets hard for your partner to recognize? If so, how could you change those mosaics? What else might help your partner learn the order of the planets?

In a paragraph, compare the true order of the planets with the order your partner placed them in.

Explanation

The planets of our solar system are very different from one another. As you learned in creating your mosaics, the planets are different colors and have important visible features, such as moons, spots, and rings.

Activity 9.5

Planet Places

The distances between objects in the night sky are too large for the human mind to easily understand. To help you grasp how huge those distances really are, you'll build a model in this activity. And all you'll need is a partner and a few easy-to-find items!

1▶ Get Ready

10 straws   Black felt-tipped marker
10 index cards   Masking tape
Partner
Large, safe, unpaved outdoor area
    (such as a playground or lawn)

2▶ Do and Wonder

Before you begin, use the marker to write the name of one of the planets on each of the nine index cards and the word *Sun* on the tenth card. Write each word in large letters in the center of the card.

Next take a few minutes to study the information below with your partner. Note that the numbers in the second (right-hand) column show each planet's *relative distance from the sun*. These numbers let us compare how far individual planets are from the sun without using actual distances in miles or kilometers. For instance, the relative distance for Mars is 7.9 and that for Mercury is 2.0. This means that Mars is almost four times as far from the sun as Mercury.

Planet	Relative Distance from the Sun
Mercury	2.0
Venus	3.7
Earth	5.2
Mars	7.9
Jupiter	26.8
Saturn	49.2
Uranus	99.2
Neptune	155.2
Pluto	204.2

You can show how far the planets are from the sun using whatever units of measurement you'd like. In this activity, you'll use a strange unit—the *stride*.

Pick a starting place on the playground or lawn. Stick a straw in the ground there, and attach the *Sun* card using the masking tape. Have your partner start slowly walking away from the *Sun,* taking steps (or strides) that are all the same length. Count each step.

The planet closest to the sun is Mercury, which has a relative distance of 2.0. So at the stride 2 position (after 2 steps), have your partner stop. Stick another straw in the ground at that point, and attach the *Mercury* card.

The planet after Mercury is Venus, which has a relative distance of 3.7. At about the stride 4 position (almost 4 steps), have your partner stop. Stick another straw in the ground, and attach the *Venus* card.

Keep counting steps and inserting straws and cards until all the planets have been marked at the proper locations.

As you look at where each planet is marked, keep in mind that the planets' orbits are ellipses (sort of flattened circles) and their distances from the sun are really averages. Sometimes planets are closer to the sun, and sometimes they're further away. In fact, Pluto is sometimes closer to the sun than Neptune.

3▶ Think and Write

What did you think when you looked over your scale model of the planets? Did anything surprise you? Answer these questions in a short paragraph.

Do some research to find the position of the asteroid belt in our solar system. Where would the asteroid belt belong in your model?

Explanation

The earth's average distance from the sun is about 93 million miles (150 million kilometers). Because it's so hard to imagine even 1 million of anything, it's just about impossible to get an idea of how large these distances really are. To solve problems like this, scientists use models. You created an outdoor model of planet positions using their relative distances from the sun.

Activity 9.4

Who? What? Benjamin Banneker, Caroline Herschel, and Mae Jemison

Are you curious about the sun, planets, moon, comets, and stars? In this activity, you'll discover some interesting things about the lives and work of three scientists who lived in very different times but all studied objects in the sky.

1▶ Get Ready

Paper and pencil
Ruler
Resource books and/or
  access to the World Wide Web

Two sheets of poster paper
Felt-tipped markers in assorted colors

2▶ Do and Wonder

In this activity, you'll do two things: (1) Gather a lot of information about the life and discoveries of a scientist, and (2) create two posters that will show what you learned.

Pick one of these scientists for your research: Benjamin Banneker, Caroline Herschel, or Mae Jemison.

To begin, read the brief biography of this scientist in the Explanation section at the end of this activity. Then use resource books and/or the World Wide Web to find more information about your scientist. Take as many notes as you can about the individual and his or her discoveries.

Now you're ready to create your posters.

Poster 1

Write the scientist's name at the top of the poster, and draw a picture of him or her below it.

Write down when and where the scientist lived.

List important facts about his or her life.

Poster 2

At the top of the poster, write the problem or question the scientist worked on.

Draw the kinds of equipment he or she used to make his or her discoveries.

If you could ask the scientist two questions about his or her life and discoveries, what would they be? Write them down.

3▶ Think and Write   Imagine that the scientist you selected was going to visit your classroom. What would you like him or her to bring to show you and your classmates? What science questions do you think you and your classmates might ask the scientist? What are two things the scientist might tell about his or her life and work?

Write one or two paragraphs about the scientist's visit to your classroom, describing what he or she would show and tell you and your classmates.

Explanation

Benjamin Banneker

Benjamin Banneker was an early American scientist who was born in 1731 on a farm in Maryland. He went to school for a few years and also taught himself algebra and geometry. Later in life, at the age of 56, he began a careful study of astronomy. When he was 60, he published a book called an *almanac,* which included information on astronomy as well as the weather and climate. This book was very useful to farmers and others who needed information that could help them decide when to plant and harvest their crops. Benjamin Banneker died in 1806.

Caroline Herschel

Caroline Herschel was born in Prussia (part of Germany) in 1750. She became an astronomer and discovered some amazing objects in the sky, including three nebulae (distant clouds that eventually form stars) and eight comets. She reported her astronomical observations in a book, for which the British Royal Astronomical Society awarded her a gold medal. The King of Prussia awarded Caroline Herschel the Gold Medal for Science in 1846. She died just two years later at the age of 98.

Mae Jemison

Mae Jemison was born on October 17, 1956, in Decatur, Alabama. She went to college at Stanford University and graduated in 1977 with two degrees: one in chemical engineering and another in African American studies. She then attended Cornell University, where she earned the degree Doctor of Medicine. Mae Jemison went on to serve in the Peace Corps, providing medical care for people in Sierra Leone and Liberia in West Africa. Then in 1987, she was accepted as a candidate to become a U.S. astronaut. She was the fifth African American astronaut and the first African American female astronaut. In August 1992, she traveled on a space shuttle mission and carried out experiments to discover how materials and living things behave in space.

Activity 9.5

When? Where? A Taking-Up-Space Puzzle

Long ago, people observed the night sky using only their eyes. Over the years, a series of inventions made it possible for people to study the sky very carefully. In this activity, you'll solve a puzzle by putting inventions and discoveries in the order in which they occurred. And when you're done with the puzzle, you can have some fun discovering whether adults at your home or school can solve it!

1▶ Get Ready

12 index cards
Pencil
Resource books and/or access to the World Wide Web

2▶ Do and Wonder

Take a look at the following list of inventions and discoveries. Write the name of each on the front of an index card. Then put the cards in a stack, with the names of the inventions and discoveries facing upward.

First human to orbit the earth

First humans on the moon

First planetlike object discovered outside our solar system

First robot vehicle traveled on Mars

First space station launched

First spacecraft landed on Mars

Hubble Space Telescope placed in orbit

Sextant

Space satellite placed in orbit

Stonehenge

Sundial

Telescope

Spread the cards out on a table so you can see each one. Think about which item was probably invented or discovered first, second, third, and so on. Here are some hints:

Think about how early in history humans would have needed each invention or discovery.

The inventions that use energy such as gas or electricity were probably invented fairly recently.

Some of the inventions and discoveries use ideas that came from previous inventions and discoveries.

Put the cards in order, from the oldest invention (at your left) to the newest (at your right).

Check your work. Look at the Explanation at the end of this activity. There, you'll find a list of the inventions and discoveries, including information about when each happened, who invented or discovered it, and what country that person was from. The inventions and discoveries are listed in order from oldest to newest. Use this information to check the order of your index cards. How did you do?

Now it's time to see how well an adult can put the inventions and discoveries in order. Find an adult family member or someone at school who's willing to try. Mix up the cards, and challenge the adult to put them in order, from oldest to newest. When he or she has finished, check the order of the cards. Then ask the adult if any of the dates surprised him or her. Also ask about what ideas he or she used to put the cards in order.

3➧ Think and Write   Write a paragraph about how *you* did in solving the puzzle. Did you have the oldest invention or discovery in the correct place? The most recent? How about those in between? When you checked the order of your cards against the correct information, what surprised you? Why?

Write another paragraph about the *adult's* success at arranging the cards.

Explanation   *Stonehenge* (2,000–1,000 B.C.E.*)—Originally believed to be a religious monument but later hypothesized to be a huge astronomical instrument; England.

*The abbreviation B.C.E. means "before the common era" (which is the same as B.C., or "before Christ").

Sundial (between 1,000 and 700 B.C.E.)—Probably by early astronomers in Egypt.

Telescope (about 1590)—Various inventors in different countries made contributions. Galileo Galilei, an Italian, is believed to be the first person to use the telescope to make careful studies of objects in the sky.

Sextant (about 1730)—Invented independently by John Hadley, an Englishman, and Thomas Godfrey, an American; ancient sailors probably used devices based on some of the same ideas.

Space satellite placed in orbit (1957)—Many Soviet inventors and designers created *Sputnik;* the former USSR (now Russia).

First human to orbit the earth (1961)—Soviet cosmonaut Yury Gagarin completed a full orbit of the earth in the *Vostok I;* the former USSR (now Russia).

First humans on the moon (1969)—American astronauts Neil Armstrong and Buzz Aldrin landed on the moon in *Apollo 11;* the United States.

First space station launched (1971)—Various Soviet inventors and designers created the *Solyut I;* the former USSR (now Russia).

First spacecraft landed on Mars (1976)—Many American inventors and designers created the *Viking I;* the United States.

Hubble Space Telescope placed in orbit (1990)—Many American inventors and designers created the Hubble, which was placed in orbit by the space shuttle *Discovery;* the United States.

First planetlike object discovered outside our solar system (1995)—Swiss astronomers Mayor and Queloz gathered evidence of a planet outside our solar system; Switzerland.

First robot vehicle traveled on Mars (1997)—The NASA *Pathfinder* probe landed on Mars, and *Sojourner,* the first robot rover, traveled over its surface; United States.

Word Play

Word Play 9.1

Planet Poetry

One way to show what you know about a science topic is to write about it. In this project, you'll write about two planets in our solar system. But you won't be writing paragraphs. You'll be writing some planet poetry instead!

1▶ Get Ready

Pencil and paper
Resource books and/or access to the World Wide Web

2▶ Do and Wonder

Select a planet from the list below, and use resource books and/or the World Wide Web to gather information about it. Be sure to write down any interesting information you discover.

Mercury	Mars	Uranus
Venus	Jupiter	Neptune
Earth	Saturn	Pluto

Next you're going to use what you learned about your planet to write a type of poem called a *cinquain* (sin-kwane). A cinquain has five lines, but they don't have to rhyme. Instead, each line says a specific thing about the planet and has a certain number of syllables. Here's what each line should do:

1. Word or words to describe the planet	2 syllables
2. More describing words	4 syllables
3. Words that tell about things happening on or around the planet	6 syllables
4. Words that tell how you feel about the planet	8 syllables
5. A synonym (word that means the same as another) for the word or words on line 1	2 syllables

3▶ Think and Write   Read the planet poems below, and decide whether each follows the pattern for a cinquain. Write a short paragraph telling what you like most about each poem.

Jupiter	**Saturn**
So large	Ring place
Made of gases	So far away
Red spot moving through clouds	Ice and rock circle high
Such a beautiful traveler	Amazing object in our sky
Giant	Show off

Explanation   Poets for centuries have been writing about all the beautiful things in the sky, such as the sun, the stars, and the moon. You were a poet in this activity, using the scientific information you learned to write a planet poem. The type of poem you wrote—a *cinquain*—is one of several types of poetry that follow certain patterns.

Word Play 9.2

A Message from the Space Shuttle

If you've ever seen the space shuttle land or take off, you know it's an amazing invention! It blasts off like a rocket and lands like a glider. Wouldn't it be exciting to take a trip on the shuttle? In this activity, you'll discover what that would be like and then tell about it by writing an electronic mail (e-mail) message to a friend.

1▶ Get Ready   Pencil and paper
Resource books and/or access to the World Wide Web
Optional: Access to e-mail

2▶ Do and Wonder   Gather information about the space shuttle using resource books and/or the World Wide Web. Try to find astronauts' descriptions of what it's like to blast off and land and what sorts of things they do during missions.

Here's some information about the space shuttle to get you started:

> The space shuttle has three main parts: (1) an orbiter that carries the crew and cargo, (2) a large external tank that carries liquid fuel, and (3) two solid-fuel rocket boosters.
>
> The space shuttle takes off like a rocket. The two solid-fuel rocket boosters separate from the shuttle shortly after take off. They fall into the sea and are recovered for reuse.
>
> Just before reaching orbit, the liquid-fuel tank separates. It breaks up as it passes through the atmosphere.
>
> The orbiter continues its flight and travels around the earth.
>
> When the astronauts have finished their tasks, they prepare the orbiter for its trip back to the earth.
>
> Small rockets are used to adjust the shuttle's speed and direction.
>
> The orbiter lands like a glider. It can land at the Kennedy Space Center in Florida or Vandenberg Air Force Base in California.

▶ Think and Write

Imagine that you are in the space shuttle, circling the earth. Write a four-paragraph e-mail message you might send to a friend. Be sure to tell about blasting off, the changing view, and living and working in a weightless environment.

Explanation

The space shuttle missions have taught us a lot about traveling and living in space. The *next* big step for the world-wide space program will be to complete the international space station. It might be the starting place for humankind's next big space adventure: traveling to, landing on, and living on Mars!

Magnificent Math 9.1

Planet Thermometers

Have you ever wondered whether there's life on other planets? Scientists are searching for life using space probes, satellites, telescopes, and in the case of Mars, even rover vehicles. One of the things they're looking for is liquid water, which could support life. In this activity, you'll learn one way to discover whether any of the planets have water.

1▶ Get Ready

Ruler
Five sheets of paper

Pencil
Watercolor marker

2▶ Do and Wonder

Draw one thermometer on each sheet of paper (five in all). Label four of them with the names of these planets: "Earth," "Mercury," "Mars," and "Venus." Label the fifth thermometer "All the Planets."

Use the data below to find the temperature range for each of the planets. (You may use Celsius or Fahrenheit temperatures.) Use the marker to color in the temperature range on each planet's thermometer. Then show all the planets' temperatures on the fifth thermometer. (Note that the temperature on Venus doesn't change very much, so just put a single temperature on its thermometer.)

Planet	Temperature Range in Degrees Fahrenheit	Temperature Range in Degrees Celsius
Earth	140 to –128	60 to –89
Mercury	806 to –328	430 to –200
Mars	81 to –220	27 to –140
Venus	864	464

3▶ Think and Write   Water is a liquid between 32 and 212 degrees Fahrenheit (0 and 100 degrees Celsius). Keep that in mind as you answer these questions in a few paragraphs: Could any planet besides Earth have liquid water on it? Do you know of any plants or animals that live in places that don't have liquid water? Do you think there might be living things somewhere that don't need water of any kind to live? Why or why not?

Explanation   How hot and cold it gets on a planet depends on many things. Most important is the amount of time the sun's rays directly strike the planet. Another thing to consider is whether the planet has an atmosphere that affects how fast it warms up or cools down. The distance a planet is from the sun *isn't* very important, except for the closest and furthest planets.

Magnificent Math 9.2

Weighing In on the Planets

To lose weight, people usually have to eat less and exercise more. But did you know that there's *another* way to lose weight? All you have to do is travel to and survive on another planet! In this activity, you'll learn how much you'd weigh in some very interesting places.

1▶ Get Ready   Pencil and paper

2▶ Do and Wonder   First of all, you need to know how much you weigh on Earth. Write it down here: _____

To find out how much you'd weigh on other planets, use the chart on the next page. For the sun and each planet in column 1, multiply your Earth weight by the number in column 2, and write that new number in column 3. That's how much you'd weigh if you lived there.

Sun	27.90	_____
Mercury	.37	_____
Venus	.88	_____
Earth	1.00	_____
Earth's moon	.16	_____
Mars	.38	_____
Jupiter	2.64	_____
Saturn	1.15	_____
Uranus	.93	_____
Neptune	1.22	_____
Pluto	.06	_____

3▶ Think and Write   Look closely at the numbers in column 3, and answer these questions in a short paragraph: Where would you weigh the least? Where would you weigh the most? Do you think how far you could jump would be different on other planets?

Explanation   Your weight on the earth depends on your mass, the earth's mass, and the distance between you and the center of the earth. Your weight on the sun or another planet would depend on the same things. So of course, your weight on the sun or another planet would be different from your weight on the earth.

Art Connections

Art Connections 9.1

String Star Sculptures

What could be more magical than being outdoors on a clear night, looking up at a sky full of twinkling stars? You'll try to copy the magic of the stars in this project by making a star sculpture with string. And if you make more than one star, you can hang them all together to make your own beautiful evening sky.

1▶ Get Ready

Note: This list shows what you need to create *one star*. If you want to make more than one, increase the amount of each material.

Piece of cardboard about 6 inches × 6 inches
    (15 centimeters × 15 centimeters)
12 straight pins
Liquid starch
Paintbrush
Spool of thin, white yarn or string
Small container of glitter or glitter spray

2▶ Do and Wonder

Stick the pins in the cardboard so they form the outline of a five-pointed star. Then stick pins at different places inside the outline.

Tie the end of the yarn around one of the pins. Then loop the yarn back and forth around all the pins until you have created a star pattern. Be sure the yarn is tight around and between the pins. Fix any loose spots by moving the pins just enough to pull the yarn tight.

Use the liquid starch and paintbrush to paint the yarn connecting the pins. You want the yarn to become quite stiff, so you're going to apply *two* coats of starch. Let the star dry after applying each coat.

Now paint the star with another *light* coat of starch, and then sprinkle it with glitter. Let the star dry completely.

Carefully remove the pins from the stiff yarn. You have made a string star!

3▶ Think and Write

The star you made has five points. Do you think the stars in our universe are really pointed like this? Answer this question in a few sentences. (Hint: We have a *real* star in our solar system. Think about its shape.)

Explanation

Our universe is filled with stars. The light we see coming from them actually left each star long ago and has been traveling through space. The light energy was released when some matter on the star was changed to energy. The starlight that comes through our atmosphere bounces around a little. So when people say that a star twinkles, they're noticing the slight changes in the path that the light took.

Safety Hints

Don't leave the pins around where others might accidentally stick themselves.

Don't do this activity around small children.

Art Connections 9.2

Moon Phase Flip Book

One of the most interesting things about the moon is that it looks so different from night to night. If you watch the moon every night for a week or so, you'll notice how much it changes shape. In this activity, you'll make a flip book that shows the changes that happen during a month in just a few seconds.

1▶ Get Ready

16 plain, white index cards
Thin, black marking pen
Stapler
Reference book that shows phases of the moon

2→ Do and Wonder

Use the reference book to find drawings or photographs of how the moon looks to people on Earth on four or five different nights of the month. Draw your own pictures of these different moons on index cards (one moon per card). Try to make all the drawings the same basic size, and center each in the middle of the card.

Place the cards in order, from the night of a new moon to a full moon.

Now make four or five more cards that take the full moon back to the night of a new moon. Add these to your collection so they follow the first set of cards.

Make more drawings that show the moon's phases between those you've already drawn. When you're done, you should have at least 16 cards.

Put all the cards in order, forming a deck that starts and ends with a new moon. With the pictures rightside up, staple the deck together at the lefthand side, forming a little book.

Holding the book in one hand, bend the pages back and quickly flip through them. You should see the moon going through its phases.

3→ Think and Write

The phases the moon goes through is only one of many patterns in nature that could be shown with a flip book. What other patterns can you think of? Write a short paragraph about how you could make a flip book for one of these patterns.

Explanation

The moon is the earth's satellite. It revolves around the earth in 29½ days and rotates on its axis just once in the same period of time. This means that from the earth, we can only see about half the moon. The moon is lit by the sun, so when we look at the moon, we see reflected sunlight. As the moon revolves, the amount of the half that we actually see changes.

Amazing but True!
BRAINSTRETCHERS

9.1   What is astrology?

Be careful not to confuse *astronomy* with *astrology*. *Astronomy* is the science that studies the stars, planets, galaxies, and universes. But *astrology* is definitely not a science! It's a set of myths based on the idea that the positions of the planets in the sky at the moment of someone's birth will affect him or her throughout life. People who believe in astrology read their horoscopes in order to find out what's predicted to happen to them that day or month or year. They are, of course, wasting their time but perhaps having fun wondering whether they'll get rich or find their true love!

9.2   What are a year, a month, a day, an hour, a minute, and a second?

Do you have time for the answers? Well, here they are:

(1) A *year* is the time it takes the earth to make one complete trip around the sun.

(2) A *month* is the time it takes the moon to make one complete trip around the earth.

(3) A *day* is the time it takes for the earth to spin once on its axis (axe-iss).

(4) An *hour* really doesn't have anything to do with the sun, the moon, or the earth. Instead, it's a human creation. Many years ago, someone divided the day into 24 equal parts and called each an *hour*. The fact is, that person could just as easily have divided the day into 3 equal parts and called each a *Fred*.

(5) If you divide an hour by 60, you get a *minute*.

(6) If you divide a minute by 60, you get a *second*.

9.3   What is the sun made of?

The sun is made of the gases hydrogen and helium. At the center of the sun, intense pressure causes hydrogen atoms to squeeze together to form helium. This process is called *nuclear fusion* and is the same thing that happens when a hydrogen bomb is tested on the earth. When nuclear fusion occurs—whether at the center of the sun or on the earth—a great deal of energy is released. The energy released from nuclear reactions at the center of the sun leave the sun as heat and light.

9.4   If you look at the sky on a clear night, how many stars can you actually see?

On a clear night, without using binoculars or a telescope, you can see between 2,000 and 3,000 stars. These stars are either very close to our solar system or distant but very bright.

9.5 What is a galaxy?

A *galaxy* is a group of hundreds of millions or even billions of stars. Even though the stars in a galaxy *seem* to be in a group when we look at them through a telescope, they may be millions and millions of miles apart. Our own sun is part of the galaxy we call the *Milky Way*. And throughout the universe, there may be billions of galaxies.

9.6 If you could see every star in the universe, how many would you see?

No one knows for sure how many stars are in the universe. But there may be billions of galaxies, and some may contain more than 1 million stars. To get a rough idea of how many stars there are, assume there are 1 billion galaxies and each has 1 billion stars. Use your math skills to multiply 1,000,000,000 × 1,000,000,000. (Be careful to keep track of all those zeroes!)

9.7 How do stars make the light we see?

The tiny points of light we see on a starry night are really ball-shaped clumps of gas and dust. As time passes, the materials in stars draw closer and closer together. While this happens, tremendous heat and pressure build up at the center of the clump. If the pressure and temperature are high enough, the hydrogen in a star changes to helium. When this occurs, enormous amounts of heat and light are released in what scientists call a *nuclear* reaction. It's the same kind of reaction that happens on the earth when a hydrogen bomb explodes. The only difference is that on a star, the reaction is far more powerful.

9.8 Why do stars twinkle?

If you've ever been out in the country or another place where the air is very clear, you may have noticed that stars seem to change in brightness as you watch them. They sort of flicker because the light they give off passes through different layers of the atmosphere and bends in different directions on the path it takes to our eyes. Some of the light we see from a single star is constantly being bent back and forth. This causes the twinkling we see.

9.9 How hot is it at the center of the sun?

The temperature at the center of the sun is probably between 18 and 36 million degrees Fahrenheit (which is about 10 and 20 million degrees Celsius). Now *that's* hot!

9.10   How long has the universe been around?

This question has many answers because scientists argue about the age of the universe all the time. The best answer right now is an estimate—a very rough estimate—that the universe is between 8 and 20 billion years old.

9.11   Is there really such a thing as a shooting star?

Yes and no. What people call *shooting stars* aren't stars at all. Rather, they're chunks of rock called *meteors* that are moving through space and enter our atmosphere because gravity attracts them. As a meteor moves through the air, it heats up because of air friction and begins to glow. So when you see a shooting star, you're watching a meteor burn up as it travels through our atmosphere. But not all meteors burn up completely. Those that reach the ground are called *meteorites* (meet-ee-or-ytes). Don't worry about getting hit by one, however. Although millions of meteors of all different sizes enter our atmosphere each day, very few ever reach the ground.

9.12   Would it be possible to make a machine that would let us travel back in time?

Why go through all the trouble of making a time machine when you already have one! To see the past, just go outside on a clear night and look up. When you look at a star that is five light-years away, you're seeing light that was emitted five years ago. In fact, you're seeing the past—how things used to be. What's even stranger is that you may be looking at stars that don't even exist anymore!

9.13   Do all the planets rotate in the same direction?

No. Venus and Uranus spin in the opposite direction of Earth and the other planets. Uranus not only spins in the opposite direction, but its axis is very tilted. If you look at Uranus with a telescope from Earth, it looks like it's spinning and orbiting while lying on its side!

9.14   My grandmother sometimes says that things happen "once in a blue moon." What in the world is a blue moon?

At times, there's so much pollution in our atmosphere that the moon seems to be a slightly different color than normal. Volcanic eruptions can also send millions of tons of tiny particles in the air, blocking some of the moon's light from reaching us. Sometimes, these particles absorb most of the light waves except the blue ones, which makes the moon have a slight bluish color. This happens very rarely—in fact, only "once in a blue moon!" (which is what that expression means).

9.15   If everything in a space station is weightless, wouldn't food like spaghetti and meatballs be really hard for astronauts to eat?

Wouldn't it be fun to see a picture of an astronaut holding a fork and chasing a meatball around the space station? You'll never see a picture like that because the foods astronauts eat are heated and served in closed, plastic containers. Any liquids in the foods get squeezed through tubes and into the astronauts' mouths. Solid foods—such as cheese, turkey, and meatballs—are all prepared on the earth and cut into bite-sized pieces. If the astronauts had to cut up their own food, the tiny crumbs they'd make would wind up floating around the spacecraft.

9.16   Is there life on Mars?

No one knows for sure whether there's life on Mars. Scientists will have a definite answer some time in the next 10 or 20 years, after more spacecraft reach the planet's surface. Until then, scientists are studying some possible hints that there *was* life on Mars long ago. For instance, some of the meteorites recovered on Earth may have come from Mars. One group of geologists says one of these meteorites shows evidence of very simple life forms, but other geologists don't agree. Another hint that there may have been life on Mars came with the discovery that there may have been water on that planet. (Since we humans need water to survive, we tend to think that all other life does, too.) Exploration by the Mars rover and photographs taken by orbiting spacecraft show evidence that great rivers of water once flowed on Mars.

9.17   What are the rings around Saturn made of?

Scientists have wondered about Saturn's rings for a long time. Just recently, spacecraft have been able to pass near or through Saturn's rings and send back a lot of information about them. Now scientists believe that the rings are made of rocks, gases, and ice.

9.18 Is the sun the only star that has planets orbiting it?

No. In recent years, astronomers using powerful radio telescopes and other instruments have discovered that other stars have planets, too.

9.19 Is there life anywhere else in our solar system or universe?

Again, no one knows for sure whether life exists anywhere but Earth. Scientists have been sending messages into space using radio waves for many years, hoping to receive an answer. So far, no one (or no thing) has answered. Keep in mind that ordinary radio and television broadcasts also travel into space. Maybe the first message we get from extraterrestrial life will be to tell us they really like the TV programs they're getting!

9.20 I heard that scientists discovered vinegar in a cloud of gas near some star. Is that really true?

Yes! Using radio telescopes, astronomers from the University of Illinois discovered molecules like those of ordinary vinegar (acetic acid) in a cloud of gas and dust called *Sagittarius B2 North*. This gas and dust cloud is 25,000 light-years away from our solar system.

9.21 What kind of pills do astronauts take?

Space capsules.

9.22 Where do astronauts leave their spaceships?

At parking meteors.

9.23 What's the biggest telephone company in space?

ET&T.

Chapter 10

Preserve and Protect

Activities

Word Play

Magnificent Math

Art Connections

Amazing but True!
Brainstretchers   [SPSP 1–11]

Part IV Ecology, Technology, and You

Ecological Sciences

Activities

The Biome Box

Did you know that you live in a biome (by-ome)? *Biomes* are places on Earth that have the same climate and types of living things. In this activity, you'll make a three-dimensional model of one of our planet's biomes.

1 ▶ Get Ready

Shoebox or other small, cardboard box
Magazines that can be cut up
Assortment of scraps of paper, cardboard, thread, yarn, cotton balls, fabric, and so on
Scissors
Watercolor paints of various colors
Felt-tipped markers of various colors
Clear tape or glue stick
Construction paper of various colors
Resource books and/or access to the World Wide Web
Index card

2 ▶ Do and Wonder

Use resource books and/or the World Wide Web to gather information about the climate and living things you would expect for one of the following biomes:

Tundra	Ocean
Grassland	Temperate forest
Ice	Mountains
Taiga	Desert
Tropical rainforest	Tropical forest

Set the box on a flat surface, laying it on one of its long sides. The open top of the box should be facing you.

You're going to create a model of your biome inside the shoebox. The idea is to make people feel like they're actually looking into this small world. Here are some ideas to get you started:

Paint the inside of the box using colors you would expect to see in this biome.

Find pictures of various living things, cut them out, and tape or glue them on the floor and walls of the model. Make your own drawings of plants and animals inside the biome, too. Arrange things to give the biome a three-dimensional look.

If birds live in your biome, hang or draw bird pictures on the top of the biome.

Finally, use the collection of scraps to add other features to your biome, such as clouds in the sky, trees, rocks, and sand dunes.

On the index card, write the name of the biome, describe its climate, and list the plants and animals that live within it. (Use the information you found in resource books and/or on the World Wide Web.) Attach the card to the outside of your biome box.

3▶ Think and Write   Imagine that you're a nature guide taking a group of people to visit a natural area in your biome. List three or four things you should mention to make sure the visitors don't harm the biome during their visit.

Explanation   The earth is a giant *ecosystem,* which is an environmental community in which everything works together. Scientists have divided the earth's ecosystem into nine *biomes,* which are areas that have particular climates, levels of precipitation and temperature, availabilities of water, and resources, plants, and animals.

Activity 10.2

Measuring Acid Rain

Is rainwater pure? Scientists worry that the rainwater in some places is absorbing pollution and becoming acidic. To measure just how acidic, scientists use several techniques. You'll use one of them in this activity to discover the acidity of a liquid.

1▶ Get Ready

¼ cup lemon juice   ¼ cup rainwater
¼ cup cola drink   ¼ cup soapy water
Marking pens   Six paper cups
½ teaspoon baking soda in ¼ cup tapwater
Blue litmus paper or pH paper (available at a pharmacy)

2▶ Do and Wonder

Using a special kind of paper strip, you're going to test six liquids to find out whether they're acids. One type of strip is blue litmus paper, which turns pink when it's put in a liquid that's acidic. The other type of strip is pH paper, which gives a reading of 7 or less if a liquid is acidic.

Pour a small amount of each liquid into one of the six cups (one liquid per cup). Write the name of the liquid on the cup.

Before testing any of the liquids, predict which ones might be acids. Then dip a short strip of blue litmus paper or pH paper in each liquid. Write down your observations. How do your results compare with your predictions?

3▶ Think and Write

Design an activity to test whether precipitation is becoming more or less acidic. In a paragraph, tell how much water to collect, what containers to use, and what information to record on graphs and charts.

Use reference books and/or the World Wide Web to discover the effects of acid rain. Write a paragraph that summarizes what you learned.

Explanation

Even pure rainwater contains carbon dioxide, which makes it a weak acid. But chemicals such as sulfur dioxide and nitrogen oxide are making rainwater more acidic. These chemicals are produced by the burning of fossil fuels by motor vehicles, certain kinds of industries, and nature itself. The result is *acid rain*, which is rainwater that contains chemicals that can dissolve minerals.

How Many People per Place?

What can scientists do to stop certain plants and animals from becoming extinct? First they have to learn whether the population of a specific plant or animal is really getting smaller. In this activity, you'll learn how to gather the information needed to determine that change. And the creatures you'll study have two eyes, two ears, a nose, and generally look a lot like you!

1▶ Get Ready

Pencil and paper
Yardstick or meterstick
Access to three or four classrooms

2▶ Do and Wonder

You're going to keep track of how many people are in several classrooms over three days. To begin, make a chart to record the information:

Label the first column "Classrooms," and then list "Classroom 1," "Classroom 2," and so on below it.

Label the second column "Area in Square Yards" (or "Square Meters").

Label columns 3, 4, and 5 "Day 1," "Day 2," and "Day 3." (Make each of these columns wide enough to fit two numbers.)

Pick three or four classrooms in your school that are the same size. Find the area of each classroom by measuring its length and width and multiplying the two numbers. For example, a classroom that's 10 yards wide and 15 yards long has an area of 150 square yards. (Do the same measuring and multiplying if you're measuring in meters.) Write the area of each classroom in column 2 of the chart.

Next find the population of each classroom by counting the number of people in it. Write down your results under "Day 1" on the chart.

To find the *population density* of each classroom, divide the number of people in the room by its area. For example, a classroom that has 20 people and an area of 150 square yards (or meters) has a population density of .13 people per square yard (or meter). Write the population density on the chart, also under "Day 1." (Use a slash to separate the two numbers, like this: 20 / .13.)

Count the number of people in each room and figure its population density for two more days. Record this information on the chart under "Day 2" and "Day 3."

3▶ Think and Write   Write a short paragraph that answers these questions: Which classroom had the highest population density? The lowest? Over the three days, did the population density increase or decrease in each classroom?

Imagine that over five years, a scientist observed changes in the population density of bluebirds. Make a hypothesis that could explain these changes:

Year 1	1 bluebird per square mile (or kilometer)
Year 2	2 bluebirds per square mile (or kilometer)
Year 3	4 bluebirds per square mile (or kilometer)
Year 4	1 bluebird per square mile (or kilometer)
Year 5	1 bluebird per square mile (or kilometer)

Explanation   Scientists find the population density of a living thing by counting or estimating the number (population) of living things and dividing it by the space it lives in. If the population density for a certain plant or animal starts to drop, it might mean that the plant or animal is using up all its resources in that environment.

Activity 10.4

Where Are the Rainforests?

If someone gave you a map and asked you to point out where the rainforests are, could you do it? If you can't right now, you'll certainly be able to after completing this activity. In it, you'll write a television commercial that could be used to tell people how to save the rainforests.

1▶ Get Ready

World map or globe
Paper and pencil
Reference books and/or access to the World Wide Web

2▶ Do and Wonder

Look closely at the map or globe, and find the 20 degrees north latitude line and the 20 degrees south latitude line. Notice which countries or parts of countries lie between these two lines. These are the countries with rainforests.

List some of the countries that might have rainforests. Is your country one of them?

Pick three countries, and do some research about the rainforests there. Use reference books and/or the World Wide Web to find information about the following:

What animals and plants live in these rainforests?

Which animals and plants are in danger?

How people are trying to save the rainforests in these countries?

3▶ Think and Write

Suppose the government of one of the countries you studied has asked you to make a television commercial about preserving the country's rainforest. Use what you've learned about the rainforests to create a commercial. It may include videotapes, still pictures, and interviews but can't be more than 3 minutes long. Describe how your commercial will begin (using 30 seconds), what the main part will say (2 minutes), and how it will end (30 seconds).

Explanation

About *half* the plant and animal species on Earth live in tropical rainforests. These regions—along with the plants and animals that live in them—are in danger because the climate they're in is excellent for farming and ranching. People destroy the rainforests to take natural resources from them and to make more land available for crops and herds.

Activity 10.5

The Rainforest's Layers of Life

There are *so many* different plants and animals living in the rainforest that you might wonder how they all fit! Amazingly enough, they fit by living in layers—from the very tops of the trees down to the ground. In this activity, you'll make a drawing that shows these layers and the plants and animals found in each.

1▶ Get Ready

Easel paper, newsprint paper, or butcher paper
Water-based markers or crayons in assorted colors
Resource books and/or access to the World Wide Web

2▶ Do and Wonder

Before starting your drawing, use reference books and/or the World Wide Web to do some research. Look for information about the layers of the rainforest and what kind of life is found in each one. Start from the bottom and go up:

   (1) *Forest floor:* Wet leaves, mosses, herbs, fungi, deer

   (2) *Understory:* Small shrubs and trees, ferns, palms, monkeys, sloths

   (3) *Canopy (can-oh-pee):* Medium-sized trees usually not more than 150 feet (about 46 meters) tall, vines, orchids, mosses on trees, air plants (which grow on branches and whose roots hang down absorbing water from the air), monkeys, sloths

   (4) *Emergent (ee-merj-int) layer:* The tops of very tall trees usually more than 250 feet (about 76 meters) tall

Use all this information to make a large drawing that shows the four layers of the rainforest. Add drawings of plants and animals, including birds and insects, to the correct layers on the drawing. Label each plant and animal as you add it.

3▶ Think and Write

Write a short paragraph about the layers of the rainforest and the plants and animals found in each one. What did you learn that might surprise others?

Explanation   The rainforest has four major layers. The bottom layer is the forest floor and is covered with plants, leaves, mosses, and fungi. The next layer is the understory, where small trees, vines, and shrubs grow. The third layer is the canopy, which is formed by branches of trees growing close together like an umbrella. The canopy stops sun and rain from directly reaching the forest floor. The top layer is the emergent layer, and it has very tall trees whose branches grow up toward the sunlight.

Activity 10.6

The Perfect City

Imagine what it would be like to live in a city with clean air, pure water, no traffic, and no pollution. You'll design a city in this activity that's perfect in almost every way. Doing this should give you ideas about how to improve your city, too.

1▶ Get Ready

Graph paper
Pencil and paper
Ruler

2▶ Do and Wonder

You're going to make a scale drawing that shows how your perfect city would look from an airplane. To get started, think about this list of what your city must include:

Your city has two rivers. One runs right through it, and the other runs along one of its edges.

Your city gets its water from one of the rivers and has a water purification plant and a sewage treatment plant.

Your city has three factories that make automobiles.

Your city has a landfill for garbage and a recycling plant for paper, plastics, metals, and glass.

People in your city can walk or bicycle to work and school.

Your city has no suburbs. Everyone has a home or apartment in the city, and most people also work and go to school in the city.

Your city's electrical energy comes from two sources: water power from a dam in one of the rivers and wind power from windmills on hilltops outside the city.

Your city has a downtown shopping area, but the streets in front of the stores aren't wide enough for cars to drive through them. Shoppers park their cars in lots near the stores and then walk from store to store.

Your city has farms and ranches and food-processing companies along its edges.

Now draw your city, including all these things. Add other things to your perfect city, if you want. Label all the parts of your city.

3▶ Think and Write   Think about how the city you designed is the same or different from the town or city you *really* live in. Write a paragraph comparing the two places. Be sure to mention any problems with air pollution, traffic, sound pollution, and water pollution in each.

Explanation   Making cities better places to live requires careful planning and making big changes in how things are done over a long period of time. Creating a brand-new city, like you did in this activity, is probably much easier than trying to change a city that already exists.

Activity 10.7

Measuring Noise Pollution

The world is often a noisy place—so much so that we may not even notice all the loud and unpleasant sounds around us. You *will* notice in this activity by measuring different types of noise pollution and seeing how they can affect you.

1▶ Get Ready

Graph paper
Assortment of colored markers or pencils

2▶ Do and Wonder

You'll be gathering information about sounds in different places. Pick five locations to study—some indoors and some outdoors.

Before you begin, make a graph to record your data. List the five places you're going to study along the horizontal axis.

Table 1   Decibel Levels of Types of Sounds

Type of Sound	Decibel Level	Examples
Barely heard	0–10	Light breathing
Faint	10–25	Someone whispering close by Quiet library
Moderate	25–50	People talking Restaurant
Loud	50–70	Vacuum cleaner Noisy playground
Very loud	70–90	Garbage disposal Lawn mower Traffic on a busy street
Deafening	90–115	Train or motorcycle passing by
Painful to ears	115–130	Nearby thunder Jet getting ready to take off
May break eardrum	130 or more	Explosion Jet taking off

Label the vertical axis "Decibels" (des-a-bells), and make a scale from 0 to 150. (Note that the loudnesses of sounds are measured in decibels.)

Visit each of the five locations, taking Table 1 and your graph along with you. Sit quietly for a minute at each place. Then pick the "Type of Sound" from the table that's closest to the loudest sound you hear in that location. Record the decibel level of that sound on your graph.

③▶ Think and Write

Sounds that are at high decibel levels can seriously injure your hearing. How else might noise pollution in or near your home or school affect you and the people around you? Write a short paragraph that answers this question.

Explanation

The loudness of a sound is measured in decibels. Sounds near 0 on the decibel scale are the quietest sounds that people with excellent hearing can hear. Listening to sounds of 90 decibels or more over a long time can make you deaf, and listening to sounds over 130 decibels can break your eardrums. Loud and annoying sounds are examples of noise pollution.

Activity 10.8

Measuring Air Pollution

Do you collect anything? Well, maybe you'd like to start a nice collection of dust or dirt. That's what scientists who study air pollution do everyday. In this activity, you'll study the air outdoors to learn how clean it is. You may be breathing in more than air!

1▶ Get Ready

Roll of white, plastic furniture repair tape (available at a hardware store)
Two rulers, each 12 inches (about 30 centimeters) in length
Two paper cups   Masking tape
Hand lens (magnifying glass)   Scissors

2▶ Do and Wonder

Cut two strips of tape, each 5 inches (about 13 centimeters) long. Tightly wrap one end of each ruler with a strip of tape so the sticky side is facing out. Overlap the ends of the tape to hold it in place.

Place a paper cup on each taped end of each ruler, but don't touch the sides of the cup to the tape. (You're using the cups to keep particles off the tape until you put the rulers outside.)

Take the rulers outside, and decide on two locations to test. Stick each ruler in the ground, or tape it to the corner of a building. Remove the paper cups. Predict which ruler will gather the most particles.

After three days, observe the tape on each ruler. Use the hand lens to count how many particles have stuck to each tape.

3▶ Think and Write

Write a short paragraph that answers these questions: Did the tapes collect about the same numbers and kinds of particles? What might be the sources of the particles you observed? Where would these particles be if *you* had been standing where the rulers were located for the last three days?

Explanation

The air contains tiny particles of dust, soot, and pollen, which can be seen with a hand lens. It may also contain particles of lead and mercury, which are too small to see. Some particles come from faraway volcanic eruptions and soil that has been blown into the air. Other sources are coal- and oil-powered electricity-generating plants along with factories, exhaust, and forest fires. Breathing in any of these particles can cause problems for your respiratory system.

Word Play

Word Play 10.1

Adopting an Endangered Animal

Hundreds of species of animals are considered endangered. In this activity, you'll help people learn more about one of these animals by writing a television commercial about it. In fact, you're going to tell people why they should adopt an endangered animal and help protect it from becoming extinct.

1▸ Get Ready

Resource books and/or access to the World Wide Web
Pencil and paper
Videocamera and tape (optional)

2▸ Do and Wonder

Find out which animals are endangered by using reference books and/or the World Wide Web. (Hint: Search for the phrase *endangered animals*.) Select one of these endangered animals, and gather information about it:

Where does it live?	What is its food supply?
How many are left?	Why is it in danger?

Use the information you gather to write the script for a television commercial. It may include videotape, still pictures, and interviews but can't be more than 3 minutes long. Describe how your commercial will begin (using 30 seconds), what the main part will say (2 minutes), and how it will end (30 seconds). Your goal is to convince people to be concerned about whether the animal survives.

3▸ Think and Write

If you have access to a videocamera, actually make your commercial. Be sure to follow the script you've written.

Contact a local public television channel, and explain this activity to them. Ask them to put your commercial on TV.

Explanation   Although many people *say* they're concerned about animals becoming extinct, few actually know which species are in danger. Showing commercials, like the one you made in this activity, is one way for people to learn about endangered species and what everyone can do to help.

Word Play 10.2

Gretta and the Vacant Lot

You're going to work some magic in this activity by turning a vacant lot into a beautiful forest! You'll do so by writing a story told by the character Gretta, who watches it all happen.

1▶ Get Ready   Reference book that has descriptions and drawings of common plants
Paper and pencil

2▶ Do and Wonder   Meet Gretta, a magical person who can live for a long, long time. Her home is in a small town that was built on land that used to be a beautiful forest. The rest of the forest still lies on the edge of town. Gretta lives across the street from the vacant lot and notices everything that happens there. In your story, you're going to tell what she observes as the vacant lot slowly becomes a forest again.

At the beginning of your story, Gretta is very sad. A beautiful old building has been torn down, all the rubble has been removed from the lot, and the only thing left is bare soil. Starting with this information, add the following details to your story:

First group of plants appear: Ragweed, Daisy fleabane, and Beggars tick. These plants aren't very tall but produce many seeds, don't need much water, can survive in direct sun, and live for one year.

Second group of plants appear: Milkweed, Black-eyed Susans, and Dandelions. These are tall plants that can store a lot of food and live for at least two years.

Third group of plants appear: Staghorn sumac and Raspberry bushes. These are shrubs that have woody stems.

Fourth group of plants appear: Maples, Beeches, and Elms. These are the trees.

3▶ Think and Write   Although this story is about plants, it would be even more interesting if Gretta also noticed insects, birds, and small animals arriving at the lot and making their homes there. Add them to your story.

Explanation   Even when people clear land, nature has a way of taking it back. As time passes, seeds and animals arrive on the land and start to live in it and on it. If a vacant lot is left alone, nature will eventually change it back to the way it looked originally—before humans cleared it.

Word Play 10.3

School Bus Rides and Spaceflights–Risky Business?

Suppose you're walking to school on a beautiful day, and a small meteorite falls out of the sky and hits you on the head! While this really *could* happen, it's not very likely. So scientists would say that walking to school has many health benefits but a very low risk of head injury from falling meteorites. You'll use your head in this activity to think about the risks and benefits of other things you do—or might do!

1▶ Get Ready   Paper and pencil   Adult and younger person to interview

2▶ Do and Wonder   You're going to interview two people—an adult and a younger person—to see what they think about the risks and benefits of two very different things humans do: ride on a school bus and travel into space.

Arrange a time and place to interview each person. When you meet, try to get him or her to talk about the risks and benefits of each activity. Use questions like these to get started:

Riding a School Bus

Can a bus driver concentrate on driving with 30 or more children talking and laughing?

Do the seats on a school bus have seatbelts or airbags?

Would our atmosphere be more polluted if every child was brought to school in a car rather than on a bus?

Would there be more or less traffic accidents if every child was brought to school in a car rather than on a bus?

Do cars, like buses, have first aid kits that could be used to help a child who was sick or injured?

Would the driveway in front of a school be more or less dangerous if children were brought to school in cars rather than on buses?

Would children be more or less likely to get into trouble riding on a school bus or in their parents' cars?

Traveling into Space

Astronauts have been killed in the past preparing for and taking spaceflights. Is space travel too dangerous?

Experiments done by and on astronauts provide information that's used to help people on the earth. Is this a good reason to travel into space?

Some of the information gathered in exploring space tells how the earth was formed. Does this make space travel worthwhile?

It costs a lot of money to design, build, and fly spacecraft. Should this money be used to feed, house, and provide better health care for the people who need these things?

The space program provides jobs for a lot of people. Is keeping them employed a good reason to keep the program going?

3 **Think and Write**   Review the notes from your interviews. Then write a paragraph that compares what the adult and the young person think about the risks and benefits of each activity.

Write another paragraph that tells what *you* think about the risks and benefits of each activity.

Explanation   Everything we do has risks *and* benefits. Most of us think only about the benefits without giving too much thought to the risks. We should really think about *both,* maybe listing them in two columns just to make sure. That way, you'll have the information you need to make good decisions that bring many benefits but have few risks.

Magnificent Math 10.1

Charting Changing Populations

The population of the earth increases by about 240,000 people *each day.* How many more people will that add in 1 year or 10 years or even 50 years? In this activity, you'll do something that scientists do to help predict how the population of the world will change.

1▶ Get Ready

Graph paper	Ruler
Masking tape	Pen or pencil

2▶ Do and Wonder

First set up your graph. Label the horizontal axis "Year," and make a scale that goes from 1500 to 2054. (Hint: Try making 1 square on the graph paper equal 25 years.) Label the vertical axis "Population," and make a scale that goes from 400,000,000 to 10,000,000,000 (that is, 400 million to 10 billion). (Hint: Try making 1 square equal 200,000,000 [200 million] people. If you find you're running out of room, try making 1 square equal 500,000,000 [500 million] people.)

Record these data on your graph:

Year	Population
1600	579,000,000
1700	679,000,000
1800	954,000,000
1850	1,094,000,000
1900	1,633,000,000
1950	2,515,000,000
1960	3,019,000,000

Year	Population
1970	3,698,000,000
1980	4,450,000,000
1985	4,854,000,000
1995	5,734,000,000
1998	6,000,000,000
2009	7,000,000,000
2021	8,000,000,000
2035	9,000,000,000
2054	10,000,000,000

3▶ Think and Write   Write a short paragraph that answers these questions: What trends do you see in how the world's population has changed? What hypotheses can you make about how scientists use these trends to predict what the population will be?

Explanation   As the population of the world keeps increasing, new sources of food and energy have to be found to care for all these people. To help plan for the future, scientists use graphs to make educated guesses about what the population will be.

Magnificent Math 10.2

The Water Wasters

Have you wasted any water today? Most of us do, unfortunately. And if you add up how much water is wasted by everyone in your family, you'll get a good idea of how much clean water goes down the drain. In this activity, you'll find out how much water the average family wastes every day. You'll also discover whether adults know how much water they use each day.

1▶ Get Ready

Sheet of writing paper
Sheet of graph paper
Two or three adults who will
    answer a few questions

Pen or pencil
Ruler

2▶ Do and Wonder

First set up your graph on the graph paper. List the types of activities along the horizontal axis. Label the vertical axis "Number of Gallons" (or "Liters"), and make units from 1 to 100 gallons (or 4 to 400 liters). (Hint: Try making 1 square on the graph paper equal 2 gallons [or 8 liters].)

Record the data below on your graph:

Amount Used by Average Family of Four

Activity	Gallons	Liters
Drinking and cooking	8	30
Dishwasher (3 loads)	15	57
Toilet (16 flushes)	96	363
Baths (4 baths)	80	303
Clothes washer (1 load)	34	130
Watering house plants	1	4
Garbage disposal	3.4	13

After you've completed your graph, find two or three adults to survey. Without showing the person your graph, ask him or her to estimate the total amount of water used by a family of four each day. Write down his or her estimate. Then ask each adult to estimate the amount of water used in each activity listed above. Write down his or her estimates.

Finally, show your graph to each adult. Ask him or her whether any of the data seem surprising.

3▶ Think and Write

Think about your survey results. Then write a paragraph that answers these questions: Which data surprised each adult? For which activity estimate was each adult the furthest off? Why do you think these estimates were so far off? Do you see any similarities among the adults' answers?

Explanation

The amount of water used by a family of four each day is about 237 gallons (948 liters)—more than most people would predict. If every family could reduce their water use, the problem of getting and keeping a supply of fresh water would be reduced, if not solved.

Art Connections

Art Connections 10.1

Storm Safety Posters

Wouldn't it be nice to live in a place that had perfect weather? But is there really such a place? Probably not. It seems every place is at risk for some sort of dangerous weather. In this activity, you'll learn what those risks are and make posters to tell others how to keep themselves safe when storms arrive.

1▶ Get Ready

Poster paint or wide-tip markers in various colors
Two sheets of poster paper
Reference books and/or access to the World Wide Web

2▶ Do and Wonder

Use reference books and/or the World Wide Web to learn about different kinds of storms and how to keep yourself safe during them. Also find drawings and photographs you can use to get ideas for your own drawings.

To get started, use this list of four kinds of storms and safety guidelines:

Thunderstorms

Try to get inside.

Avoid going near open doors and windows and metal objects.

Don't use electrical appliances or the telephone.

If you're caught outside, stay away from hilltops and tall trees, and don't use or be near metal objects such as fishing poles, baseball bats, golf clubs, and flagpoles.

Tornadoes

Go inside and into a storm cellar or other underground shelter.

Stay away from windows.

Take shelter under heavy furniture, such as a workbench.

Have a portable radio available for news about the storm.

If you're caught outside, try to find a low place where you can lie flat until the storm passes.

Hurricanes

If you live in an area that gets hurricanes, keep an emergency supply of clothing and blankets, a portable radio with extra batteries, water, and food that won't spoil.

Keep in mind that most damage to people and property comes from strong winds, waves, and drenching rains.

If you live near the shore of an ocean or lake, head for shelter on higher ground.

Stay indoors and away from windows and doors until the storm passes.

Blizzards

Have emergency supplies of food and water available along with a flashlight and portable radio (with extra batteries).

If you're outdoors when a blizzard starts, try to get inside a heated shelter.

Be careful when you walk outside, as there may be ice under the snow.

If you must be outside, be sure that your face and other exposed parts of your body are covered to prevent frostbite.

Don't shovel snow unless you're very used to vigorous exercise.

After you've gathered enough information, design and make a poster for each type of storm that tells people what they should do to be safe. Each poster should include a drawing and give four to six safety tips.

3▶ Think and Write   Show your posters to several adults and school friends. Ask each person which poster does the best job of presenting your storm safety message. Then write a paragraph about what people said about your posters.

Interview two or three adults to find out which kinds of storms are likely to occur in your area. Write a paragraph about what you find out.

Explanation   Most places have pleasant weather sometimes and not-so-pleasant weather other times. When the not-so-pleasant weather involves violent storms, the situation can be dangerous. People should know what types of storms usually occur where they live and how to keep safe when these storms arrive.

Art Connections 10.2

Designing an Energy-Saving House

Do you know if your home or school is an energy saver or an energy waster? The answer may depend on how old the building is. Many modern buildings are designed so they waste very little energy. In this activity, you'll design and build a cardboard model of an energy-saving house.

1▶ Get Ready

One sheet of cardboard at least 8½ × 11 inches
  (22 × 28 centimeters)
Four sheets of oak tag or other heavy paper at least
  8½ × 11 inches (22 × 28 centimeters)
  OR eight index cards

Compass	Masking tape
One sheet of graph paper	Scissors
Tempera paint in assorted colors	Ruler
Paintbrushes	Pencil

2▶ Do and Wonder

Take the sheet of cardboard, which will be the yard for your house. Use the compass to find the directions North, South, East, and West. Label each direction along the correct edge of the cardboard (N, S, E, and W). Then move the cardboard so the N is pointing north.

Using a pencil, lightly draw the path the sun takes as it rises in the east and sets in the west. And if you know the direction from which the wind usually blows in your area, draw that on the cardboard, too.

Now design your house on the graph paper. Use the following questions to help guide your design:

> How do buildings lose energy in the winter and gain energy in the summer?

> How many windows and doors should the house have, and where should they go?

> What devices will capture the sun's heat energy for heating or change heat energy into electrical energy?

> Would a windmill be useful in changing wind energy to electrical energy?

> How can dark and light colors be used on the walls and roof to absorb or reflect light energy?

> How will trees keep window and door areas cool in the summer?

After you've finished designing your house on graph paper, you're going to build it with parts cut from oak tag, heavy paper, or index cards. First draw the walls, roof, energy-collecting devices, and trees on the oak tag, heavy paper, or index cards. Paint them with the colors you selected in your design. After the parts have dried, cut them out.

Assemble the parts of the house on the cardboard yard. Use tape to hold things together. If the parts of the house are too thin to stand up, reinforce them with paper scraps.

3 ▶ Think and Write   Think about your energy-saving house and the special design features you created to save energy. In a short paragraph, explain how your house will save energy and money over the years.

Explanation   Buildings gain and lose energy through their walls, roofs, windows, and doors. Insulating a building can slow down the rate at which it heats up or cools off, which can also save energy. Other energy-saving ideas include using wind power and solar energy, using certain colors to absorb or reflect energy, and planting trees to protect the areas around doors and windows.

Amazing but True!
BRAINSTRETCHERS

10.1   Can acid rain burn right through my umbrella?

No, and it won't burn through your hat or your head, either. Acid raid is ordinary rain that's become polluted with sulfur dioxide and nitrogen dioxide. These chemicals come from the burning of fuels to heat businesses and homes, the exhaust from motor vehicles, and erupting volcanoes. Rainwater that comes in contact with these chemicals becomes a very weak acid. And even though that acid isn't powerful enough to burn through your umbrella, if enough of it falls as rain, it will pollute the environment, killing living things in freshwater lakes along with nearby plants and trees.

10.2   What is hazardous waste?

Some people's idea of hazardous waste is a garbage can you can trip over. But to scientists, *hazardous waste* is anything that people dispose of that can be dangerous to plants and animals living in the environment. There are a lot of examples of hazardous waste, including paint, gasoline, engine oil, and pesticides.

10.3   What does the word *toxic* mean?

If something is *toxic,* it contains a substance that can harm or perhaps kill living things. You may have heard this word used to describe a poison, which is a good example of a toxic substance. Or maybe your mother has used it to describe what you're like in a really bad mood! (Of course, she was just teasing.)

10.4   What is the EPA?

EPA (pronounced "E-P-A," not "eepah") is the abbreviation for the Environmental Protection Agency, which is an agency of the U.S. government. The EPA's job is to make sure people and businesses follow laws protecting the environment. For example, if a gas station has leaky underground storage tanks and the EPA finds out about it, the owner will be expected to fix the problem or else get in big trouble.

10.5   Is there really a kind of scientist called a *garbologist?*

Yes, there are scientists who are interested in finding out what people and businesses throw away and what happens to that garbage after it's buried in a landfill. And some of these scientists do call themselves *garbologists.* Maybe you could think of a better name for these scientists. How about *trash trackers?*

10.6   What is the ozone layer?

Look up. It's above your head. Actually, you can't see the ozone layer because it's *far* above your head and invisible. But it's there, doing a very important job. The *ozone layer* is a very thin layer of ozone gas about 15 miles (24 kilometers) above the earth's surface. It absorbs some of the sun's harmful rays and prevents them from reaching the earth. Scientists are concerned that air pollution is making parts of the ozone layer disappear. In fact, there are already holes in parts of the layer. If the ozone layer gets very thin or disappears, all life on the earth will be threatened.

10.7   I was watching a television program about trees, and they kept talking about "the forest station." What did they mean?

The term you heard was probably *deforestation,* which means people are cutting down trees and not replanting seedlings to take their place. Deforestation can be a big problem because life on the earth depends on green plants and trees producing oxygen. Plants and trees also take in carbon dioxide, which improves the air we breathe, and their roots hold soil in place, preventing erosion. If too much deforestation takes place, all life on the earth will be endangered.

10.8   The container my french fries came in had the word *biodegradable* on it. What does that mean?

Do you think that message is about the french fries or the container? Actually, both are *biodegradable* (by-oh-dee-grade-ah-bull), but the message is about the container. It means that if the container is thrown away and buried in a landfill, it will rot and become part of the earth. If you tried to dig it up years from now, you wouldn't find it. If you found the french fries instead, you were smart to throw them away!

10.9   What was the worst chemical pollution accident in the world?

The worst chemical pollution accident happened in 1984 in Bhopal, India. An explosion at an American-owned chemical plant released a deadly gas that killed about 2,600 people and made up to 300,000 more sick for a long time. Even the leaves of nearby plants and trees turned a yellowish color.

10.10   What was the worst oil spill in the world?

In March 1989, an oil tanker called the Exxon *Valdez* struck a reef and spilled 11 million gallons of oil into Prince William Sound, which is off the southern part of Alaska. The oil covered the shoreline and killed many birds, fish, and animals. The courts made Exxon pay millions of dollars to clean up the area so wildlife could live there again.

10.11   What was the worst nuclear accident in the world?

In April 1986, two huge explosions destroyed the nuclear reactor at an electric power plant in Chernobyl in the former Soviet Union, releasing dangerous radioactive material into the air. Thirty-one people were killed immediately by the explosion and radiation, and over 200 people had to get medical assistance for radiation poisoning.

Another 135,000 people in small towns and villages as far as 20 miles (about 32 kilometers) from the plant had to move further away to avoid being poisoned by the radiation. Even so, doctors predict that over the next 60 years, 20,000 to 40,000 of these people will die from cancer, which is caused by being exposed to radiation.

10.12   What was the worst nuclear accident in the United States?

In March 1979, cooling fluid from a nuclear reactor escaped from the center of the reactor core at the Three Mile Island electric power station near Harrisburg, Pennsylvania. The accident didn't kill anyone, and only a small amount of radioactive material entered the air. But the reactor was severely damaged, and parts of it were so radioactive that workers couldn't go near them without risking being poisoned. Following the accident, the plant was permanently shut down.

10.13   Every day, millions of animals and plants die and decompose on the earth's surface. So why doesn't nature get polluted?

This is an excellent question! Nature doesn't get polluted because it begins recycling the substances in animals and plants as soon as they die. For instance, animals called *scavengers* immediately begin feeding on the dead animals and plants. In addition, plants such as molds start to grow on the dead plants and animals, releasing nutrients and water that can be used by living things. Nature is the best recycler of all!

10.14   What birds are scavengers?

Many birds are scavengers, including buzzards, condors, crows, and sea gulls.

10.15   What fish are scavengers?

Sharks are scavengers because they eat dead and injured fish. Eels also eat dead fish and shellfish. Catfish travel along the bottoms of lakes and ponds to scavenge for food.

10.16   What mammals are scavengers?

Many mammals are scavengers. In fact, many hunt for their own food and also scavenge. For example, lions can easily kill their own prey but also steal prey that has been killed or injured by other animals. A pack of hyenas can also hunt or steal the prey captured by other animals. And if you've ever seen a raccoon, you've seen a scavenger that's very successful if it lives near humans. Raccoons love to invade garbage cans to get leftover food and other trash.

10.17 Who was Rachel Carson?

Rachel Carson was an American biologist who wrote one of the first books about the dangers of pollution. That book was published in 1962 and had a very sad title—*Silent Spring*. Rachel Carson wanted to warn people that if they didn't save the environment, the beautiful springtime would grow silent and all life on our planet would be in danger.

10.18 What's the best way to conserve water when you're in a bathtub?

Don't turn on the water.

10.19 Why do lions eat raw meat?

Because they don't know how to cook.

Chapter 11

Imagine and Invent

Activities

Making the Coolest Ice Cream [S&T 1]

Making the Perfect Paint [S&T 1]

Making a Terrific Toothpaste [S&T 4]

Making Water Safe to Drink [S&T 5]

Who? What? Thomas Alva Edison
and Philip Emeagwali [HNS 2]

When? Where? An Inventions-
around-the-House Puzzle [HNS 3]

Word Play

Robo Pets [S&T 2]

What a Wonder-Filled World! [S&T 2]

Bionic People Parts [S&T 3]

Magnificent Math

Invention Timeline [HNS 3]

Cruising on the Concorde! [S&T 5]

Art Connections

That's My Thaumatrope! [S&T 4]

For the Birds! [S&T 4]

Amazing but True!
Brainstretchers [S&T 1–5]

Activities

Making the Coolest Ice Cream

Doesn't making ice cream sound like a fun job? Believe it or not, making ice cream is also a very scientific job. In this activity, you'll use some important scientific ideas to make ice cream and then change the recipe to create your own brand.

1▶ Get Ready

Two sandwich-sized, zipper-top plastic bags
Two gallon-sized (3.7 liter), zipper-top plastic bags
1 cup (about 250 milliliters) very cold chocolate milk
2 tablespoons sugar
½ teaspoon vanilla flavoring
Coarse salt (Available in large supermarkets and hardware stores. You may use rock salt as long as it's pure sodium chloride.)
About 6 quarts (6 liters) miniature ice cubes, crushed ice, or regular ice cubes
Measuring spoons and cups
Plastic spoon for tasting
Watch or clock

2▶ Do and Wonder

Original Ice Cream

To make the ice cream mixture, add the following to the sandwich bag: 1 tablespoon sugar, ½ cup (about 125 milliliters) chocolate milk, and ¼ teaspoon vanilla flavoring. Seal the bag *tightly,* and then shake it to mix the contents together.

278

Next prepare your ice cream freezer. Add the following to the gallon (3.7 liter) bag: 2 tablespoons of coarse salt and enough crushed ice, miniature ice cubes, or regular ice cubes to fill the bag between half and three-fourths full. Seal the bag tightly, and shake it to mix the ice and salt.

Set the small, sealed bag with the ice cream mixture into the center of the large, sealed bag with the ice and salt mixture. Write down the time.

Shake the small bag and turn it over and over until you can see that the ice cream has hardened. (This will take at least 15 minutes.) When you're sure the ice cream is firm, write down the time.

Remove the ice cream from the bag and taste it. Observe its flavor and texture.

Your Improved Ice Cream

Now create your own brand of ice cream by changing the recipe and the procedure you used for freezing it. For example, maybe add different flavorings and ingredients to the ice cream mixture and more or less salt to the ice and salt mixture.

How long did it take your improved ice cream to freeze? How does it taste? What's the texture like?

3▶ Think and Write   In a short paragraph, compare the taste of the original ice cream with the taste of your improved brand. Also compare the textures and freezing times of the two ice creams. Finally, describe what else you might do to improve the taste and texture of your ice cream.

Explanation   The freezing temperature of water is 32 degrees Fahrenheit (or 0 degrees Celsius). Adding salt to water lowers its freezing temperature. When salt is placed on ice, a reaction occurs that moves some energy from the environment to the ice, causing it to melt. Anything near the melting ice loses some of its heat energy and gets colder. In making ice cream, the liquid ice cream mixture gets colder and harder.

Safety Hint   Don't use any other salt-containing products besides coarse table salt or rock salt that's pure sodium chloride. Other ice-melting products contain chemicals that are unsafe to handle and should never be used near food.

Activity 11.2

Making the Perfect Paint

Have you ever wondered what paint is made of? It probably contains a lot of chemicals, right? Not necessarily. You'll make paint out of some everyday materials in this activity and then experiment to see whether you can improve it.

1▶ Get Ready

Small, heavy-duty freezer bag	Plastic spoon
Small container of white glue	White paper
Rolling pin	Access to water
Two sticks of chalk of the same color	
Paintbrush (The size and type used for painting pictures.)	

2▶ Do and Wonder

Original Paint Recipe

First make the pigment (coloring material). Put the sticks of chalk in the plastic bag, and seal it tightly. Move the rolling pin back and forth over the bag, crushing the chalk into a fine powder. Then open the bag and add a few drops of water. Stir it with the spoon to form a paste.

Next add 1 tablespoon of white glue to the paste and mix it thoroughly. Finally, stir ¼ cup of warm water into the mixture.

You're done making the paint. Now use it to paint a picture.

Observe the quality of the paint. How's the color? The texture? How well does it go onto the paper?

Your Improved Paint Recipe

Create your own improved brand of paint by changing the ingredients or the procedures used to make it. Paint a picture using it.

Again, observe the quality of the paint.

3▶ Think and Write

In a short paragraph, compare the color, texture, and other properties of the first paint to those of your improved paint. Did your improved recipe really make better paint?

Explanation

Paint is made of solid particles of a coloring material called *pigment* that float in a liquid. In this activity, the pigment came from the colored chalk you ground up and mixed with liquid glue and water. The scientific name for a mixture of solid particles and liquid is *colloid* (coh-loyd).

Making a Terrific Toothpaste

There are *so many* different kinds of toothpaste that you could easily get confused when trying to buy one. Some toothpastes are striped, some have interesting tastes, some contain fluoride, and some come in a pump, not a tube! The question is, how well do they work? In this activity, you'll make your own toothpaste, try it, and then work on improving the recipe.

1 ▶ Get Ready

Package of unflavored Tums antacid tablets
Small box of baking soda
Assorted liquid food colors
Assorted liquid food flavors (for example,
  vanilla and orange)
Plastic spoon
Measuring spoons
Two sandwich bags
Clean dish towel
Two clean, clear, plastic cups
Rolling pin
Access to water

2 ▶ Do and Wonder

Toothpaste Recipe

To begin, you'll need to grind up some Tums to form a fine powder. Put two or three in the sandwich bag, and then seal it tightly. Break up the Tums by tapping on them through the bag. When they're in pieces, put the towel over the bag and then move the rolling pin back and forth over it, crushing the Tums into a fine powder. Keep adding, breaking, and crushing Tums like this until you've made about ½ teaspoon of powder.

Put the powder into a plastic cup, and add ¼ teaspoon of baking soda. Then mix in two or three drops of water to make a paste.

You've made your own toothpaste! Write down your observations. What does it taste like? What does it smell like? What is its texture like?

Your Improved Toothpaste Recipe

Study the original recipe and your observations to get ideas for improving the toothpaste. Think about using different amounts of substances, adding a flavor, and changing the color.

Make a new batch of toothpaste, test it, and write down your observations.

3▶ Think and Write

In a short paragraph, compare the original toothpaste you made with your own improved brand. How are they similar and different?

In another paragraph, make a hypothesis that explains why toothpaste makers limit the amount of grinding material (called an *abrasive*) used in their products.

Explanation

Toothpaste is made of a combination of substances. It usually contains a fine material, called an *abrasive,* that grinds and pushes deposits of plaque and tartar off your teeth. Some toothpastes also contain fluoride, which helps prevent holes called *cavities* from developing in your teeth. In addition, toothpastes usually contain a little soap along with a flavor and a color. The simple toothpaste you made used calcium carbonate (from the Tums) as an abrasive and baking soda to remove stains and reduce mouth acids.

Activity 11.4

Making Water Safe to Drink

In this activity, you'll create a model of a water treatment plant, which will help you understand how water is made safe to drink. Keep in mind that your water treatment plant is just a *model;* it doesn't really work. So if the water you started with was polluted, the water that leaves your model will be polluted, too.

1▶ Get Ready

Four clear, thin-walled, flexible plastic cups
    (These are sometimes called *airline cups*.)
Several tablespoons of soil
Two large, empty coffee cans, plastic containers,
    or small buckets, each of which can hold at least
    1 quart (about 1 liter) of water
Access to water
Liquid food coloring
Push pin
2 cups of aquarium sand or clean sandbox sand
2 cups of aquarium gravel or washed gravel found outdoors
Package of alum (a pickling chemical found in the spice
    section of a supermarket)
Two or three paper coffee filters
Tablespoon
Teaspoon
Water-based marker
Masking tape
Scissors

2▶ Do and Wonder

To begin, you'll need to prepare two kinds of dirty water. For the first kind, put about 1 quart (1 liter) of water into one of the containers. Mix in about 2 tablespoons of soil or as much as is needed to make the water look slightly muddy. Use the masking tape and marker to label this container "Dirty Water."

Pour about half of this dirty water into the second container. Add enough food coloring so you see the color of the water change. (The food coloring represents chemical pollution.) Label this container "Dirty and Polluted Water."

Water Treatment Plant 1

To construct your water treatment plant, first take the push pin and make 5 to 10 holes in the bottom of one of the plastic cups. Then line the bottom and sides of the cup with a paper coffee filter. (You may need to cut the filter to fit.) Use a bit of tape to hold the filter in place. Add gravel to the cup until its about one-fourth filled. Then pour enough sand over the gravel so the cup is about half filled. Use the masking tape and marker to label this cup "Water Filter."

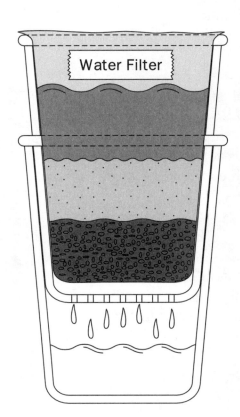

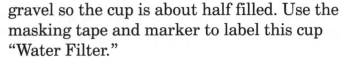

The first step in preparing the water for treatment is to get as much of it as possible in contact with oxygen from the air. This process is called *aeration* (air-ay-shun). To aerate the water, pour about ½ cup of "Dirty Water" from one cup to another three or four times.

The next steps in preparing the water are called *coagulation* (co-ag-you-lay-shun) and *sedimentation* (said-uh-men-tay-shun). To complete these steps, stir 1 teaspoon of alum into the ½ cup of water you've already aerated. Stir the water and observe the contents of the cup.

Now carefully pour the water from this cup into the cup containing the filter. Try not to disturb any of the material at the bottom of the first cup. Catch the water that flows through the filter in a third cup.

Write down your observations.

In a real water treatment plant, there would be one more step in the process. Small amounts of chlorine would be added to the water to kill any bacteria and plant material that remained. You won't be doing this step.

Now treat ½ cup of the "Dirty and Polluted Water" using your water treatment plant. Start by aerating the water (see second item above), and continue through the rest of the steps. Be sure to write down your observations.

Water Treatment Plant 2

Invent an improved water treatment plant by changing or adding layers of sand and gravel to the filter.

Test ½ cup each of "Dirty Water" and "Dirty and Polluted Water," following the same steps listed on page 284.

Write down your observations.

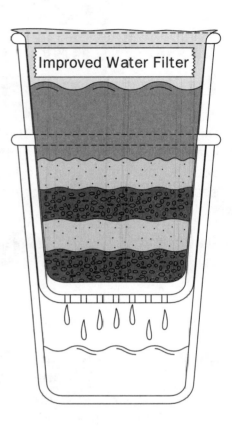

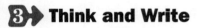 **Think and Write**   In one paragraph, compare the first and second water treatment plant models. Be sure to describe what changes you made to the filter in the second model and how well each model worked.

Explanation   The rainwater that falls to the ground eventually reaches underground reservoirs as well as streams, rivers, lakes, and oceans. Some of this water is captured and used for drinking water. However, it may have picked up soil particles, bits of organic matter, bacteria, and chemical pollutants along the way. These harmful materials are removed by a water treatment plant, which filters the water and treats it with chemicals that kill harmful organisms.

Safety Hint   Remember that you have made a *model* water treatment plant. It doesn't really work. So even if the water that comes out the filter is clear, it's still not safe to drink.

Who? What? Thomas Alva Edison and Philip Emeagwali

Get ready to be amazed as you learn about the life and work of an inventor who did things that others thought were impossible. In this activity, you'll learn about Thomas Alva Edison or Philip Emeagwali, each of whom earned the title of *genius*.

1▶ Get Ready

Paper and pencil
Ruler
Resource books and/or
   access to the World Wide Web

Two sheets of poster paper
Felt-tipped markers in assorted colors

2▶ Do and Wonder

In this activity, you'll do two things: (1) Gather a lot of information about the life and discoveries of a scientist, and (2) create two posters that will show what you learned.

Pick one of these scientists for your research: Thomas Alva Edison or Philip Emeagwali.

To begin, read the brief biography of this scientist in the Explanation section at the end of this activity. Then use resource books and/or the World Wide Web to find more information about your scientist. Take as many notes as you can about the individual and his discoveries.

Now you're ready to create your posters.

Poster 1

Write the scientist's name at the top of the poster, and draw a picture of him below it.

Write down when and where the scientist lived.

List important facts about his life.

Poster 2

At the top of the poster, write the problem or question the scientist worked on.

Draw the kinds of equipment he used to make his discoveries.

If you could ask the scientist two questions about his life and discoveries, what would they be? Write them down.

3 **Think and Write**   Imagine that the scientist you selected was going to visit your classroom. What would you like him to bring to show you and your classmates? What science questions do you think you and your classmates might ask the scientist? What are two things the scientist might tell about his life and work?

Write one or two paragraphs about the scientist's visit to your classroom, describing what he would show and tell you and your classmates.

Explanation

Thomas Alva Edison

Thomas Edison was born in Milan, Ohio, in 1847. From the start, he was a very curious child. By the age of 10, he had created a small science laboratory in the basement of his home. His early experiments were in chemistry, building batteries, and constructing a telegraph. As a young adult, he invented devices that helped send information about stock prices from place to place. Using the money he earned from these inventions, Thomas Edison built a laboratory in Menlo Park, New Jersey. There, he created and improved on all sorts of inventions, such as light bulbs, motion picture cameras, and projectors. Perhaps most important of all, he invented a way of generating and sending electricity to homes and businesses. During his life, Thomas Edison created over 1,000 more inventions. He still holds more U.S. patents than any other American. He died in 1931.

Philip Emeagwali

Philip Emeagwali was born in 1955 in Akure, Nigeria, the son of parents from the Igbo tribe. He was educated in England and received five degrees in four different areas of study: one bachelor's degree, three master's degrees, and a doctorate in scientific computing. During his career, he has been very successful in many different fields. But he is especially known for his brilliant ways of thinking about, designing, and programming computers. Philip Emeagwali received the Gordon Bell Prize for designing one of the fastest computers ever, which he called *Hyperball*. He is also well known for designing a computer program that describes how oil flows underground.

Activity 11.6

When? Where? An Inventions-around-the-House Puzzle

Take a quick look around the room, and pick out 10 objects. Even though they're all in the room now, were they invented at about the same time? Could you put them in order from the object invented first to the one invented last? That's what you're going to do in this activity, using a list of 10 common household inventions.

1▶ Get Ready

10 index cards
Pencil
Resource books and/or access to the World Wide Web
Adult to survey at home or at school

2▶ Do and Wonder

Take a look at the following list of inventions. Write the name of each on the front of an index card. Then put the cards in a stack, with the names of the inventions facing upward.

Bicycle	Hang glider
Bifocal glasses	Lawn mower
Can opener (not electrical)	Motorcycle
Canned food	Porcelain false teeth
Hair dryer	Vacuum cleaner

Spread the cards out on a table so you can see each one. Think about which item was probably invented first, second, third, and so on. Here are some hints:

Think about how early in history humans would have needed each invention.

The inventions that use energy such as gas or electricity were probably invented fairly recently.

Some of the inventions use ideas that came from previous inventions.

Put the cards in order, from the oldest invention (at your left) to the newest (at your right).

Check your work. Look at the Explanation at the end of this activity. There, you'll find a list of the inventions, including information about when each was invented, who invented it, and what country the inventor was from. The inventions are listed in order from oldest to newest. Use this information to check the order of your index cards. How did you do?

Now it's time to see how well an adult can put the inventions in order. Find an adult family member or someone at school who's willing to try. Mix up the cards, and challenge the adult to put them in order, from oldest to newest. When he or she has finished, check the order of the cards. Then ask the adult if any of the dates surprised him or her. Also ask about what ideas he or she used to put the cards in order.

3 **Think and Write**

Write a paragraph about how *you* did in solving the puzzle. Did you have the oldest invention in the correct place? The most recent invention? How about the inventions in between? When you checked the order of your cards against the correct information, what surprised you? Why?

Write another paragraph about the *adult's* success at arranging the cards.

Explanation

Porcelain false teeth (1770)—Alex Duchateau; France

Bifocal glasses (1784)—Benjamin Franklin; United States

Canned food (1811)—Nicolas Appert; France

Lawn mower (1830)—Edwin Budding; England

Bicycle (1839)—Kirkpatrick Macmillan; Scotland

Can opener (1855)—Robert Yeates; England

Motorcycle (1885)—Gottlieb Daimler; Germany

Hang glider (1891)—Otto Lilienthal; Germany

Vacuum cleaner (1901)—Hubert Cecil Booth; England

Hair dryer (1920)—Racine Universal Motor Company; United States

Word Play

Word Play 11.1

Robo Pets

Imagine that you're one of a group of scientists and their families who have been sent to Mars to build a space colony. You've arrived with plenty of food, equipment, and materials to live under a clear dome on the planet's surface. Unfortunately, there was no room on the spaceship for any pets. Now all the children in the colony are sad—some are even crying! In this activity, it will be *your* job to design pet robots for the children. And you're going to call these very special toys *Robo Pets!*

1▶ Get Ready   Paper and pencil

2▶ Do and Wonder   Think about what a robotic pet would be like—part animal and part machine. Use these questions to help plan your Robo Pet:

> Will it be able to do any tricks?
>
> How will it communicate?
>
> Will it have to be fed?
>
> Will it have to be cleaned?
>
> Will it need to sleep?
>
> What will make a child like a Robo Pet as much as the pet he or she left back on Earth?

Now design and draw your own Robo Pet. Label its computer brain, the electric motors that move the body parts, and the wires connecting the brain to the motors. (If you want, you can use solar-powered electric motors.)

3▶ Think and Write   Name your Robo Pet, and then write a paragraph describing it. Be sure to mention what a child would really like about this pet.

Explanation   A robot is a machine that can do a task. Its brain is a computer chip. Today most robots are used to do jobs that are boring or dangerous. In this activity, you used your imagination to design and write about a Robo Pet. Perhaps in the future, people will have pets that look and act just like the one you designed.

Word Play 11.2

What a Wonder-Filled World!

What would it be like to live in a world where we had inventions to help us save energy, recycle materials, and keep the air, water, and land clean? Your job in this activity will be to use your imagination to create inventions that will do exactly those things.

1▶ Get Ready Paper and pencil

2▶ Do and Wonder People create inventions to solve problems. Use this list of problems to start thinking about possible inventions you can create:

> People litter the roadsides by throwing garbage out car windows.
>
> People forget to turn lights off when they leave a room.
>
> By driving motor vehicles, people pollute the air.
>
> People waste water when they take showers.
>
> People use chemicals to kill weeds and pests in their gardens and lawns.
>
> People's garbage cans are sometimes knocked over and spilled by dogs and other animals looking for food scraps.
>
> People use salt to clear the ice from sidewalks and roads, and that salt is sometimes carried into streams, rivers, and lakes.
>
> People waste a lot of water by watering their lawns and gardens.

Select the two problems that most interest you. Or think of two other problems that you'd like to solve with inventions.

Design and draw each invention on a sheet of paper. Label its important parts, and give it a name.

3▶ Think and Write Write the directions that people will need to use each of your inventions. Imagine that each set of directions is part of an instruction book that will be attached to the invention. Try to make the directions complete yet simple and easy to follow.

Explanation   Although our world is a wonderful, beautiful place, it does have its problems. To solve these problems, we have to find better ways to control pollution and save energy and other resources. Perhaps inventions like yours will someday help people make the world a better place—and then keep it that way!

Word Play 11.3

Bionic People Parts

Some amazing inventions have made it possible for doctors to actually replace parts of the human body. These parts are made of special materials called *biomaterials.* In this activity, you'll discover and write about how these bionic parts are made and used.

1▶ Get Ready   Paper and pencil
Resource books and/or access to the World Wide Web

2▶ Do and Wonder   Use resource books and/or the World Wide Web to learn about these bionic body parts:

Knee joints	Tendons	Ligaments
Hip joints	Skin	Eye lenses
Ankles		

For each bionic part, try to find answers to these questions:

What biomaterials are used to make it?

What does it look like?

How do doctors use it to help make a patient's life better?

3▶ Think and Write   Imagine that the cost of making and placing bionic body parts in people goes way down in the future, so that anyone could afford them. Do you think people will start getting careless about their health because spare parts will be available to fix what ails them? If someone had all of his or her body parts replaced, would he or she still be a human being? Use the information you discovered to answer these questions in a paragraph.

Explanation   Scientists have been doing experiments for many years to discover ways of helping people with diseased or injured body parts. So far, scientists have found ways to use organs donated by others and how to make replacements for some body parts.

Magnificent Math 11.1

Invention Timeline

This activity will help you learn when some very interesting things were invented by organizing the information on a timeline. You'll also get to see how well adults can estimate when inventions were made!

1▶ Get Ready

Ruler
Pencil
Sheet of newsprint or chartpaper
Two or three adults who will answer survey questions

2▶ Do and Wonder

Using a pencil and ruler, draw a line across the bottom of your paper. Then decide on a scale that will let you fit 400 years across the line. Mark units on your timeline to show every 25 years from 1600 to 2000.

Look at the following list of inventions and the approximate year each was invented. For each invention, write its name at the correct date on the timeline:

Invention	Year	Invention	Year
Bagel	1610	35 mm camera	1914
Sandwich	1770	Zipper	1914
Piano	1700	Jet engine	1928
Battery	1800	Pop-up toaster	1930
Electric motor	1821	Parking meter	1935
Lawn mower	1830	Microwave oven	1946
Bicycle	1839	Credit card	1950
Saxophone	1846	Videotape	1956
Stapler	1868	Electric toothbrush	1961
Chewing gum	1872	Skateboard	1962
Typewriter	1873	Space station	1971
Cash register	1879	Home video game	1972
Hang glider	1891	Personal computer	1978
Vacuum cleaner	1901	Artificial heart	1982

After you've finished making your timeline, find two or three adults to survey. Without showing him or her your timeline, ask each adult to guess at the years in which at least five items were invented. Write down each person's answers.

After you've surveyed each adult, show him or her the timeline. Repeat his or her estimates of dates, and then show the actual year each item was invented.

3▶ Think and Write   Write a short paragraph that answers these questions: How well did the adults do with their guesses? Were there any patterns in the adults' answers? Why might someone think an invention is older or newer than it really is?

Explanation   The dates given for the inventions are from *Smithsonian Timeline of Inventions,* by Richard Platt (New York: Dorling Kindersley Publishers, 1991), pp. 22–61.

Magnificent Math 11.2

Cruising on the Concorde!

Many military jets can fly faster than the speed of sound, but only one passenger plane can—the *Concorde.* In this activity, you'll calculate how long it would take this amazing airplane to fly you from one place to another.

1▶ Get Ready   Globe   Paper and pencil

2▶ Do and Wonder   Locate London and Singapore on the globe. Use your finger to trace the path an airplane would fly from one city to the other. The distance between London and Singapore is 6,743 miles (10,852 kilometers), and the Concorde can cruise at a speed of 1,354 miles per hour (2,179 kilometers per hour). How long would it take you to fly from London to Singapore (counting just time in the air)?

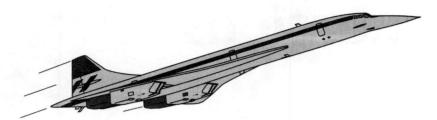

Now trace the path a plane would fly from London to Washington, D.C. Using the distance scale on the globe, estimate the distance between these two cities. Then figure out how long it would take the Concorde to fly from one city to the other (again, just time in the air).

3▶ Think and Write   Imagine that in the future, it will be possible to refuel the Concorde while flying. Using the distance scale on the globe (and what you know about the plane's speed), figure out how long it would take for the Concorde to fly around the world nonstop.

Explanation   The Concorde is the world's first supersonic airliner. It was invented by British and French engineers, who got many of their ideas by looking at how supersonic military aircraft were designed and built. The Concorde took its first flight in 1969 and went into commercial service seven years later.

Art Connections

Art Connections 11.1

That's My Thaumatrope!

What a great word: *thaumatrope* (thaw-ma-trope). But what does it mean? It's a device that tricks your mind into thinking a picture is moving. It was invented long before moving pictures. In this activity, you'll make your own thaumatrope out of simple materials.

1 ▶ Get Ready

Two or three white paper plates
Watercolor markers in assorted colors
Unsharpened round pencil (not six-sided)
Scissors
Ruler
Masking tape
Sharpened pencil (of any type)

2 ▶ Do and Wonder

Cut the edges off each paper plate to make a flat circle about 5 inches (13 centimeters) across.

Use the sharpened pencil to lightly draw an animal on one side of a paper circle. Then turn the circle over and draw where the animal lives on the other side. For example:

A bird / A branch

A frog / A lily pad

A monkey / A tree

Tape the circle firmly to the eraser end of the unsharpened pencil. Be sure the tape doesn't cover your drawings.

Now hold the pencil between your palms, and rub them back and forth quickly so you can see both the front and back of the paper circle. What do you observe?

Make changes to your drawings until the images of the animal and where it lives fit well together. When you're satisfied, use the markers to color your drawings.

Make other thaumatropes of different animals and places—perhaps endangered species and their environments.

3▶ Think and Write   Use what you learned making the two-sided thaumatrope to design one that would create more than one image. Draw a picture of your invention, and label its parts. Also write a short paragraph to explain how it works.

Explanation   The thaumatrope creates an optical illusion. Your brain seems to hang on, just for a short time, to each image you see. This means you'll still see an object after it's been removed from in front of your eyes. If another image comes into view while your brain is still hanging on to the previous image, you'll see the images together. And if the images are slightly different, they'll blend together.

Art Connections 11.2

For the Birds!

Most bird feeders are made of painted wood or plastic. In this activity, you'll make some bird feeders out of natural materials. You'll also create your own bird food mixture to attract birds to your feeder.

1▶ Get Ready   ½ grapefruit or orange with "meat" and juices removed
Two or three small pine cones that have opened
Metal or plastic bowl about 6 inches (15 centimeters) across
    (2 quart or 2 liter size)
Sharpened pencil (to make holes)
Six eggshells
½ pound (about ¼ kilogram) bird seed
1 pound (about ½ kilogram) inexpensive peanut butter
Strong string or yarn
Metal spoon
Roll of aluminum foil
Stove with oven and an adult helper
Metal baking tray and potholder
Reference books with nutritional information

2️⃣ Do and Wonder
Do this step with your adult helper: Crush the eggshells and put them on a sheet of aluminum foil. Place the half grapefruit or orange on the foil, as well. Put the foil on the baking tray, and bake both at 200 degrees Fahrenheit (93 degrees Celsius) for 1 hour. Use the potholder to remove the tray, and then let it cool down.

After the half grapefruit or orange has cooled down, carefully poke three holes through the rim of the rind about ¾ inch (2 centimeters) down from the top edge. Make the holes equal distances apart.

Cut three 8 inch (about 20 centimeter) lengths of string. Run one string through each hole. Bring the ends of the strings together, and knot them securely. This is how you'll hang the bowl.

Next make the food mixture. Mix the peanut butter, bird seed, and baked crushed eggshells. Form some of the mixture into a ball that will fit into the rind bowl. Put the ball into the bowl, and hang the bowl from a tree branch.

Stuff any of the leftover food mixture into the pine cones. Tie a string to each, and hang it from a tree branch.

3️⃣ Think and Write
Using a resource book about food and nutrition, find out which nutrients the birds will get from eating the bird seed, peanut butter, and eggshell mixture. Write a short paragraph that tells what you learned.

Explanation
You may have seen just a few species of birds living near your home or school. If you live in or near a city, you've probably seen blue jays, starlings, pigeons, and perhaps crows. The growth of towns and cities has changed the environment so much that other species of birds can no longer live there. A bird feeder will attract other species that happen to be passing through your area. These birds may stay around as long as there are food and water and good weather.

Amazing but True!
BRAINSTRETCHERS

11.1	Why is there a line right through the middle of some people's glasses?
11.2	Where's the motor in a rollercoaster car?
11.3	How are photographs developed from film?
11.4	How does a Thermos (or vacuum) bottle make things hot or cold?
11.5	Who invented the Ferris wheel?
11.6	Whenever there's an airplane crash, people are always searching for the "black box." What is it?
11.7	Does the word *scuba* come from the name of a fish?
11.8	Who invented the computer?
11.9	Who was the first computer programmer?
11.10	Why are the letters on the keys of my computer keyboard all mixed up?
11.11	What important scientific discoveries and inventions happened by accident?
11.12	Was the American president Thomas Jefferson really an inventor?
11.13	What did the scientist and inventor Percy Julian invent?
11.14	Who was the first woman named to the National Inventors Hall of Fame?
11.15	What is a patent?
11.16	What did the inventor of the brakeless carousel call this invention?
11.17	Who invented spaghetti?

11.1 Why is there a line right through the middle of some people's glasses?

First of all, these kinds of glasses are called *bifocals* (buy-fo-kulls). They were supposedly invented by Benjamin Franklin. Bifocals have two different kinds of lenses, which are useful to people who are nearsighted when they're young but become farsighted when they get older. They need the top lens to see things that are far away and the bottom lens to see things that are close. If these people didn't have bifocals, they'd need to have two pairs of glasses with them all the time. Anyway, the line you think you see is just the place the lenses meet.

11.2   Where's the motor in a rollercoaster car?

Actually, the motor's not in the rollercoaster car. It's part of the wooden or metal platform that holds the rollercoaster track in place. At the beginning of the ride, the motor pulls on a chain attached to the rollercoaster car. This moves the car to the top of the first hill. Hooks inside the track then release the car at the top of the hill, and gravity pulls it down. The energy of the car going down the hill also carries it up the next hill. The hills in basic rollercoaster rides are all smaller than the first hill, since the cars never have as much energy as they had at the top of the first hill.

11.3   How are photographs developed from film?

The film is unrolled in what's called a *dark room* (which is a place without normal light) and placed in some liquid chemicals. The chemicals change the film so that whatever was light colored in the scene you photographed becomes dark and whatever was dark colored becomes light. This new image is called a *negative*. Light is then sent through the negative and onto a sheet of photographic paper. When the paper is bathed in other chemicals, a picture eventually forms. The areas that were dark and light in the negative are reversed again, which means light and dark colors are back where they're supposed to be!

11.4   How does a Thermos (or vacuum) bottle make things hot or cold?

Actually, a Thermos bottle doesn't *make* things hot or cold. But it will keep hot things hot and cold things cold for a long time. A Thermos bottle is an excellent insulator, which means it slows the flow of heat energy into and out of the bottle. If you could take one apart, you'd find a plastic or metal container outside and a glass bottle inside. Some of the air is removed from the space between the glass bottle and the inside wall of the Thermos when it's made. That space is a vacuum, which slows the flow of heat energy.

11.5   Who invented the Ferris wheel?

Would you be surprised to learn that it was a person named *Ferris*? George Washington Gale Ferris was an American bridge builder. He entered a contest to build a spectacular ride for a great festival that was going to be held in 1893. Ferris invented and then had built a giant revolving wheel whose top was 825 feet (251.5 meters) above the ground. Attached to the wheel were 36 hanging metal platforms called *cars* that could each hold 60 people. A ride on George Ferris's wheel cost 50 cents and lasted for 20 minutes.

11.6   Whenever there's an airplane crash, people are always searching for the "black box." What is it?

The *black box* is a very strong steel and plastic case that contains a recording of data showing the speed, direction, altitude, and other important information about the airplane just before it crashed. If investigators can find the black box, they may be able to figure out why the plane went down. If you're ever part of the search for a black box, keep this in mind: Black boxes are actually *bright orange* in color!

11.7   Does the word *scuba* come from the name of a fish?

No, there's no scuba fish! Rather, *scuba* is an abbreviation for "self-contained underwater breathing apparatus." The scuba equipment used by divers was invented by Jacques Cousteau and Emile Gagnan. Cousteau was a diver, so he knew exactly what kinds of equipment were needed to make ocean diving safe. And Gagnan was an engineer, so he was able to build the equipment. What a team!

11.8   Who invented the computer?

This question is difficult to answer because people have been using machines to do calculations for thousands of years. Hundreds of years ago, Blaise Pascal (1623–1662) made a simple device that could add and subtract. A little later, Gottfried Wilhelm Leibniz (1646–1716) invented a machine that could do multiplication. More than a century later, Charles Babbage (1792–1871) developed plans for a machine that could do complicated math problems. Unfortunately, he kept changing the design and never received the funds needed to build the machine. The first computer that could actually solve important problems was the *Collossus,* which was based on the ideas of Alan M. Turing, designed by Max Newman, and built by T. H. Flowers. It was used during World War II to crack German codes. The first large electronic computer, called *ENIAC,* was built at the University of Pennsylvania by John Prosper Eckert, Jr., and John William Mauchly between 1943 and 1946.

11.9   Who was the first computer programmer?

That honor should probably go to two people, both women. The first programmer was Lady Ada Lovelace, who lived in the 1800s. She was a mathematician and a close friend of Charles Babbage. While he was designing his calculating machine, Lady Lovelace worked on how to get information into the machine. In the twentieth century, the honor for being the first programmer of a modern computer goes to Commodore Grace Murray Hopper. She created the first program for a computer used by the U.S. Navy called the *Mark I*.

11.10   Why are the letters on the keys of my computer keyboard all mixed up?

You're very observant! You've probably also noticed that the first six keys in the top row of letters spell out *QUERTY*. The QUERTY keyboard was designed by Christopher Sholes in the late 1800s for use in typewriters. He discovered that putting the keys in alphabetical order just didn't work. People would press the keys of the most commonly used letters at the same time and from the same area of the keyboard. This jammed up parts of the typewriter! Sholes found a new pattern that spread out the letters, so the ones that are usually used together get struck from different places. This QUERTY keyboard worked much better, so it became the standard for typewriters. And now it's the standard for computer keyboards, too.

11.11   What important scientific discoveries and inventions happened by accident?

Accidents that produce discoveries or inventions usually happen when someone is trying to discover or invent one thing but ends up discovering or inventing something else. It's not as though someone who's trying to invent a new kind of lawn mower accidentally discovers a cure for cancer instead. The accidental discovery or invention is usually related to what the person was really working on. One such accident discovered a process called *vulcanization* (vul-ken-eh-zay-shun), through which liquid rubber is hardened into a substance that can be used to make tires and other things. Other accidental discoveries and inventions include penicillin, air conditioning, x-rays, dynamite, and the fabric rayon.

11.12   Was the American president Thomas Jefferson really an inventor?

Thomas Jefferson (1743–1826) did invent a few things, including the swivel chair, a device for measuring how far you've walked, and an improvement for part of a plow. He never received patents for any of his inventions, however, so he didn't really own them.

11.13 What did the scientist and inventor Percy Julian invent?

Percy Julian (1899–1975), the grandson of a former slave, created medicines and discovered other important uses for plant materials. One of his most important discoveries was a way to produce the powerful drug physostigmine (fye-sas-teg-meen), which was used to treat people with a disease that caused blindness. He also invented ways to make medicines to treat arthritis and other diseases. During his lifetime, Percy Julian obtained 130 patents.

11.14 Who was the first woman named to the National Inventors Hall of Fame?

Gertrude Belle Elion (1918–1999) was selected for this honor based on her valuable research. The work she did led to creating drugs for treating people with leukemia and blood infections and for helping people prepare for kidney transplants.

11.15 What is a patent?

A *patent* is a license granted to an inventor to protect his or her rights to use, make, and sell whatever he or she has invented. The inventor has to register the invention with the government patent office and must be able to prove that the product is unique and original. Only one patent is given for each type of invention. And if two people invent the same thing, whoever gets the patent wins!

11.16 What did the inventor of the brakeless carousel call this invention?

The merry-go-round and round and round . . .

11.17 Who invented spaghetti?

A guy who really used his noodle.

Activities for National Science Education Content Standards K–8

Content Standard A: Science as Inquiry*

All students should develop:
- Abilities necessary to do scientific inquiry
- Understandings about scientific inquiry

Content Standard B: Physical Science [PS]

Standard	W & W Symbol	W & W Activity	Page Number
➡ Grades K–4			
Properties of objects and materials	[PS 1]	Balloon Blower-Upper	2
		Candy Testing	4
		Eggshell Excitement	5
		Boro Slime: Make It, Test It	28
		Starch Slime: Make It, Test It	30
		Oobleck—Regular and Alien: Make It, Test It	32
Positions and motions of objects	[PS 2]	Marbles and Surfaces	43
		Seashell Mobiles	46
Light, heat, electricity, and magnetism	[PS 3]	Spectacular Spectrums	56
		Weird Lenses	59
		Racing Ice Cubes	61
		Measuring Magnet Power	71
		Smart Battery Shopping	72
		Rainbows Outside *and* Inside	74
		Solar Energy Prints	75
➡ Grades 5–8			
Properties and changes of properties in matter	[PS 4]	Make a Fizzler	7
		Nice Spice	8
		Split (Yes, *Split*) Milk	10
		Starch Detective	11
		Superfoam	13

*This general standard is the foundation of all the NSE standards. Since it is emphasized in all the *Whizbangers and Wonderments* activities, it is not identified for each one. Be aware that some of the NSE K–4 standards are also 5–8 standards, which is why some standards are listed twice. Also, the bracketed symbols in column 2 of this chart were prepared for this book by this author.

Content Standard C: Life Science [LS]

➡ Grades K–4

➡ Grades 5–8

Content Standard D: Earth and Space Sciences [ESS]

➺ Grades K–4

➺ Grades 5–8

Content Standard E: Science and Technology [S&T]

➤ Grades K–4

➤ Grades 5–8

Content Standard F: Science in Personal and Social Perspectives [SPSP]

➤ Grades K–4

Content Standard G: History and Nature of Science [HNS]

National Science Education Content Standards K–8*

Unifying Concepts and Processes

Standard: As a result of activities in grades K–12, all students should develop understandings and abilities aligned with the following concepts and processes.

Systems, order, and organization

Evidence, models, and explanation

Constancy, change, and measurement

Evolution and equilibrium

Form and function

Content Standards: K–4

Science as Inquiry**

Content Standard A: As a result of activities in grades K–4, all students should develop

- Abilities necessary to do scientific inquiry
- Understanding about scientific inquiry

Physical Science [PS]

Content Standard B: As a result of the activities in grades K–4, all students should develop an understanding of

- Properties of objects and materials [PS 1]
- Position and motion of objects [PS 2]
- Light, heat, electricity and magnetism [PS 3]

Life Science [LS]

Content Standard C: As a result of the activities in grades K–4, all students should develop an understanding of

- The characteristics of organisms [LS 1]
- Life cycles of organisms [LS 2]
- Organisms and environments [LS 3]

Earth and Space Sciences [ESS]

Content Standard D: As a result of the activities in grades K–4, all students should develop an understanding of

- Properties of earth materials [ESS 1]
- Objects in the sky [ESS 2]
- Changes in earth and sky [ESS 3]

Science and Technology [S&T]

Content Standard E: As a result of the activities in grades K–4, all students should develop an understanding of

- Abilities of technological design [S&T 1]
- Understanding about science and technology [S&T 2]
- Ability to distinguish between natural objects and objects made by humans [S&T 3]

*From the National Research Council, *National Science Education Standards* (Washington, DC: National Academy Press, 1996), pp. 109, 110. Reprinted with permission of National Academy Press. Note that *Whizbangers and Wonderments* focuses on just the K–8 content standards. Also, the bracketed symbols to the right of the standards were prepared for this book by this author.

**This general standard is the foundation of all the NSE Standards. Since it is emphasized in all the *Whizbangers and Wonderments* activities, it is not identified for each one.

Science in Personal and Social Perspectives [SPSP]

Content Standard F: As a result of the activities in grades K–4, all students should develop an understanding of

- Personal health [SPSP 1]
- Characteristics and changes in populations [SPSP 2]
- Types of resources [SPSP 3]
- Changes in environments [SPSP 4]
- Science and technology in local challenges [SPSP 5]

History and Nature of Science [HNS]

Content Standard G: As a result of the activities in grades K–4, all students should develop an understanding of

- Science as a human endeavor [HNS 1]

Content Standards: 5–8

Science as Inquiry

Content Standard A: As a result of their activities in grades 5–8, all students should develop

- Abilities necessary to do scientific inquiry
- Understandings about scientific inquiry

Physical Science [PS]

Content Standard B: As a result of their activities in grades 5–8, all students should develop an understanding of

- Properties and changes of properties in matter [PS 4]
- Motion and forces [PS 5]
- Transfer of energy [PS 6]

Life Science [LS]

Content Standard C: As a result of their activities in grades 5–8, all students should develop an understanding of

- Structure and function in living systems [LS 4]
- Reproduction and heredity [LS 5]
- Regulation and behavior [LS 6]
- Population and ecosystems [LS 7]
- Diversity and adaptations of organisms [LS 8]

Earth and Space Sciences [ES]

Content Standard D: As a result of their activities in grades 5–8, all students should develop an understanding of

- Structure of the earth system [ES 4]
- Earth's history [ES 5]
- Earth in the solar system [ES 6]

Science and Technology [S&T]

Content Standard E: As a result of the activities in grades 5–8, all students should develop an understanding of

- Abilities of technological design [S&T 4]
- Understanding about science and technology [S&T 5]

Science in Personal and Social Perspectives [SPSP]

Content Standard F: As a result of the activities in grades 5–8, all students should develop an understanding of

- Personal health [SPSP 6]
- Populations, resources, and environments [SPSP 7]
- Natural hazards [SPSP 8]
- Risks and benefits [SPSP 9]
- Changes in environments [SPSP 10]
- Science and technology in society [SPSP 11]

History and Nature of Science [HNS]

Content Standard G: As a result of the activities in grades 5–8, all students should develop an understanding of

- Science as a human endeavor [HNS 2]
- Nature of science [HNS 3]
- History of science [HNS 4]

Index

312